UNMASKED!
THE STORY OF
SOVIET ESPIONAGE

UN MASKED!

THE STORY OF
SOVIET ESPIONAGE

Ronald Seth

Hawthorn Books, Inc □ New York

Author's Note

My motive for writing this book is a simple one. Since the end of the Second World War we have had our attention drawn by a series of dramatic incidents—the Gouzenko defection in Canada, the Pavlov defection in Australia, the Nunn May, Fuchs, Pontecorvo, Lonsdale, Blake and Vassall cases in particular—to the vast ramifications of Soviet espionage. The responsible authorities have lost no opportunity to impress upon us, via mass communication media, the threat which Russian spies and pro-Russian traitors represent to us in the nuclear age, and only the utterly complacent can fail to have been moved by the information which has been offered.

Regarding it all quite dispassionately, however, it seems to me that the picture represented has been somewhat distorted. I have been led to this view because I have found in conversation that very few of my friends, who are not espionage experts, do not appreciate that massive though the postwar Soviet spying effort has been, it is little greater than the prewar effort.

I think, too, that the sensationalism which has accompanied Soviet espionage revelations has also been an error of judgment. Whenever a nuclear spy scare has erupted, an atmosphere of near panic has immediately enveloped it, like a kind of transparent smoke-screen emitted, not by the general public—though it has inevitably involved them—but by politicians of one function or another. Panic warps judgment; in the face of such a threat calmness is essential if countermovement is to be effective; and I personally believe that if the public were armed with the full picture of Soviet espionage the panic or, at any rate, the movement toward panic, would be counteracted to advantage.

It has not been only the politicians and the press which have been guilty in this respect. Several books on Soviet espionage have appeared in the last twenty years, and I cannot find one of them untinged by some degree of sensationalism. In many cases they are also factually at fault. The public, therefore, has no calmly presented casebook of Soviet spying on which to draw. It is to remove this lack that I have written this book.

I cannot claim to have dealt exhaustively with Soviet espionage. To be able to do so would require several volumes this size. I hope, however, that I have succeeded in my twin aims of presenting my material dispassionately and of giving an over-all picture of Soviet espionage during the forty years of its activity.

R. S.

Contents

PART I

Development and Organization

☐ The Russian Tradition
of
Secret Service

According to legend, about the middle of the ninth century A.D., the Russians, concentrated in the trading community of Novgorod, sent the following message to a chief of the Varangians called Rurik, saying, "Our land is great and beautiful, but there is no order in it. Come and rule over us!" Whether legend or not, a Rurik did found a dynasty which welded the numerous small principalities over the course of the next five hundred years into a single nation under the aegis of Moscow.

This period was followed by a Tartar invasion under Batu Khan; they broke up the consolidated empire and ruled over it for two and a half centuries until expelled by Ivan the Great in 1492. The grandson of Ivan the Great was Ivan the Terrible, a contemporary of Queen Elizabeth I. From Ivan's reign spring the principles of autocratic government besides which the Stuart theory of the Divine Right of Kings becomes a mere wraith.

Ivan owed his sobriquet, the Terrible, to his ruthlessness and cruelty, though he was, in fact, a very able ruler. Because of his opposition to the privileged classes he was in constant danger of assassination, and to protect himself he formed a Praetorian Guard, called the Oprichniks.

The Oprichniks have a particular place here, for they are the forerunners of the Okhrana, the Cheka, the OGPU, the NKVD and MGB—the secret police through the centuries whose sole function has been the physical protection of the rulers of Russia, whether the régime has been autocratic-despotic or socialist-despotic. That the ruler of Russia needed the protection of the Oprichniks is understandable when it is appreciated that there was scarcely one who did not rule without excess of one kind or another, all of which militated against the well-being and happiness of the mass of their subjects.

This is particularly true of the Romanovs, the dynasty founded by the boyar Michael Romanov in 1612, which ruled without a break until the advent of the Bolsheviks. In the hundred and fifty years preceding the murder of the last tsar in 1918, three tsars had been assassinated. But even those tsars who had died natural deaths had never been free from the possibility of meeting a violent end.

From this state of affairs two observations can be drawn. One: the fear of assassination and the strong possibility of its happening made it essential for the tsars to be protected by a secret police, which would know of all plots before they came to fruition. Two, which is the corollary of the first: the long centuries of subjugation had so preconditioned the great mass of the Russian people to the tyranny of the secret police that their unchanged lot in this respect from the advent of their new leaders until the end of the Stalin era was made acceptable by the very fact that they had never known any freedom from such tyranny; that they had, in fact, merely exchanged one tyranny for another, which differed from it in no great way.

Probably no other country, with the possible exception of Prussia during the reign of the great Wilhelm Stieber as Bismarck's Director of Intelligence (fl. 1850–92), has been so subjected to the pressures of secret service as has Russia. Certainly this is true of the last one hundred and fifty years.

But the tsars, from Ivan the Terrible, had felt compelled to preserve their lives just a little longer by the protective watchfulness of their secret guards; it was Nicholas I who laid the foundations of the system which even today influences the espionage machine of modern Soviet Russia.

This tsar had none of the liberal leanings that his brother Alexander I had been tempted to give expression to, and the revolt of the *Dekabristi*, as they subsequently became known, at the very beginning of his reign uprooted any similar ideas, if there had ever been any, from his mind. He put down the revolt swiftly and harshly, hanged the leaders and sent over a hundred others, all officers and young men of good family, into exile in Siberia.

This was the first time that exile in Siberia, which was to become one of the main weapons of all subsequent national security organizations in Russia, was employed as a punishment, and it seems to have been the progenitor of a number of innovations in the tsarist attempts to rule by suppression.

Determined to be prepared in the future for any upheaval which might threaten his throne, Nicholas caused to be set up a Special Corps of Gendarmerie, in charge of which he put Count Constantin Benckendorff—not to be confused with his son, Count Alexander Benckendorff, who was Russian Ambassador in London from 1908 until his death in 1917. Benckendorff carried out the wishes of his master so well that he spread terror and fear not only into the hearts and minds of the ordinary people, but also among every official of the administration. In spite of this, however, Nicholas was not satisfied, and created yet another organization known as the Third Section, whose chief had the power of sending into exile any Russian citizen, no matter what his rank, without specifying a reason and at a few hours' notice. From the decisions of the Third Section there was no appeal.

Nicholas' successor was perhaps the most humane of all the occupants of the Russian throne. He began his reign, as we have seen, with the best of intentions which he tried his best to make practicable in his interpretation of the functions of monarchy. He dissolved the Special Corps of Gendarmerie and the Third Section, and released all the latter's prisoners who were still alive.

But Alexander II's liberalism did not go far enough for large

numbers of his disappointed people and, when an attempt was
made to assassinate him, he responded with a form of government almost as harsh as his predecessor's had been. When, as
a result, a revolutionary movement, far more widespread and
active than any similar movement had previously been, came
into being, he had to resort to the same kind of protection as that
with which former tsars had surrounded themselves. It was to
no avail, however, and on March 13, 1881, a bomb exploded
under his carriage, which, while it did not harm him, wounded
and killed a number of his retinue. As he dismounted to inquire
after the casualties, a second bomb was thrown, and his son
Nicholas II mounted his throne.

Nicholas II, perhaps naturally in view of the complete failure
of his father's liberalism, showed himself to be the most violent
reactionary, and reverted to an autocratic form of government
surpassed by no other tsar. To combat the revolutionaries, who
stepped up their activities as the harshness of the régime increased, he organized at fabulous expense and by tremendous
efforts a state police force which was given the title of Department of State Protection, taking from the Russian form of this,
Okhrannoye Otdyelyenye, its infamous name, the Okhrana.

By this time the revolutionaries had not only organized themselves within the boundaries of Russia, but abroad, and the Okhrana
was responsible for keeping under surveillance both home- and
foreign-based conspirators. To do this it introduced the most
stringent passport regulations and sent its agents to every known
refuge of the self-exiled conspirators in Europe. This was a feature
not normally found in secret police activity, but it has left a lasting
mark on Russian espionage organization, for even today foreign
espionage responsibilities fall to the department of government elsewhere more usually concerned with internal security—the Ministry
(or Committee) of State Security.

At home the Okhrana attempted to do its work by a system of
mass observation. This, of its very nature, called for a colossal
number of agents of all kinds, and an organization far larger
than any similar one before or since. Both in its structure and in
its working it was a ludicrous institution, whose mountainous

labors consistently produced ridiculous mice. Its chiefs were members of the aristocracy and bureaucrats, to whom not only remaining in office but achieving promotion, rather than protecting the régime, was their sole goal. This led to rivalries within the organization which seriously militated against any significant results it ought to have achieved.

In addition the non-co-operation of their opponents was a constant source of worry to these egoistic policemen, for though the revolutionaries increased in numbers as the harshness of Nicholas' rule was extended, they broke out into what could be termed dangerous and menacing activity only occasionally. Since, by their definition, a man could demonstrate his worth, both for retention in office and for promotion, solely by the results he achieved, the long periods of revolutionary quiescence were not at all to the Okhrana's taste. To obtain action, they made extensive use of a type of agent which self-respecting security organizations will employ only as a last resort—the *agent provocateur*. This unsavory character, whose task is to pretend friendship in order to betray, to provoke speech which may be interpreted as having meanings far from the speaker's true thoughts, they sent out among their fellow citizens at home and abroad.

The lengths to which they went to produce results were for the most part laughable. When the Bolsheviks, their former victims, came to power they made public the secret police archives, and these read like fantasies told by the village idiot. But fantasies or not, by the very wickedness of their working, they inspired terror and dread among the entirely innocent.

The story which Vassall (see page 299) told of his initial involvement with Soviet espionage—which anyone who knows anything of the operation of that organization can accept as entirely credible—indicates that the Okhrana's influence is still coloring the activities of the Russian security forces in this respect. Nor is this the only sphere of resemblance, for the Soviet organization today still relies for its success on a fantastically large number of agents.

The Okhrana lumbered its way across the Russian domestic scene for thirty-five years. It was not equipped to prevent the events for which it had been created, and it ended in a failure which crowned all its failures when Nicholas met his death in the Ekaterinburg cellar in 1918.

Despite all its faults, however, it maintained the tradition of centuries. It was a tradition followed by no other country in Europe, and was not to come to an end with the Okhrana's demise.

☐ The Beginnings
of
Soviet Foreign Espionage

The men who took over the ordering and conduct of affairs in Russia in 1917 had had long experience of the particular pressures of a secret police as their number one adversary. They were aware of the shortcomings of the Okhrana, and were equally alive to the necessity of having protection for themselves, for they would have had to be blind indeed not to recognize that, though they might have shaken free from the iron fist of tsarism, there were large numbers among their compatriots who did not agree with their ideologies or approve of their rule.

In their clandestine activities, too, they had had practical experience of espionage work, for in order to outwit the Okhrana they had had themselves to engage in extensive undercover operations. Having had no professional instruction they had been compelled to gain a working knowledge at second hand or rely on common sense. Since common sense forms the basis of that special kind of security which is an essential ingredient of successful espionage, one would think that they would have been well equipped to set up an organization which would have all the merits of good espionage, and none of the demerits of traditional Russian espionage. That they did none of these things necessi-

tates a brief examination of the work they undertook as revolutionaries and a further consideration of what seems to be the
peculiar Russian approach to, or conception of, espionage.

Despite the often ludicrous activities of the Okhrana, the revolutionary party within Russia was consistently hampered by it
in its attempts to weld itself into a party of force and effective
action. The main difficulty was to discover who might be the
security agent who had succeeded in infiltrating himself into
their councils only to pass to his superiors all he could learn of
their identities and plans. The infamous double-agent, Eugene
Azeff, who began his career as an Okhrana *agent provocateur*
while still a student, gained promotion until he was regarded by
his chief as one of their most successful operators. At the same
time, and for more than twenty years, Azeff led the revolutionary
terrorist organization *Narodnaya Volya,* for whom he planned
assassinations and with his own hands made the bombs, subsequently betraying his trusting revolutionary colleagues to his
Okhrana masters.

There were others like him, though not so successful, and
together they discovered the identities of almost all the outstanding leaders—Lenin, Trotsky, and the Zhitlovsky husband-and-
wife team, for example. When these leaders were released or
escaped from prison or exile, it was necessary for them to seek
refuge abroad in order to be active at all.

These prominent men and women were joined by hosts of
lesser Party members who looked upon themselves as planners
or formulators of theory, as instigators of action rather than men
of action, who would plan and guide the destinies of the Party,
direct the Revolution and return to the Fatherland to take charge
of the country's affairs under the new order.

The wisdom of seeking a haven abroad from which to conduct affairs is really too self-evident to need more than a statement of its fact. The émigré groups congregated in most of the
European capitals, Vienna, Munich, Paris, Zurich and London
among them, and there set up bureaus.

As almost inevitably happens when a new movement, led by
single-minded men of purpose, passes from incipience to a more

mature stage of development, there sprang up within the Party in exile divergencies of opinion both as to formulas and to action. These need not be considered here, except that the differences made contact between groups a necessity, and between each group and the Party in Russia essential, for it was the Party in Russia which was to be the army of the Revolution.

This situation, then, called for the constant movement of couriers between groups, and between groups and Russia, and it was in this way that both sections of the Party gained their first experience in purely espionage activity. (The activities of the Party inside Russia were conducted along clandestine lines, admittedly, but such rudimentary security was observed that they cannot really fall into the classification of espionage activity.) It was of such great importance that messages from the émigré leaders should reach their followers in Russia, and for the reactions of the latter to reach the leaders, that all the precautions of the secret service courier had to be employed to ensure success. Of all the activities of this kind it was those of Lenin's *Iskra* organization which provided the most extensive and the most useful experience.

After his release from exile in Siberia after ten years, Lenin had escaped from Russia and made his way to Germany. Here he founded *Iskra*—"The Spark" from which the flame would spring—a newspaper in which he set out everything pertaining to Party affairs, particularly to doctrine. Tens of thousands of copies of *Iskra*—together with propaganda pamphlets, instructions, arms and explosives—were smuggled at irregular intervals across the frontiers into Russia, and, once successfully inside the borders, were distributed by chains of equally competent agents throughout the length and breadth of the country.

Nor was the experience of either section of the party confined merely to espionage activity. The Okhrana made constant and successful efforts to infiltrate the various organizations at home and abroad. Two outstanding examples of this success were the attendance of Okhrana agents, in the guise of delegates, at the Congress of the Russian Social Democratic Party in Zurich in 1897; while the chairman of the Revolutionary committee in Moscow in 1910 was a police agent named Kukushkin. The

Revolutionaries were aware of attempts by the Okhrana to join their ranks, and were constantly on the watch for such infiltrators, thus gaining valuable experience in counterespionage.

The Revolutionaries adopted the same tactics. They had many agents safely ensconced in all tsarist government departments, including the Police, the War Office and a great many units of the Army, many years before the hour became ripe for the Revolution to be launched.

Thus, when the time came, the new rulers could call upon a very large body of men practiced in espionage and counterespionage activities—though their experience was somewhat restricted—to form the nucleus of the first Soviet secret service.

As to the conception of the requirements of watchfulness which their situation demanded, those at the helm saw their country as vast, its population numerous, and their enemies an unknown quantity for the most part. Lacking really professional experience in this field, as in nearly every other aspect of government, they believed that a vast body of agents was required to protect them and the régime; and when the moment came, they called for an organization which, in this respect, outmatched the Okhrana itself, and that other organization notable for this same feature, the Prussian secret service of Wilhelm Stieber.

Among the founder members of the Bolsheviki, the "Old Bolsheviks," there was one man who stood out from all the rest for his experience in clandestine activities of all kinds. He was a former Polish aristocrat, the son of a great landed family, Felix Dzershinsky. He had first joined the movement as a student, becoming a member of the Socialist Revolutionary Party, which he left after a short time to join the ideologically more acceptable Social Democratic Labor Party. When the split between the Bolsheviks and the Mensheviks came in 1903, he cast his lot with the Bolsheviks, the faction of Lenin. It was to Dzershinsky that Lenin turned in 1917 to organize the formation of a secret service.

Dzershinsky's first task was to seal off all lines of communication. This he did so successfully that a number of members of the

Kerensky administration learned that neither they nor their party, the Mensheviks, were any longer in office only some hours after Lenin and the Bolsheviks had taken over.

From this moment on, Dzershinsky applied himself to his duties at a spanking pace. On December 20, 1917, just two months after he had taken up the reins, and six weeks after his party had seized power, he raised the status of the Security Sub-committee to the Extraordinary Commission for the Struggle against Counterrevolution and Sabotage. From the initials of the first two words of its Russian title—*Chrezvychaynaya Komissiya* (*Ch-K*)—it took its diminutive Cheka.

The functions required of the Cheka were twofold. It was to organize a political police force to keep in check the activities of all counterrevolutionaries (that is, everyone hostile to the new régime), and to organize an Intelligence service to counteract the activities of White Army spies, and the secret agents of foreign countries, such as Sir Paul Duke and Sir Robert Bruce Lockhart, and their fellow agents of the two main "intervention-ist" states, America and France; and second, to organize a secret service abroad. Such was the opposition to the régime within Russia, however, that the main effort of the Cheka in the first half-dozen years of Bolshevik rule had to be concentrated on the maintenance of internal security, with the result that the second objective suffered, and the organization of a foreign secret serv-ice was greatly slowed down.

Though this was a grave setback for Lenin's plans for a world revolution which would place Communism in the seat of power in every country, he did not allow any marking time. If the Cheka could not at once become an instrument of world revolu-tion, until it could an organization must be set up which would be a rallying point for all foreign Communists and prepare the way for the more intensive work of the Cheka when the time came. So it was that the Communist International, or Comin-tern, came into being in 1919. As a rallying point it was a flop, but as an organization for laying the foundations of espionage abroad it had a greater success, though even in this field it was not particularly remarkable.

The struggle with the White Russian forces came to an end early in 1922, and on February 11 of that year the Cheka was renamed the State Political Administration (*Gosudarstvennoye Politicheskoye Upravlenye*), the GPU, an organization which, in its time, was to be more feared than the Okhrana or Cheka had ever been. With its commitments at home lightened by the end of the Civil War, it began immediately to turn its attention to activities abroad.

For the next two years it was feeling its way in co-operation with the Comintern, but by 1924, coinciding with the Soviet Union's opening of diplomatic relations with Great Britain, it had established its networks and refined its organization so that Soviet Russian foreign espionage, on the scale to which we have now become accustomed, may be dated from this year. This development was marked by yet another change in its name, and it now became *Obiedinennoye Gosudarstvennoye Politicheskoye Upravlenye*, OGPU.

The OGPU operated for ten years, but when it was dissolved in July 1934, its functions were taken over by a department of the People's Commissariat for Internal Affairs (NKVD). This arrangement continued until five months before the German-Russian war broke out, and the department was raised to a Commissariat, becoming known as the People's Commissariat for State Security (NKGB). The NKGB, however, was short-lived, and exactly a month after Hitler's invasion of Russian territory, it was demoted and became a department of the NKVD once more. For eighteen months it functioned thus, and then in April 1943 it was once more elevated to a Commissariat; and when all Commissariats were renamed Ministries in March 1946, it changed its title from NKGB to MGB. After the fall of its infamous chief, Lavrenti Beria, following the death of his protector Stalin in 1953, the MGB was again united to the Ministry of Internal Affairs. This lasted for a year, and then in March 1954 it became a separate unit again under yet another new title, the Committee of State Security (KGB) and still functions as such.

Now, all these changes both in status and name did not affect its role, which has always provided something of a puzzle for the uninitiated in the democracies. In the latter, two distinct organizations, functioning individually and with a clear-cut division of responsibility, have been charged with the two complements of security: an organization for tracking down foreign spies operating inside the country (counterespionage), and an organization for maintaining espionage in foreign countries. Thus, in France the first is represented by the Deuxième Bureau, the second by Intelligence; in the U.S.A., by the FBI and by the CIA; and in Great Britain by MI5, which, despite its military prefix, is an autonomy responsible only to the Prime Minister (as is the case with the French Deuxième—at times the Cinquième—Bureau), and Intelligence, popularly known as the British Secret Service.

What strikes the Western observer as odd about the Russian system is that foreign espionage should be the responsibility of a department of state charged with the maintenance of *internal* security. The Russians have always argued, however, that their foreign espionage is not an external, that is to say, an offensive activity, but is designed simply to defend the security of the State; in other words, its activities are defensive. Logically this contention of the Soviet is not without foundation, but whatever the definition may be, and however the espionage organs are controlled, the final effect of the system is that it is no less productive of results than are the dual systems elsewhere. Indeed, a good case could be made out for its superiority over the dual system, for counterespionage and espionage both have a common basis; counterespionage merely sets spies to catch spies, and its spy-catchers use much the same methods of operation as the spies they are out to catch.

If it had ever been the intention of the Soviet leaders to promote their Secret Service on dualistic lines—which it never was —their experience of the Comintern's espionage activities would undoubtedly have persuaded them to think again. For not only did the Comintern fail to attract the workers of the world to the Communist camp in worth-while numbers, but the controllers and planners of Comintern clandestine operations showed themselves peculiarly inept in this aspect of their work.

Concentrating on the rapid take-over of power by the Communists in furtherance of world revolution, they supported uprisings in a number of European countries, all of which failed miserably, and ended in almost complete annihilation of Communist supporters by the forces of democracy and at least one other form of totalitarianism. These events—the suppression of the Spartakist uprising in Berlin; the overthrow of the Bavarian Soviet Republic, in three weeks; the collapse of the Béla Kun régime in Hungary; and the frustration by Mussolini and his fascists of efforts by the Italian Communists to provoke civil war—all added up to a formidable blot on the Comintern's copybook, so formidable that they gave rise to mounting uneasiness bordering on panic in Moscow.

It was at what must have seemed like a moment of dire peril for the world-revolution concept, that the collapse of the White Russian counterrevolution relieved the Cheka of much of the pressure put on it at home, and made it possible for it to turn its attention to activities abroad. Still under the over-all leadership of Dzershinsky, the newly established Foreign Department (INO) was placed under the direction of First Vice-Chairman of the Cheka, M. A. Triliser, a veteran Communist with long experience of underground operations.

The INO, under Triliser's keen eye and hand, moved in on the Comintern's field of operation, and gradually milked from it most of the purely Intelligence tasks which it had formerly undertaken. Eventually the only clandestine activities in which the Comintern was permitted to involve itself were the dissemination of propaganda and the provocation of agitation.

While the INO of the OGPU (as it had now become) was easing itself in, a certain transformation—meant at the time to be temporary—in the general Soviet approach to the non-Communist Powers was simultaneously taking place, a transformation which was to have an effect upon the consequent organization of the INO since it introduced new fields for espionage. The internal economic situation of the New Russia, and particularly the extremely grave shortage of food, compelled Lenin and his co-leaders to abandon some of the basic principles of revolutionary Communism. Between three and four thousand factories were handed back to private ownership, and, to assist in the reorganization of industry, foreign capital was to be attracted and the aid of foreign technicians sought. In the train of this policy, trade with the capitalists who were to supply the money and the technical know-how automatically followed, and this, as will be explained more fully in due course, opened new avenues for INO activity.

But the abandonment of isolation also had to bring with it the creation of diplomatic missions abroad, as well as the appointment of trade delegations, and here, too, the OGPU saw opportunities. The Comintern could never have made use of these opportunities—it was not designed to—but the INO could. However, despite the fact that the INO now took over Comintern agents, it took time to organize the new *apparats*, and two years passed before the INO could swing into action on a wide front.

From 1924, however, it can be said that Soviet espionage has never looked back. Conceived on a vast scale to aid a world-wide concept, in sheer numbers the Soviet secret service has, until recently, outpaced every other national espionage agency. (It would seem that the CIA is now numerically equal to it.) Its results, at least until the last decade and a half, were startlingly incommensurate with the effort made, for it achieved no really major coup until the treachery of Nunn May and Fuchs allowed it to present its government with atomic secrets which wiped out a ten-year lag in nuclear technology. It was the existence of so immense an organization, and its apparently feeble operation, which led the non-Communist Powers to despise and deride the Soviet attempt to spy; and it was this derisive attitude which led those same Powers into the great error of not keeping a watchful eye on the standard of Soviet espionage achievement and made them careless of their own standards of counterespionage.

This attitude has now changed; the shock of humiliation is an effective transmogrifier. Now the "menace of Soviet espionage" is a manifestation of a hyperwariness of Russia's hidden power. But while awareness is a good and necessary thing there are some who see in the current sensitivity a danger to be watched, for out of it emerges a fear which threatens to curtail man's fundamental liberties, and in the process prepare the ground for the fulfillment of the original Leninist concept of a Communist world more surely than by the acquisition of a Soviet spy ring of the most secret of secrets.

Lenin hoped to achieve the rapid fulfillment of his heart's desire. When he saw that this was not to be, he was not tempted to abandon his views altogether, but prophesied that world Communist domination would be achieved in time. As an agent for the completion of these designs Soviet espionage has today assumed an outstanding role, a role which it has built up over forty years. But forty years is a mere split second in the history of mankind, and the achievement is, therefore, correspondingly remarkable.

The true nature of the pinnacle on which Soviet espionage stands today can be seen only if its progress upward can be followed; and it is this which the present account will attempt to do.

Before we advance, however, to a consideration of the specific activities by which the rising progress was made, it is necessary to become acquainted with the spadework which dug the foundations on which the pinnacle rests; such mundane matters, for example, as organization, recruitment and training and at least one more colorful component of this uniquely based secret service.*

* In this book I shall be recounting the history of the OGPU, the NKGB, the MVD or the KGB—whichever it was called. But to forestall my more critical readers I feel I must reveal that I am aware of the existence of another, and very important, Russian espionage organization. This agency is the Fourth Department of the General Staff of the Red Army, more widely known as the Chief Intelligence Administration, the GRU.

This department was created by Trotsky when he was Commissar for War between 1918 and 1925, and was intended by him to be the chief Intelligence agency of the Soviet Union.

It very closely resembles the military Intelligence departments of other Powers, using the various Service attachés and their staffs as its main agents.

The superiority of the GRU over other espionage agencies was never achieved, and the organization with which I am concerned was always considered the main agency. The GRU did not become really prominent until the Second World War made the gathering of truly military intelligence essential.

But here again we come upon a somewhat strange state of affairs. The dividing line between the GRU and the KGB—to use its present style—has never been clearly defined, and there are many instances in which the activities of the two organizations have overlapped.

The KGB has always been considered the "master" agency. It has had the right to screen the personnel of the GRU, and has maintained its own informers within the ranks of the GRU; while the GRU is denied reciprocal rights with regard to the KGB.

The Army has been loath to accept this position, but has been able to do nothing about it; but it has constantly set itself up in rivalry against the KGB. The only period in which there has been any co-operation between the two agencies was during the Second World War. As soon as the war was over, the KGB quickly won back its superiority. It is because the KGB has always had this superiority that I have concentrated on it; but there will be one or two cases in which I shall refer to the activities of the GRU, and when this happens I will identify them.

☐ Organization and Administration

The organization of the KGB has been built up over the years, as the scope of activities increased and experience made clear what was necessary for the carrying out of policy laid down from time to time, and the steps necessary for the achievement of the ends demanded by the hierarchy. At various times in the last forty years there have been changes, but these have had little effect on the over-all functioning of the organization, except perhaps in operational efficiency, and though it is not possible to give a detailed description of the setup as it is today, the broad outlines of the main organization—which is all that is needed for our purpose of making the accounts of activities which constitute the greater part of this book comprehensible—can be given.

The headquarters of the Soviet secret service—colloquially known as the Center—is divided into two directorates, each led by a director who has deputy-ministerial rank.

The First Directorate, as it is called, is roughly analogous with the Intelligence agencies found elsewhere; but the Second Directorate is indigenous only to Soviet Russia.

Though the First Directorate has the subtitle of the Directorate of Counterespionage, its functions are—somewhat paradoxically to Western ears, for reasons set out in the previous chapter—to employ agents abroad to collect strategic and general intelligence, and to co-ordinate the activities of and assess the results achieved by the much smaller and more specialized Intelligence agencies of the Ministry of Foreign Affairs or External Trade, among other activities.

The First Directorate is divided into six main divisions, of which the first is the Foreign Division, whose functions make it the most important. It controls all secret agents, sets the tasks, and assembles the results returned by the networks. In addition, it directs Intelligence research and disseminates the information collected.

The second division is the Operational Division. Under the guidance of the Foreign Division, it directs, as the name implies, the actual operations of the agents, controls the networks, selects the agents to be sent abroad or advises about the recruitment or otherwise of potential agent material which its recruiting officers abroad submit to it. It maintains special agents in every Russian Embassy, Consulate or other official mission or delegation abroad. It maintains contact between the networks, where this is necessary; and it organizes communications.

The Communications Division is responsible for the practical maintenance of communications. In addition, if an agent is compromised and must make a rapid departure from the scene, or if he escapes after arrest, this division organizes the escape route. It was this section of Soviet Intelligence which arranged the escape routes of Pontecorvo and of Burgess and Maclean to Russia.

The Secret Division is in fact the documentation service. It is its function to supply every kind of forged document an agent is likely to need, and for this purpose maintains what must be the most extensive collection of genuine documents in existence.

Besides its forgery department, it can produce any uniform, map or badge it may be asked for. One of its sections is responsible for preparing "cover" stories; while yet another provides the necessary codes, secret inks, microdot apparatus and radio links which agents may require.

The Information Division does exactly what its name suggests. It collects every scrap of information on the social, cultural, economic and political situation that it can lay hands on, in every country in which it operates. Every newspaper, down to the most obscure journals, is read by it; rumors are collected and sifted; and it listens to broadcast programs on a world-wide scale.

The most interesting section of this division is undoubtedly the Index, which is probably unique, at all events in so far as its detail goes. The Nazi Gestapo had much the same kind of organization, but it was not nearly so detailed or so all-embracing as the KGB's Index.

The Index is a vast collection of biographies of everyone who might, even very remotely, be of use at some time or another to Soviet espionage. Besides information about parentage, place and date of birth, education and educational achievement, career, family details, friends, and the usual items which might be useful in gauging the background and intelligence of a man or woman, a record is also kept of a man's political views and affiliations, his relations with his employers, his financial circumstances (how much he earns, whether he owns an automobile or a house, and so on), his debts (most important), whether he is a good family man if married, or a philanderer whether married or single, if he drinks, and how much, whether his wife has any influence on his actions, and all the "dirt" which can be raked up about him, which is almost as important as a full account of his debts or of his political leanings and maturity of judgment. The main object is to discover weaknesses as well as strengths, since weaknesses may be played upon or used as blackmail to induce a reluctant collaborator to collaborate.

The Index was first introduced into the Russian secret service by the Okhrana, when it was trying to keep the Revolutionaries in check, and it was copied by the Revolutionaries in their attempt to assess loyalty of members and ferret out possible Okhrana infiltrators. It was taken up and expanded by Mikhail Triliser when he became the first chief of the INO. In the two decades before the 1917 Revolution he had been in charge of the Party's archives. From Triliser's comparatively small beginnings, it expanded until it became the most potent weapon in the hands of the notorious Beria, and the basis of his tremendous power over all the other members of the Soviet hierarchy, Stalin not excepted.

The Index contains the names and particulars not only of men and women who might be of possible use to Soviet espionage, but of those, too, whose integrity is complete and whose loyalty to their own country unswerving. This may be taken as an undeniable sign that the doctrine of world domination is still an important tenet of Communism, if such a sign were needed. If, and when, the world revolution takes place, it is these men and women of integrity and loyalty who will be the first victims of the purge which must follow.

It is estimated that at least two hundred and fifty people are employed in keeping the Index up to date. Its accuracy in all its factual information has been testified to on many occasions.

The sixth and least important Division of the First Directorate is the Recruiting and Training Division, the work of which will be referred to in subsequent chapters.

The Second Directorate, as has already been indicated, will not be found to have a counterpart outside Soviet Russia or its satellites, for the simple reason that the greater part of its functions would not be tolerated in a democracy.

The Propaganda Division possesses functions which its innocuous name tends to conceal. Its main aim is to weaken, disrupt and eventually destroy the forces of law and order in the non-Communist states, and thereby pave the way for Communist government. To this end it maintains contact with national Communist Parties, and is particularly active where these Parties have been suppressed by official action. It employs its own agents whose main tasks are to gather political intelligence and to create subversive groups which will come into action when necessary, and while waiting will work quietly but ceaselessly to undermine the existing order.

The Individual Division is the alter ego of that section of Internal State Security which keeps a check on the reliability, according to Party requirements, of Soviet citizens resident at home. This division keeps a similar check on the reliability of all Soviet citizens working abroad, from ambassadors down to embassy chauffeurs (who may even be high-ranking members of the First Directorate's Foreign Division). Every diplomatic and consular mission, every delegation, every party of athletes, actors, dancers, singers, musicians who travel outside the Soviet Union, has agents of the Individual Division attached to it. Sometimes these agents are made to look somewhat foolish, by such people as Nureyev, the ballet dancer, and others who escape from their supervision in order to seek political asylum. Agents of this division also keep surveillance on agents working for any of the other divisions and sections of Soviet espionage.

The postwar expansion of Communism to the countries of Eastern Europe is the *raison d'être* of the Allied Division. The security police and espionage services of Poland, Czechoslovakia, Romania, Hungary and Bulgaria are supervised by Russian representatives of the KGB. In the case of East Germany these departments are actually directed by Russian officials, and the same used to be true of Albania until the latter split with the U.S.S.R. over the question of de-Stalinization. Though each country carries out espionage on its own account, it operates also on behalf of Soviet espionage, with the effect of greatly increasing the scope of the latter's activity. In many instances intelligence gathered by agents of satellite nations goes direct to Moscow, and the country of origin of the agent may never become aware of it.

The Allied Division went into action on the heels of the Russian liberating armies. That it could do so was the result of long-term planning by the Russians, which provides a good example of the thoroughness and doggedness of purpose with which Communist world domination is pursued. It may be safely assumed that Russian secret service is already training men in every country who will be able, when the time comes, to step into positions of power, like Boleslav Rutkovski, Poland's first Communist President, Piotyr Groza, the Romanian Prime Minister, and Klement Gottwald, President of Czechoslovakia, who were all KGB-trained, and at some time had been active agents.

For a long time, also, Soviet espionage has been keeping a watchful eye on the Chinese through the Foreign Division of the First Directorate and the Allied Division of the Second Directorate, who have shared the responsibility for the control of the Chinese Section, which employs a number of Chinese Communists more Moscow-orientated than toward Peking. Outposts of the Chinese Section also operate in North and South Vietnam, Laos and Cambodia, while the outpost in Harbin, a traditional center of Russian espionage in the Far East, controls networks in Shanghai, Nanking and Fuchow, to collect and collate the information provided by networks in Japan and Formosa.

The fourth major division of the Second Directorate is the Special Division. This is one of the oldest departments of Soviet espionage, set up by Dzershinsky to liquidate the enemies of the Revolution by violence and murder in such obstinate cases where other forms of persuasion were not effective. Between 1932 and 1936 it was the personal instrument of Stalin for ridding himself of all opponents. In this role it was directed by Nicolai Yezhov. In the Second World War it was known as Bureau 1, and was responsible for carrying out Stalin's "scorched earth" policy in the face of the German advance. Because of its specialized functions it has always been an independent department, even since its formal incorporation in the OGPU-KGB, which took place during the reorganization of the espionage services under Genrik Yagoda in 1934.

The section responsible for the kidnapings and murders of deviationists and other potential enemies of Communism is the infamous Section Nine, the Section for Terror and Diversion. Though there is a grain of truth in the Bond image—that is to say, other secret services from time to time resort to murder and kidnaping to achieve their aims—the Soviet secret service is the only one which today keeps a special organization for the liquidation of its enemies, with the possible exception of Red China. Details of its work will be given in a subsequent chapter.

The operation of Soviet espionage "in the field" may be said to fall into two quite separate and watertight compartments, though the results of both compartments reach the same destination. The first is the members of embassy, legation and consulate staffs and the selected personnel of the many delegations, such as trade missions and cultural missions, which have always been a favorite Russian mode of maintaining relations with foreign powers.

The second is the independent networks and individual agents. These follow the classic lines insofar as the organization of the network is concerned; that is to say, a network will consist of one or two cells, operating quite independently of one another and unaware of each other's existence. The cell comprises three or four agents, each of whom will have his (or her) own particular function—collecting information, courier, radio operator and so on.

Between the Center in Moscow and all the espionage agencies operating in a certain country there is a key figure—the Resident Director. Though his actual powers are limited, he fills an important role, for he is a kind of central pivot, and the channel through which, with certain exceptions, all instructions and funds emanating from the Center are passed to the networks and lone agents, and through which a return service of all the intelligence gathered by all the networks is passed to the Center. He also has links with the Soviet Embassy and with the national Communist Party, through whom he maintains contact with the friendship and cultural societies which supply information of a general kind which would not ordinarily be termed intelligence. In a large country there may be two or more Resident Directors.

In most espionage organizations documentation is kept to the absolute minimum. If all written records can be dispensed with, so much the better. This principle is followed in the effort to maintain the greatest degree of security. In this respect the Soviet organization differs also. The Resident Director is required to keep a full record of all his transactions, the reason being that when he is superseded—and this appears to happen fairly frequently—his successor will have no difficulty in taking up the reins. This one aspect of Soviet spying is indicative of the general organization of the service, which is, fundamentally, a bureaucracy, a reflection of Russian government administration as a whole.

It is the vast amount of paperwork which is demanded from networks and individual agents that is partially responsible for the great numbers of agents of all categories found to be necessary to produce any information at all. Since all the paperwork produced by the networks must be studied if it is to have a *raison d'être,* headquarters must necessarily engage a staff of comparable size. It has been estimated that Soviet espionage as a whole employs about a hundred thousand operators of one kind or another. These include professional agents and all the back-room personnel required to keep them in the field. (The American CIA is reckoned to employ about the same number.) To the Russian service must be added, however, several hundred thousand amateurs scattered throughout the world upon whose services it can call in time of need. One expert has put this number at three quarters of a million, but suggests that even this vast figure may be an underestimate.

Actual figures, however, must always remain a matter of speculation. In any case, the Soviet espionage activity is world wide, and if achievement had been commensurate with numbers, by this time the world should have been entirely Communist. Fortunately for the non-Communist Powers, there have been flaws in the organization and training which have reduced successes to a handful of spectacular coups; on the other hand, taking Soviet plodding determination and almost oriental patience into consideration, it is suggested that the long-term effects of Russian espionage activity have still to be felt. Herein lies the danger; herein lies the need for constant vigilance.

☐ Recruitment

Soviet espionage, as we have already seen, presents many dissimilarities in its approach to its task, in its organization and in its activities, when compared with analogous organizations elsewhere. In the selection of its agents it presents yet another.

The employment of such vast numbers of agents naturally calls for a recruitment policy which will not be found necessary in smaller organizations. But this policy is assisted by the goals which Soviet espionage sets itself and by the ideological loyalty which Communism inspires, a loyalty which has a far firmer grip upon its adherents than democracy has upon its followers, since, compared to the vagueness of such democratic principles as freedom of speech, freedom of the individual, parliamentary government and so on, Communism lays down, with inflexible firmness, exactly where a man stands in his private life and in his relation to the State. There are no shades of Communism. A Communist in America or Great Britain or, despite the differences between the Chinese and the Russians, China, is fundamentally indistinguishable from the Russian Communist. This fact opens up possibilities for the recruitment of agents denied to other organizations.

The operatives of Soviet espionage fall into three categories. There is the hard core of professional, trained agents of Russian nationality; there is the foreigner whose sincere adherence to Communism has been tested over a long period and whose work presents him with useful espionage opportunities; and there is the third category of amateurs who can be called upon for specific tasks should the need arise.

Recruitment for the first category offers no difficulties. In every organized facet of Russian life—the armed services, the universities and colleges, the Workers' Faculties, in the Party organs, and particularly in the Young Communist League (Komsomol)—there are political commissars whose job is to keep a watchful eye on the "political reliability" of those citizens who come under their surveillance. This is the State's method of ensuring that no dissatisfaction gives rise to contagious defection; in other words, it assures the security of the Party and the administration, by making certain that no "weak" Communist is left in a position where he may influence others, and that only the best Communists obtain the best positions.

In addition to this main task, the commissar is required to keep his eyes and ears open for young men and women who might be potential agent material. When a commissar comes upon such a likely young man or young woman, he passes the information to the Division for Observation and Distribution. Somewhere or other, either in the Index or in the records of his local police office, there is bound to be a file upon him, and if a study of his dossier reveals that to his natural and personal qualifications he brings a family background which is also impeccable according to Communist standards, he will have passed the first stage.

He is now subjected to a month's special observation by a KGB agent attached to whatever institution he may belong. Up to the time that the agent reports upon him—and if the agent's report is against him—he will not know that he has been selected as a possible spy. If the agent's report is favorable, he will now be called before a Selection Commission. Here he will learn that he is being considered as a candidate for one of the KGB's departments, and in consequence of his conditioning he will greet the news with enthusiasm. There have been very rare cases where the candidate's reactions have disappointed the board. Not only is the candidate at once told that the interview is finished: his career is also finished; for his lack of enthusiasm has clearly indicated that he is fundamentally politically unreliable.

On passing the board, the candidate is told that he will serve a probationary period and undergo training, which may take anything from two to four years. He will still not be told that he is being trained as a spy, and he is not expected to reveal that he may have guessed what is in store for him. The first he will officially know is when he is posted to some fairly lowly post with a diplomatic mission abroad. His subsequent promotion will thereafter be subject to how he acquits himself at each stage.

This hard core probably represents five per cent of the operatives of the service. They are the backbone, the Resident Directors, the organizers, the men who give the orders transmitted by Moscow.

The second category for the most part is comprised of men and women of foreign nationality, who are loyal Communists, and who operate either in their own country or in a foreign country. The Index has classified them as politically thoroughly reliable, and they are recruited for a specific task for which their contacts and background make them suitable candidates. They have no choice in the matter of their selection; they are given orders and expected to obey them. If they refuse at this point, their membership in any Communist Party is denied them, and they can consider themselves fortunate if they are not liquidated.

The experience of Alexander Foote, the Englishman, who, after an outstanding career as a Soviet spy in Switzerland, renounced Communism and returned to respectability in England, illustrates this.

Foote, the son of an English middle-class family, was born in 1905. His early years of manhood, therefore, coincided with the unsettled and unsettling interwar years. He had had a good education, but the restlessness engendered by the insecurity of the times affected him, as it did so many other young men, and he drifted from job to job. Like so many other young men of his class and education, too, he drifted toward Communism, wherein he believed he saw a panacea for the ills of Western civilization. But though he attended discussion groups and meetings, he never joined the Communist Party. In fact, though he was to be a Soviet agent for ten years, he was never at any time a Party member.

When the Spanish Civil War broke out, he was received into the International Brigade on the recommendation of two prominent British Communists. There he was appointed battalion transport officer, but since he was not a Party member he was not given commissioned rank. In this capacity he served for two years and was then sent on leave to England to attend the Communist Party Congress, held at Birmingham in 1938.

Before going on leave, he had been told that when he returned it would be as the driver of a Red Cross truck which was to run between England and Spain at regular intervals, carrying medical supplies and comforts. In fact, he never returned to Spain, for when he reported for instructions to Communist Party H.Q. in King Street, London, after the Congress, he was told that a request had been received for someone to be recommended for a dangerous assignment abroad. The Party leaders had discussed a number of people, and their choice had fallen on Foote.

Though no one could tell him more than this, Foote accepted the proposal. Had he refused there is no doubt that that would have been the end of his association with the Communist Party. On reporting to an address in St. John's Wood, he was received by a respectable housewife who recruited him into Soviet Intelligence, though he did not know it and was not to make the discovery for some time. He knew that he was not working for the British Communists, but believed that he might be in the employ of the German Communist Party or the Comintern.

Following instructions given him by the housewife, he traveled to Geneva, and on the day following his arrival he made contact with a woman outside the General Post Office there. After contact was made, the woman introduced herself by her

cover name Sonia, and over coffee told Foote that further rendezvous would be made. At the final one of these, he was told
that he was to go to Munich to prepare political reports on
Germany, and at the end of three months to report back to
Sonia in Geneva.

When Foote's qualifications for espionage are considered, the
conclusion must be reached that they did not amount to much.
Before joining the International Brigade he had been a motor
mechanic and motor-bicycle salesman. He spoke no foreign language fluently, though he had some not very good French, a
little worse Spanish and a few elementary phrases of German.
When he went to Munich, and even subsequently, he had received no training in security, he knew nothing about codes or
secret writing, and he was quite inexperienced in operating a
radio transmitter.

On the credit side, however, he was a common-sense Englishman; and he had the ability to sum up a situation rapidly and
accurately. These must have constituted his appeal to the directors of the KGB; nevertheless, he could not be rated higher than
merely reasonable agent material. The assessment was confirmed by the results of his research in Munich and the correct-
ness and conciseness of the report which he submitted. This
assignment appears to have been a test; had he bungled it, he
would have been dismissed.

Shortly after Foote returned to Geneva, the Second World War
broke out, and Sonia was instructed to withdraw all her agents
from Germany. (Her real name was Ursula-Maria Hamburger, a
member of the German Communist Party, who, with her husband, Rudolf, had worked for many years as a Soviet agent in the
Far East and Poland. She was in charge of a network operating
in Germany, being based herself, for the sake of security, in
Switzerland.) She was to remain in Switzerland, however, and
instruct Foote and another Englishman, William Phillips, in the
arts and skills of radio transmitting.

Foote proved a painstaking pupil, and soon became proficient
in radio operating and in the mysteries of coding and decoding.

But apart from a little instruction in security procedure, this was the only training he received.

At this time the Soviet network in Switzerland was controlled by its Resident Director, Alexander Rado. Rado was a Hungarian by birth and a Communist of long standing, having been a member of Béla Kun's group. He was just nineteen when the Kun revolution failed, and he fled to Moscow where he was welcomed in the highest circles of the Comintern. Since that time, 1919, he had carried out extremely useful undercover work for Russia, and had been appointed Resident Director in Switzerland in 1936.

It was to Rado's network that Foote was assigned as soon as he was proficient in operating a radio transmitter. Now, but not until now, was he told that he was a member of Soviet espionage. There is no indication at all in his account which he published after his defection that the thought of refusing the dangerous work occurred to him.

Foote was so successful as an agent that in time he was promoted to be Rado's understudy as Resident Director. This, however, was due solely to wartime conditions, for since 1930 agents of the first rank have generally been Russians who have passed through one of the training schools. Rado owed his appointment in 1936 to the facts that he had been Moscow-trained and that he had a long and honorable record of Communist clandestine activity.

The amateurs of the third category are the Nunn Mays and the Fuchses, the George Blakes and the Vassalls, and, because they represent the greatest proportion of trapped agents, they are the more widely known to the general public.

There are two types of amateur which appeal to the Soviet spy master. The first is the man who is in a position to supply interesting and important intelligence and who has a good deal of sympathy with Communist ideals. The second is the man, also in a position to supply first-rate information, who has a skeleton in his cupboard of such hideousness that he will be susceptible to blackmail. The first are the Blakes; the second are the Vassalls.

The method of recruiting varies with each type. The first may already be connected with some group which openly professes sympathy with Communist ideas, though not with out-and-out Communism; friendship societies, cultural groups and so on. In this case the approach is simple. The "victim" is persuaded to join a study group, and here, without his knowing it, he is cunningly conditioned. If his reaction to the conditioning is satisfactory, by degrees the task for which he has been chosen is little by little put to him, and with such skill that one might almost describe it as subliminal. Then, when he has been fully "developed," frankness is brought into play, by which time the victim has been conditioned to double-thinking to a degree in which he sincerely believes that he will be helping his own country by betraying the secrets to which he has access rather than benefiting Soviet espionage.

Naturally, this kind of development can only be successful where the candidate is already in some sympathy with Communist ideals or is violently opposed to the form of government in his own country. Unless this sympathy is present before the attempt is begun, it will never be started.

There is little need to go into the method of recruitment of the second type in great detail. His weakness is exploited, he is placed in an extremely compromising position and then threats of exposure are made, with the alternative of pandering to the weakness if the candidate is sensible and agrees to co-operate.

Where the candidate in either group is not in contact with a fellow-traveling organization, efforts will be made to get in touch with him socially. The agents employed in this kind of approach have been specially trained in this art, and though they must many times fail to enroll their candidates by these means, they apparently regard such efforts to be well worth while, for they have been using the technique for many years, and were still using it a year or two ago.

The training which the amateur agent receives is merely a little instruction in the technique of making contacts and passing material. Their contact man will be a well-trained professional agent so that the likelihood of anything going radically wrong is very small. In any case, common sense regulates the greater part of the actual espionage activity which such a spy will be called upon to perform, and, as nearly all are intelligent men and women whose usefulness is likely to be limited to a fairly short period of time, the realistic view is taken that it would be pointless to involve this type of agent in a protracted period of training.

Where the potential usefulness of the agent is outstanding and the period over which he could operate if he were carefully trained could be prolonged beyond the average life of this type of agent, then more intensive training is given. Though it has never been revealed, everything points to the fact that Vassall, who had had no espionage experience before he began to operate for Soviet Intelligence, must have received this more intensive training. That he was able to evade discovery for the considerable period of eight years is a very strong clue in this direction. No amateur who had not been given more than the rudiments of espionage and especially security techniques could possibly have existed in the role for so long.

It is the trained professional nevertheless who contributes most to the success of Soviet espionage. The numbers of Russian nationals taken *flagrante delicto* spying are extraordinarily few. Only three come readily to mind: Valentin Gubitchev, who was Judith Coplon's contact man in America; Colonel Abel, who was detected by the FBI; and Gordon Lonsdale, who fell to the agents of MI5 and the Special Branch. It is safe to say that Gubitchev would never have been detected if Judith Coplon had not been suspected; Colonel Abel operated for nine years before the FBI got wind of his trail; while Gordon Lonsdale had to thank Harry Houghton's rank stupidity and his own carelessness for his downfall.

These facts compel one to the conclusion that the training given to the professional agents is thorough; and so it is. It nevertheless produces a kind of agent who would never be acceptable to the masters of British espionage, as we shall now see.

☐ Training and Technique

The candidates who pass the board of the Selection Commission fall naturally into two categories—those who are studying at some institute of higher education (university, technical college, officers' academy or NCOs' training school) and those whose education has been or is being completed at a Workers' Faculty or some other course of comparable standing, such as night schools in engineering, photography, radio, and so on. Those in the first category are automatically earmarked for advanced training (they will be required to finish whatever course of study they are engaged in at the moment, before beginning their espionage training); those in the second are given what is called intermediate training.

The advanced training recruit is destined to become a member of the élite corps of agents who fill the posts in embassies, become Resident Directors or the leaders of networks, the specialists given the task of obtaining intelligence of the highest importance. But the practice of espionage requires a number of back-room assistants, men who are never seen, who never engage in actual spying activity, but who are important elements all the same—the radio experts, the microphotography experts, the encoders and decipherers—since they are the technicians of the organizations. These roles are filled by the intermediate training recruits.

Quite rightly, the Center requires all its operatives in all categories to be young men in the best of health, and the physical condition of the candidate receives the first attention. His training, whether he is an advanced student or an intermediate one, begins with an intensive course of physical training at schools which specialize in this subject. Here his body is brought to the highest peak of physical fitness of which it is capable. At the same time he is taught elementary unarmed combat, the use of firearms, and such other practical subjects as automobile and motorcycle driving. Subsequently, at whatever school he may attend, he will spend a fair proportion of his time keeping his body in trim. Soviet espionage has produced some of Russia's leading athletes and sportsmen.

When his course in physical training has been completed, the recruit will begin his specialist studies. His subsequent role has already been decided by the Division for Recruiting and Training of the First Directorate, who will have taken into consideration not only his intellectual attainments, but such things as his physical appearance and any natural abilities he has been found to possess. Two general courses, however, must be completed by every candidate; one in the foreign languages assigned to him, the other in spying technique.

The courses which he is required to follow are provided by schools specializing in one subject. For example, if the recruit is destined for one particular country, he will become a student at the school which specializes in imparting the fullest knowledge of every aspect of that country, its politics or economics, the customs of the people and so on. Or, if he is to specialize in one aspect of espionage—the gathering of economic or technical intelligence, for instance—he will enter the school designed to prepare him for carrying out his special assignments as successfully as possible. If he is to become a radio operator or a coding expert, he will be drafted to schools which teach only these subjects.

In this respect, the Soviet system of training agents differs very little from those of other Intelligence agencies, except perhaps the British, who rely on the common sense and individuality of their agents to produce the results required to a degree which fascinates and appalls many another organization. If he requires technical know-how of one kind or another, radio operating, for example, the British will give their recruit just enough training to allow him to perform this function tolerably well; and he will also be given a little elementary information about the observance of security. For the most part, however, he must rely on his own initiative to produce his results, and the fact that the British service conceals behind its façade of true secrecy some of the greatest espionage coups in history indicates that this haphazard system of training suits the British temperament and flair eminently well.

The Soviet system, on the other hand—and in this it resembles very closely the former Nazi German, and even the Kaiserine German, system—produces such highly trained agents that if they are confronted by any situation not "in the book" they are totally unable to cope with it. The training systems of both Colonel Walter Nicolai and Dr. Elsbeth Schragmüller of the First World War and of all the various Nazi espionage agencies of the thirties and the Second World War, demanded absolute obedience to orders and in so doing produced agents who were incapable of using their own initiative. They lost countless spies from this cause alone.

But if the Nazis demanded absolute obedience, the Russians demand it in an even higher degree. The subservience to Party and State discipline controls the Russian's life in every aspect. The *Manual of Organization* issued by the Central Committee of the Russian Communist Party states: "The Party demands everything from these comrades. . . . The professional revolutionary cannot be demoralized. Nothing can shake him. Whatever is demanded of him, he will undertake it." And so well has the Soviet citizen been imbued with these principles and so conditioned by the punishments meted out for weakness or disobedience, that all initiative has been dissipated. He will obey orders, but if orders are not forthcoming he will not act on his own. Until 1941 this fear even operated in the Army. On June 21, 1941, when the German armies crossed the River Bug, the Russian units opposite sent urgent signals *en clair,* saying plaintively, "We are being fired on. What shall we do?" A day later the German troops found the vital Kodena bridge intact, and when they interrogated the Russian officer responsible for its defense, whom they had taken prisoner, and asked him why he had not blown the bridge as soon as the first German units came in sight, he replied, "I had no orders to do so, and I could not find a superior officer prepared to give me such an order without permission of Command."

The recruit, therefore, is conditioned to obey long before he is drafted into espionage, and since throughout all his training the strictest obedience is exacted from him, he emerges, at the end of it, a highly trained spy, but possessing several grave limitations. The minuteness of detail in which his training is imparted to him is designed to overcome these limitations, but probably in no other field of activity is the unexpected as likely to turn up as it is in the practice of espionage. Because he was untrained to cope with the unforeseen many a good Soviet spy has been lost.

And this obedience is underlined by yet a third general course which all recruits are required to follow: an intensive course in political indoctrination to which is attached a study of revolutionary activities designed to imbue the candidate with a patriotism *par excellence,* as a weapon against seduction by democratic ideologies and by Western ways of life; and to produce a body of men highly trained in subversive activity of all kinds who simultaneously with their espionage duties can, if the opportunity arises, further the aims of revolution.

It is not possible to say with certainty how many schools are maintained by the Division of Recruitment and Training, but it is thought that there are between twenty and thirty. The recruits are formed into small groups, and all the members of one group will be trained for one specific role. The group will keep together throughout training, and arrangements are made so that only one group attends at a time. The object of this is to restrict the agent's contacts to as small a number of fellow agents as possible; that is to say, it is a security measure.

Equally strict security measures apply within the group itself. Each agent is given a cover name by which he is known to the other members of his group and to his instructors. He is forbidden on pain of dismissal and dire punishment to divulge his own name to anyone. All letters coming to him at school are opened by one or two censors who alone know each student's true identity. They are read and, if approved, are passed on to the student without envelopes. Any letters he may write must be submitted to the censors, who undertake to pass them on if their contents are approved.

Once he has joined a school, the student may not leave it again on his own, but must go with other members of the group accompanied by a member of the staff. He may receive visits from two relatives once a month, and wives (the organization approves of married agents since wives and children provide excellent hostages for the good behavior of the agent working abroad) may attend the monthly dance given in the school hall. Girl friends, however, are not permitted to visit the school at any time; an embargo which seems to be the outcome of the impossibility of checking up on an individual in a short time. At the dances the hospitality is very generous, the object being to keep the student as materially happy as possible. To this end, students are relieved of all financial responsibility for their families and themselves, the family being paid a monthly allowance directly by the Ministry of the Interior, the student a small monthly allowance for pocket money.

Having completed his course satisfactorily, the student now becomes a probationer and is attached to a unit of the Security Police in Russia. During this period he will be required to undertake tasks which all help to give him practical experience and to break him gradually for his future work and life. He may, for example, be required to keep certain foreign diplomats under surveillance, or he may be required to become an Intourist guide to foreign visitors (to bring him into contact with the foreign bourgeoisie), or to attend parties of foreign Communists, or trade unionists, or delegates to conferences as guide and general factotum. He may also be sent to a customs or frontier guard post, where he will be subjected to tests and tricks, to test his practical reactions and his political reliability. He will also be sent on certain exercises to test his ingenuity, such as probing the security of an airfield or a plant engaged in secret work.

Safely through this stage, he is brought before another board. Here again the conditions of his service are read to him and he signs an oath to observe them. It has been made very clear to him that if he now breaks any one of the conditions of service he may forfeit his life and that a similar fate may overtake all his relatives.

He is now ready to go out into the field. He may be assigned to an embassy staff, or he may be sent as a replacement to a network. But whichever it is, he will have assumed not only a new name, but an entirely new identity. This latter he will have assimilated so completely that he may, in time, have some difficulty in remembering who he really is.

The network follows much the same pattern wherever it operates. It will consist of a number of cells, each of which is engaged on some specific task. At the head of the network is the Resident Director, who is the channel of communication between the Center in Moscow and the various components of the network. He receives the instructions for the network and passes them on to the cells and agents; he receives the money required to keep the network functioning (and is required to keep a very strict account of how he spends it); and all the intelligence gathered by the network is passed to him for onward transmission to Moscow. Contact with Moscow is by radio, though in certain circumstances it may be by word of mouth or letter, in which case a courier is used. Contact between the cell or agent and the Resident Director is through a go-between or cut-out, or courier. The Resident Director comes into contact with no one except his cut-out and his radio operator, though in the latter case he may, and frequently does, employ a cut-out to contact with the operator.

In peace time, except in times of emergency, the radio operator makes two wireless contacts a month—in the jargon, works two schedules—with Moscow. Sometimes he acts as the network's expert encoder, in which case he will receive the Resident Director's material *en clair* and encode it, though more often than not it will come to him already encoded in the R.D.'s own code. Neither code will be used by any other operative in the whole organization.

For long reports, microfilm is now being extensively used by Soviet Intelligence. This requires a microphotographer to be attached to the network. If the microfilm is used, it may be sent to Moscow attached to ostensibly innocuous letters transmitted through the ordinary post, or it may be sent to an address in a neighboring country for forwarding by the Military Attaché in that country by diplomatic bag. This contact with the Military Attaché is two-way, the center on occasion using it when direct wireless contact may be considered unsuitable, and for the passing on of funds.

Normally the agents are paid in the currency of the country in which they are working, but rates of pay are reckoned in American dollars. A Resident Director receives anything between $225 and $450 a month, according to the social position which his cover requires him to maintain. A radio operator may receive between $85 and $170 a month, but most other agents are paid by results. Occasionally an agent of long standing is put on a salaried basis. Bonuses are paid for special achievement. On the whole, the rates of pay are low; often, if the agent has an income from his cover occupation, he is allowed only the special expenses incurred in his spying. The Soviet has adopted this system in the belief—in many cases proved right—that nothing raises suspicion more quickly than a clerk or a journalist living above his income for that job. On the other hand cases have come to light when the payment of agents has been so high as to appear to be out of all relation to the duties performed. Vladimir

Petrov, who defected in Australia where he was a member of the Russian embassy staff, was paid the equivalent of £A450 a month, which is about the salary of the British Director of Security Services.

But if salaries are not paid out in the field, regular amounts are credited to the agents' accounts in Moscow. These can accrue, if the agent has a reasonably extended run of activity, to quite a sizable nest egg for when he has to be withdrawn from service, for it is over and above the allowances paid to his family if he is married.

The operation of the network on the ground will become clearer in subsequent chapters when the work of specific networks is described, but it will be useful here to give brief details of the practical functioning of agents in the field.

Despite the few outstanding cases—particularly the Lonsdale case—in which the lax observance of normal security precautions led to the detection of the network (Harry Houghton's [see p. 285] rash overspending in the public houses around Portland, and Lonsdale's own strange behavior in making personal contact with the Krogers instead of working through cut-outs) the Soviet insistence on security is almost obsessional.

The present writer must confess to having great sympathy with the Center's point of view in this connection. More spies have been caught through faulty security than for any other reason, and it should be totally clear to anyone who has made the slightest study of the history of espionage that the often irksome attention to security detail is repaid many hundreds per cent in immunity from detection. Nevertheless, however great the emphasis that should be placed upon security observance, the lengths to which Soviet agents are required to take it strikes one as fantastic. One might even be tempted to put forward the theory that it is this official insistence which in the long run causes even the most skillful agents to kick over the traces and rush headlong into ruin in so doing.

This insistence on security appears in every aspect of Soviet espionage operation, but it is probably best seen in the arrangements which are made for meetings between agents and contacts. These are, in any case, kept down to the minimum, but when they have to take place the procedure is minutely detailed.

The respectable housewife in the St. John's Wood flat, for example, gave Alexander Foote the following instruction for meeting his contact in Geneva.

"On the day following your arrival in Geneva, you will be outside the General Post Office exactly on the stroke of twelve midday. You will wear a white scarf outside your coat so that it is plainly visible, and in your right hand—not your left, remember—in your right hand you will carry a leather belt. A second or two after the clock has struck twelve, a woman will approach you. In one hand she will be carrying a string bag in which you will be able to see a parcel wrapped in green wrapping paper; and in the other hand she will carry an orange. The woman will come up to you and will open the conversation by asking 'Excuse me, but where did you buy that belt,' and you will reply, 'At an ironmonger's in Paris,'"—and it all fell out as Foote had been told it would.

The greatest insistence is placed on the agents' being absolutely on time for their rendezvous. If one fails to arrive exactly on time, the other must not wait lest he attract attention. Arrangements will have been made for a second attempt to make contact at a later date.

Nor is it only in making contact that security is absolutely insisted upon. To avoid frequent meetings of individuals, "postboxes" are arranged. These are places in which written information may be hidden by the agent and picked up later by the contact. Some of the "postboxes" devised by the Soviet service are so melodramatic that they seem to have been lifted from sensational fiction. In one case in Sweden, the postbox was a rusty tin can hidden in an out-of-the-way place on the outskirts of Stockholm. Sometimes the reference sections of public libraries are used; the agent marks up his message in code in a prearranged book, and the contact will enter the library later and copy the message from the book. Hairpins arranged in a certain way on a wire fence have also passed on a message.

Every aspect of a network's internal edifice and operation is so constructed as to conceal the identities of as many operatives as possible, and this is so successfully done that even if a network is exposed by a defector, the authorities cannot be certain that they have the complete network in the bag; indeed, it will be almost certain that they have not. Even though Igor Gouzenko brought a mass of documents relating to the atomic spy ring in Canada and the U.S.A. over with him, nearly eight years later the Ottawa authorities discovered the fact that a parallel network had continued to work unperturbed and undisturbed by the betrayal of Zabotin's network.

For all its strangenesses, there can be no room to doubt that Soviet espionage is today one of the most potent weapons not only of the U.S.S.R. but of the Communist world. It spreads its tentacles everywhere, and as each year passes it introduces into its armory new weapons all aimed at the eventual achievement of world Communist supremacy. If this aim is to be thwarted then the antidote must be applied stringently.

The application of this antidote is not, as might be at first supposed, the sole responsibility of the counterespionage agencies alone. In her summing-up of the Vassall Tribunal, Dame Rebecca West has written:

> The public should realize that the problem of security is now so acute that they must do their part in preserving their own safety. Parliament and the Press alike must abandon party interests and instruct the community with one voice in the extent and kind and possible effects of enemy espionage.

Our aim here is to do much the same. By studying Soviet espionage achievement in the past we may, it is hoped, acquire some idea of what to expect in the future, bearing in mind developments both in operating techniques and in political atmospheres.

PART II

Between the Wars

□ France

The reader in whose memory the events of the immediate post-First World War years have faded will probably recall with surprise that as early as 1922 the Soviet Union and Germany signed the Treaty of Rapallo, by which the two countries canceled their claims to war indemnities and offered each other the position of "most favored nation" in the economic sphere. The Soviet Union would have liked to include clauses arranging for military co-operation between herself and Germany, but this was thwarted by the intervention of France.

This intervention was for Russia just another unfriendly act toward her on the part of France. It had been with French arms and French financial assistance that Poland had been saved from becoming overrun by Russia and incorporated in the Union of Soviet Socialist Republics; it had been France who had engaged in an identical role in the protection of Romania and saved that country from a similar fate; it was France who dominated the European scene and who, besides these acts, made her opposition to the Soviet Union very plain. Not until Great Britain and Italy had done so did France grant diplomatic recognition to Russia.

Of all the Allied Powers who had been involved in the war,

France was being the most active in the development of munitions and aircraft, both of which the Soviet Union lacked, and the technical know-how of producing them. So, from the enmity which she exhibited and the military strength she was building up, France became a very desirable target for Russian espionage.

But between the decision to spy upon France and the implementation of that decision there was fixed a fairly wide chasm. Up to the establishment of an embassy in Paris, Soviet Intelligence had to rely, through the Comintern, on the French Communist Party; and herein lay the difficulty.

The independence which the Titoist and the Hodja régimes in Yugoslavia and Albania respectively exhibit today set them apart from the usual run of Communist régimes. It had always been the intention of the Russian Communist Party to direct the world revolution according to their own designs, and this entailed a complete subservience to the whims of Moscow of all the other national Communist Parties, in the same way that Satellite régimes today are required to toe the Kremlin line.

In the early period after the First World War the French Communist Party demonstrated, like Tito, that they had minds and ideas of their own. They were not a large Party, and they did not include in their membership enough men of outstanding intellect and Marxist-Leninist views to give the Party either strength or influence within a country in which the old institutions of government had not been influenced by the internal upheavals which had taken place in, say, Italy and Germany.

Of all the leading Parties of the International, the French Party was odd man out. Its delegates attended Congresses and subscribed to the resolutions passed, but this turned out to be merely lip service. On their return to France the delegates and their Party went their own way. Soon there were complaints from above that the Central Committee of the French Party was not following the line laid down by the Comintern, but these complaints had little effect on the French leaders, who were of the opinion that the International should be an alliance and not the subservient tools of the Russian Party.

As will be described in the following chapter, the advance post of Soviet espionage had been established in Berlin, and it was from Berlin that agents recruited by headquarters for work in Germany, Belgium and France were directed. At this time, the organization's lack of trained professionals made it imperative that the few—mostly Poles and Jews—should receive the assistance of the members of the local Parties. In this aspect of international Party relations the French held divergent views as well. Spying was contrary to the tenets of French trade unionism, and since it was in the factories that the information which Russian Intelligence so badly wanted was to be found, the response for subagents was not enthusiastic. This is not to say that there was no response at all; but it does explain why the achievements of Russian espionage in France at this time were not outstanding. In addition, the few men who did agree to co-operate were quite without knowledge of the skills and techniques essential to active spying, and the counterespionage agencies were professionals in the world class; a juxtaposition which made the situation even more unproductive than it might have been.

Among those who did agree to co-operate in the pre-1924 era were Henri Coudon and his mistress Marthe Morrisonnaud, who interested themselves in obtaining details of French aircraft. They had been operating only a few months when counterespionage arrested them in possession of a secret report on aviation problems. Another operating in the same field, and who had better luck, was Joseph Tomasi, general secretary of the Motorcar and Aircraft Workers' Union. He was not a full-time agent, however, and produced little intelligence, but he was able to avoid suspicion for two years, and when at last counterespionage did pick up his trail, he managed to avoid capture and reached Moscow, where he died in 1926.

The first breakthrough of significance came in 1924 when Jean Cremet, secretary of the St. Nazaire branch of the Shipbuilders' Union, a post which he held together with the secretaryship of the Metalworkers' Union, was selected as leader of the French network, which, up to this time, was a euphemism.

Cremet, who was also a member of the French Central Committee, was a "Moscow man," a fact which probably blinded the Russians to any other shortcomings he may have possessed.

For three years, without the knowledge of his Party colleagues, he organized what could truly be called networks in all the important targets all over France, in the munitions, aircraft and naval shipbuilding industries. Though by now the Soviet Embassy was establishing itself in Paris and the Russian direction of espionage in France was sheltering there, Cremet was regarded so highly in the Center that he visited Moscow to report personally, and his intermediate reports were sent by courier to Berlin, from where they were forwarded.

This arrangement lasted until late in 1925, when the Center appointed a Resident Director for France. The man they chose was an agent of some experience called Uzdanski, who had served in Warsaw and Vienna.

In Paris, Uzdanski adopted the cover of artist, and the cover name of Abraham Bernstein. His cut-out was a young Lithuanian student, Stefan Grodnicki.

The Center's instructions to Uzdanski were concise. He was to inform the French networks that every scrap of information connected with artillery and shells, aircraft, naval construction, troop movements and tanks was required in Moscow. It was a tall order, and its execution required the organization of extensive networks. Uzdanski, however, found that not only did Cremet's existing organization provide a firm foundation on which to build, but Cremet's contacts were so widely flung that almost single-handed he could produce the rest of what was needed.

All went well for about a year, and then Cremet ran into difficulties with an "orthodox" French Communist, a man named Cochelin. Cochelin, who worked in the arsenals at Versailles, was approached by Cremet and asked to supply information about tanks and explosives. The first time Cochelin refused to co-operate, but undeterred, Cremet made a second advance. Again Cochelin refused, but not quite so decisively as on the first occasion. It would appear that he had made up his mind that if he were asked again he would, despite his being a militant Communist, report the matter to the Ministry of War. This he now did.

The counterespionage service had already become aware that espionage was being carried out at the College of Military Studies at Versailles, and that the Russians were responsible. In view of the embarrassment that would inevitably be caused to the newly established Soviet Embassy if steps were taken, reluctance to act held the French authorities back.

But Cochelin's information was too serious to permit the luxury of considering the finer feelings of the Russians to be taken into account any longer. It was decided that when action was taken the evidence must be unshakable, and Cochelin was persuaded to help produce such evidence.

On February 5, 1927, Cochelin accepted a list of questions from Cremet; the answers were concocted by the Ministry of War, and passed to Uzdanski through his cut-out Grodnicki by Cochelin at a meeting near the Madeleine, which was observed by counterespionage. The French agents followed Grodnicki, who led them to Uzdanski, and both men were arrested. Over the next few days Cremet, his mistress, Louise Clarac, and their chief assistants were arrested.

The arrests created one of those scandals much loved by the French, and the affair served as a warning to other nations that the protestations of the Soviet government of friendliness toward other countries and a total lack of interest in any nation's internal affairs were meaningless.

Having uncovered the secret menace, the French Government decided that it could afford to be lenient with the culprits. But they seem to have misunderstood the comparative importance of the roles of Uzdanski and Grodnicki, for the latter was given five years imprisonment, while the former received only three. A similar light sentence was inflicted on Cremet and Louise Clarac, in their absence, for they had been able to escape to Russia.

The trial, which was conducted amidst great Communist outcries that the whole business had been fabricated in order to discredit the Party and Russia, had revealed the scope of Russia's espionage activities. Despite this, however, one network was untouched by the affair and continued to operate for another year.

This was a network which had been established in the printing works of the College of Military Studies at Versailles by Cremet, and which passed copies of every secret military document which came through their hands to Soviet Intelligence. They eventually came to grief because they had not the experience to judge the character of one of the men whom they approached for additional information about the Army and Air Force mobilization orders.

The corporal, who was offered money for the information, reported to the authorities, and the agent who had approached him was arrested. He confessed and revealed the names of all the other ten members of the network; that he could do so illustrates the ignorance of espionage techniques of these amateurs. Only the Russian who had taken over from Uzdanski escaped, and he only did so because he had followed espionage procedure and identified himself only by his cover name, Paul, and had even managed to disguise himself so that no description could be made to fit any known Russian.

Though the Soviet Union's prestige had received a heavy blow from the Uzdanski-Cremet affair, neither the Kremlin nor the Center saw any reason for discontinuing to spy in France, or elsewhere. Certain adjustments were made in organization—the embassies were to have no further dealings with national Communist agencies, for instance—but efforts to keep abreast with all secret developments were to continue.

To replace Uzdanski and Cremet there now appeared on the French scene a man whose true identity has never been discovered, though a good deal has come to light concerning his background. He was an Old Guard Bolshevik who had suffered exile in Siberia, and had engaged in clandestine activities for some years before the Revolution. In 1929 he was reputed to be in his middle forties.

He was the Paul to whom the network at St. Cyr had handed

the fruits of their labors. Later he was identified with a man who called himself General Muraille, but even this led to no clue as to his real name.

Being an Old Guard Bolshevik, he was strongly imbued with the concept of world revolution and all his efforts in the field of espionage were devoted to clearing the path to this goal. Since the French Party was not revolutionary enough for his tastes, he held it in slight regard, and it was probably this which prompted him to practice the espionage technique of strict concealment under cover names, revealing his identity to no one, for in his fairly long career he consistently evaded the watchful eye of counterespionage, until finally betrayed.

Paul's orders from the Center were identical with those which had been given to Cremet and Uzdanski—he was to discover all he could about the French military situation, with special attention to new weapons, particularly aircraft. Despite his own aversion to the French Party and Moscow's orders that the local Parties were not to be recruited for espionage, he found that without being able to call on his source of manpower he could not operate. So, with Moscow's permission, he contacted the leader of the French Party, Henri Barbé, to whom he explained that he had been assigned the task of selecting likely young people for a course of Marxist-Leninist study in the Russian capital. Having no cause to doubt him, Barbé put him in touch with youth organizations.

Within a short time Paul had set up networks composed of young men he found in the youth organizations, who had not the same outlook as their seniors and were ready to co-operate. Though he had his spies in aircraft factories and naval dockyards, it was the munitions industry centered on Lyons which interested him most. From the latter he was successful in obtaining blueprints of the newest designs for aircraft.

Paul did not, however, rely upon the younger generation entirely, and it was his association with an older Communist, Vincent Vedovini, who worked as an engineer in the naval arsenal at Marseilles, which led to his eventual discovery. Having completed several lists of questions for Paul, Vedovini decided, for idealistic reasons, that he had had enough spying, and handed the latest list to the police with information to enable them to identify Paul.

Paul, however, was forewarned and escaped abroad. In the spring of the following year, confident that he had the ability to escape the notice of French counterespionage, he returned to France, and was immediately arrested.

At his trial in September 1931, Paul denied that he had engaged in espionage, and, when asked to explain the documentary proofs which had been turned up by the investigation and Vedovini's evidence, he claimed that he was a writer and had been merely collecting information for a novel. The court did not believe this, and sentenced him to three years. On his release, he returned to Russia and was lost sight of.

As a result of this case Henri Barbé was summoned to Moscow, where an attempt was made to induce him to take over espionage activity in France. This he firmly refused to do, saying that it was not an activity in which French Communists believed they should indulge. He held out against all persuasions and arguments; but in so doing he rang his own knell. Within a short time he was replaced by Thorez and Duclos, who were Moscow men.

Under Thorez and Duclos, a system was evolved for gathering information by a means already proved in Russia, though used for quite different purposes. When the Communists took over the reins of power in Russia, they suppressed all the old newspapers and founded new ones. With the old papers went also the old journalists, and the new papers discovered that they had insufficient sources of information. To supply this lack they instituted a scheme called Workers' Correspondents (Rabcor), under which anyone who wished could send to the newspapers any item of information which it was thought would interest them.

A Rabcor system was now inaugurated in France, and the correspondents were encouraged to submit every kind of information, especially that dealing with the French war industry. The information received was carefully sifted and all those items which had particular interest to Intelligence were sent to the

embassy, while the harmless ones were reproduced in the newspapers. This proved a most useful source of Intelligence information.

In this Rabcor activity a young Communist student called
Riquier was appointed by Duclos to the staff of *L'Humanité*, the
French Communist newspaper, to act as sieve and go-between
with Soviet espionage. The latter was now being led by a Pole,
Izaia Bir, who, having been exiled from his native land, had gone
to Toulouse to study engineering, and had then been drawn into
the Soviet net. Bir's lieutenant was another Polish émigré, a
young man in his middle twenties called Alter Strom, who had
first come to Paris in 1929.

Under the direction of these two men the Soviet organization
in France quickly made good the damage which the Paul affair
had wreaked, and their success was based almost entirely on the
information supplied by the unsuspecting Rabcor.

Nor was it only the worker-correspondents themselves who
were ignorant of the uses to which their information was being
put. For a long time Riquier, the go-between, did not suspect
that he was engaging in espionage; but when it did suddenly
dawn on him in February 1932, he immediately got in touch
with the police.

Co-operating with the police, Riquier continued to work on
L'Humanité, as though nothing had happened. But in the meantime, the police went to work to discover as much as they could
about the organization, and when they decided they had enough
evidence to break it up, they provided Riquier with certain documents to plant on Bir, who was then arrested with them in his
possession. Duclos took the hint, and fled abroad, where he remained until granted an amnesty in 1933.

Bir was sentenced to three years' imprisonment, and his French
accomplices to a year. His lieutenant, Strom, also received three
years.

Disasters like this were, it would seem, now taken for granted
by the Center. They certainly did nothing to reduce the espionage effort in France, and though their agents were constantly
coming to grief, there was no apparent difficulty in replacing

them. The French, too, were also becoming a little bored by the seemingly ceaseless trickle of spy trials which the newspapers reported, and were no longer scandalized by them. The counter-espionage authorities, however, maintained an unbroken watch.

But while this stream of agents passed across the French screen, one or two outstanding networks were being built up, composed of agents of an entirely different caliber from the Pauls and the Birs, agents who profited by the lessons which the Center had learned from the disasters of the late twenties and early years of the thirties.

Outstanding among these new agents were several who held American passports, like Chkalov, alias Lydia Stahl, a Russian by birth, who had emigrated to the United States at the time of the Revolution, became naturalized, and who, when her only son died in 1919, returned to Europe, where she settled in Paris. There she came into contact with Communists and was won over; before long she was engaged in espionage for the Soviet Union until she was brought to grief, together with the other members of her really professional network, by the defection of an American, Robert Switz.

Switz was the son of a wealthy American family, a dilettante of unformed idealism until, attracted by Communism, he gravitated toward the Greenwich Village leftist pseudo-intellectuals. Here he was skillfully indoctrinated, and when pronounced converted, was invited to become an agent for Soviet espionage in America. After a trip to Moscow in 1931, he married a nineteen-year-old girl, Marjorie Tilly, who not only agreed to work for the network of which her husband was a member, but very quickly became one of its most important members.

Both were trained in photography so that they might replace Lydia Stahl, who had been operating in the United States since 1928 but was earmarked to return to Paris. In July 1933, the Switzes followed Lydia to France, for the accession of the Nazis to power had necessitated a reorganization of the Berlin center and the consequent reorganization of the leading networks operating in Western Europe.

Markovich, who was Resident Director of the French networks, though he operated from Berlin, visited Paris in the following month to explain the reorganization to Switz and to give him his tasks. By this time, however, the French counterespionage had discovered the espionage role of Lydia Stahl through the confession of one of her friends, Ingrid Bostrom, who had been arrested in Finland. During their investigation of Stahl's background, they had discovered the existence of her network, and because Switz had made contact with her soon after his arrival, he too was watched, and his meeting with Markovich observed. As the role of Markovich was also known, the French authorities decided to pounce while they could lay hands on him. He managed to escape, however, but the remainder of the network, including Stahl, the Switzes and other leading agents, were arrested.

Though most of the agents had been found in possession of compromising material, the French still did not believe that they had enough evidence to satisfy the courts, and for the next three months they continued their investigations. Then one day two parcels of film were left at the French Consulate in Geneva by an unknown person, and on the films were found Switz's fingerprints.

Confronted with this, Switz decided to talk. He had already begun to be a prey to disillusionment, and he saw no reason why he should suffer for a cause in which he no longer wholeheartedly believed. He made a full confession, and five others followed his example, with the result that twenty-nine agents were arrested and the networks entirely smashed.

As relations with Russia had now changed considerably, the French Government decided that it would be a grave embarrassment if a *cause célèbre* were made of the affair. So the trial was held in secret and light sentences imposed, the Switzes being allowed to go free for the help they had given to the authorities.

During the late twenties and early thirties, the prominent role which France had filled on the international stage had begun to dwindle, and soon French internal politics had reached that point at which Will Rogers could state that his chief diversion in Paris was to go to the Quai d'Orsay to watch the Government change. French military developments were also beginning to lag behind those of Britain and America, and in any case, the presence of French Communists in the French Government made espionage scarcely necessary.

A far more worth-while target was, therefore, the rival totalitarian Germany, since it was likely to be a potential enemy, and the more rewarding United States. For these reasons Russian espionage activity in France was reduced to negligible proportions.

☐ Germany

To the Soviet leaders in 1918, the achievement of world revolution was not a long-term ideal, but one to be attained as quickly as possible. In the confusions which overtook such a large part of eastern and southeastern Europe after the armistice they believed the ground to be already prepared for a speedy victory, and nowhere did this seem more likely than in Germany.

The German proletariat had had a record of clandestine activity which, in length of time, almost equaled that of Russia, while in the more militant field, inspired by the second French revolution, they had led the Russians. Though the attempt to throw off the autocratic yoke of the Prussian domination failed, the German Socialists remained throughout the next half century potential revolutionaries.

This became clear in the first month of the last year of the war, when popular risings broke out in Hamburg, Munich and elsewhere, and though these were temporarily put down, the revolutionary movements gathered momentum between January and November 1918. On October 3, 1918, when defeat had become a certainty and the despair of the masses had reached the danger point, another kind of bloodless revolution gave

Germany her first parliamentary government under Prince Max of Baden. It brought Socialists into the cabinet, but could not prevent the proletarian revolt which had been simmering underground for so long.

This revolution, which started by creating workers' and soldiers' soviets on the Moscow pattern, was inspired by the *Spartakusbewegung* (named after Spartacus, who led the Servile War against Rome in 73 to 71 B.C.), a group of extreme left-wing Socialists. Influenced by the success of the Bolshevists in Russia, the Spartakists attempted to set up a proletarian dictatorship. But the less extreme Social Democrats found support from the bourgeois elements and what was left of the armed forces, and the revolt was rapidly crushed by force.

After the deaths of the Spartakist leaders Karl Liebknecht and Rosa Luxemburg at the hands of Noske, the right-wing Socialist Minister of the Interior, in 1919, the movement lost drive and impetus. Nevertheless, out of it grew a strong German Communist Party. Though the Spartakist attempt was the most serious one, and might have succeeded had they had a better organization, during the next eighteen months or so the German Communists kept up attempts to persuade the proletariat to seize power. These efforts were unsuccessful because any force they might have had was dissipated by the outbreaks of violence being un-co-ordinated, and the government had little difficulty in suppressing them with bloodshed.

But the government itself was running into difficulties of another kind. When the terms of the Versailles Treaty were presented to it, the Democrats refused to sign, and the Cabinet resigned. However, the Socialists and the Roman Catholic Center Party were able to form a coalition, and the Socialist Müller, and Bell of the Center, put their signatures to the Versailles Treaty.

The national assembly, which, since the election of the constituent assembly in 1919, had met in the theater at Weimar, now moved to Berlin, and the Democrats rejoined the government. For the next nine months there was comparative peace, and then there was an attempt by irregular armed forces, known as the Kapp *Putsch*, to seize Berlin on March 13, 1920. The members of the Cabinet, however, escaped to Stuttgart, and from there they frustrated the reactionary attempt by proclaiming a general strike. A Communist revolt in the Ruhr followed, and because in its suppression German forces had technically infringed the armistice terms, French troops occupied Frankfurt. This was the last serious outbreak, though the life of the nation was to be punctuated for some time to come by great industrial unrest, which at times broke out into violence.

Considered against this background, it is not surprising that the Soviet leaders, firm in the belief that world revolution was only just over the near horizon, should see in Germany an attractive place for establishing an advance post from which revolutionary activity might be planned and from which espionage activity might be directed against Western Europe more effectively than from more distant Moscow. In the last chapter we saw how the Center in Berlin controlled espionage in France; but this was only secondary in importance to that which it directed in Germany itself, for, though France was the leading European power at this time, Germany presented other attractive possibilities, possibilities in which the Soviet Union, making desperate efforts to establish an industrial life, was more selfishly interested.

Russian aims in Germany, therefore, were twofold: to do all it could to bring about a Communist-controlled state, and to obtain every scrap of information it could about the industrial developments by which the technically minded Germans were trying to rebuild their shattered country. It was to further these aims, and as a temporary measure to gain a friend in a friendless world, that Russia suggested the re-establishment of diplomatic relations in 1920, and which, two years later, led to the agreement at Rapallo. These two events were to make possible the quite formidable espionage successes which Russia was to achieve in Germany until the coming of the Nazi era. Without them the achievement could not have been half so great.

The period of greatest effort may be set at 1920 to 1925. It was, perhaps, a coincidence that this period saw Soviet espionage organization and methods emerge from its amateur status into the flowering of the highly professional agency which has been described in Part I. Because of the aims of the Soviet leadership to set world revolution on the firm basis of a Communist Germany, the GRU, the military Intelligence agency, was more active here than elsewhere.

Military espionage had two lines of activity, one of which cannot, in fact, be termed espionage at all. This was the Russian plan to direct the organization of a new German Army. Former German officers were to be won over to the Russian side, and these were to form the nucleus of the new army. Germany was divided into six military districts, each in charge of a German Communist assisted by a Russian adviser supplied by the Center. The goal of the district organization was to build up an underground military force which, when fully ready, could emerge, join with the Russians, impose a Communist régime upon Germany and then confront the rest of Europe. It was a novel and well-thought-out plan, but it collapsed in October 1923 when the strikes and risings of that month found the German forces overwhelmingly loyal to their government. Cutting their losses, the Russians rethought their approach to military espionage, and there shortly emerged a new military agency with instructions to gather real military intelligence and to operate on proper espionage lines.

For the next few years this plan was strictly adhered to, and though the initial successes were not outstanding, except in the volume of information obtained, the last two or three years before the advent of the Nazis brought some really worth-while results. The sphere of the Soviet Union's greatest interest in the military field was here, as it had been in France, the aircraft industry, in which important strides were being made.

To build up a concentrated effort in this field, a leading Soviet engineer, Alexandrovski, was sent to Germany in 1927 to collect every scrap of information about the aircraft industry that could be obtained. Even before he arrived, he had an important contact in the industry, a young aircraft expert called Eduard

Ludwig, who, in 1924, had worked in Junkers' Moscow office. During his stay of about a year, he had been contacted by Soviet Intelligence who had held out promises of reward if, on his return to Germany, he would co-operate with them. This he agreed to do.

On going back to Germany in 1925, he left Junkers after a short time, and took a job with Dornier, where he remained just long enough to learn exactly what was happening there, and their future plans, before taking a post in the Aeronautical Research Institute in Berlin. By 1927 he knew all there was to know about the German aircraft industry, and when Alexandrovski arrived in Berlin he was prepared to receive his instructions.

Unfortunately, or fortunately according to which side one views it from, the co-operation did not last long. Alexandrovski's go-between with Ludwig was a Latvian called Scheibe, through whom the Russian engineer asked the German expert to supply him with documents relating to secret aircraft engines from the files of the Aeronautical Research Institute. Ludwig complied, handed the documents to Scheibe, who passed them to a man called Ernst Huttinger to be photographed. But before the copies could be made, the authorities at the Institute discovered they were missing. The subsequent investigation led them to Ludwig, and in July 1928 he, Huttinger and Scheibe were arrested. Alexandrovski made good his escape.

The German authorities discriminated between military and industrial espionage, and treated the former as meriting severe penalties. So, Scheibe was imprisoned for six years, Ludwig for five and the photographer for three.

A number of cases of lesser importance now began to reveal to the German authorities that the Russians were conducting military espionage against them on a wide scale. They were embarrassed by it, because since 1925, under the Soviet plan to attract the help of foreign technicians to help organize Russian industry, collaboration between the two countries had become increasingly close. Nevertheless, friendship cannot justify the making of important national secrets a free gift, and the German counterespionage service maintained an unremitting alert, pulling in a bag of smaller fry over the next year or two.

Their next important coup they brought off in 1931, as the result of the defection of a Communist writer called Hans Schirmer.

In 1928 the Germans had laid down the keel of the first cruiser to be built under the terms of the Versailles Treaty. Since its size was restricted, the naval ship designers had spent many years' study so that the new ship should make up for lack of tonnage with the latest technical developments. The cruiser was an obvious target for Soviet espionage, and as early as the spring of 1929 one small cell of Russian agents had been uncovered.

For the next year German counterespionage made no discoveries, and quite possibly might never have done so but for Hans Schirmer. In February 1930, Schirmer, very unwisely it could have turned out, wrote a letter to "The Chief of the Espionage Division, The Communist Party Center, Hamburg," in which he claimed that as a former worker in the Hamburg naval dockyards he was able to supply information of interest which he could obtain through the contacts he still had in the yards.

Somewhat oddly, he received a reply asking for more information before contact was made with him. This he refused to give except face to face, and it was eventually arranged that he should meet a man called Herbert Sanger.

Sanger was the cover name of Lothar Hofmann, a Russian agent of long standing, who, when the German counterespionage had arrested the first cell, had been assigned to Hamburg to organize a successor. He was a professional spy, and while this accounts for the immunity of his group for nearly eighteen months, it makes his contact with Schirmer somewhat difficult to understand.

At their meeting Hofmann told Schirmer that "they" already had good contacts in the docks, though they could do with information about the political leanings of naval officers and men. No conclusive arrangement had been made when the two men parted, though Hofmann did give Schirmer an address to which he could write, instead of the dangerous method he had used to make initial contact.

Months passed, and Schirmer heard nothing from Hofmann, and this cold-shouldering appears to have upset the writer, for in October 1930 he went to naval counterespionage and told them of his contact with Hofmann. He also made them an offer to co-operate with them to expose Hofmann, and this offer was accepted.

On the instructions of counterespionage, Schirmer wrote to Hofmann and told him that he was now in possession of documents of great interest. Hofmann rose to the bait, and over the next few months he met Schirmer to receive the faked documents provided by counterespionage. In the meantime counterespionage had uncovered Hofmann's activities and discovered who his agents were, and in May 1931 they pounced, and arrested the lot. Their success, however, came too late to undo the harm which the network had done, for in the two years in which they had been active every detail of the new cruiser had been passed to the Russians.

Outstanding among the successes of the GRU must be counted their enrollment as agents of the daughters of General Kurt von Hammerstein, one of the German military hierarchy, who in 1930 was appointed Chief of the Oberkommando des Heeres (Army High Command). Quite a large percentage of the German officer corps favored military collaboration with Soviet Russia at this period, and among these was General Hammerstein, who made a number of visits to Moscow for discussions with Soviet military leaders.

Hammerstein had two daughters who held far more progressive political views than their conservative father. These views naturally became known to Soviet Intelligence, and Werner Hirsch, editor of a German Communist journal, *The Red Flag,* was detailed to get to know them well, and if they appeared receptive, first to indoctrinate them and then enroll their services as agents.

Hirsch carried out his instructions so successfully that within a comparatively short time both girls were passing to the GRU every military document of value which their father brought home with him. They also reported the contents of all conversations of a military nature which took place in their home. They engaged in these activities for several years, and, according to one source, "were among the best Communist agents operating in the German Army."

Though military espionage had begun with high hopes, and though it produced a good deal of useful information, the effort which it was required to exert was paltry compared with the effort which was made in the field of industrial espionage. In this field, the base for activity was the Soviet Trade Delegation, the Handelsvertretung, which had its vast headquarters in the Lindenstrasse, Berlin.

Whenever the Soviet Union established diplomatic relations with a country, more important than the setting up of an embassy was the establishment of a permanent trade organization. The Handelsvertretung in Berlin had its counterparts in Arcos in London, and Amtorg in the United States. In its legal role the trade delegation was highly important to the Soviet Union; and according to the enthusiasm of the political leaders of the host country, of varying degrees of importance to the industries of that country as well. In Great Britain in the middle twenties, enthusiasm was not very great, and Arcos was not, therefore, a very significant organism in the relations between the two countries. In Germany, however, where the return to normality rested upon the rehabilitation of the war-shattered industry—in which exports to whatever country were an essential factor—the Handelsvertretung was an extremely important organization. So the Germans did not, like the British vis-à-vis Arcos, regard the very numerous staff of the Lindenstrasse offices with suspicion. This, and the very lenient official view of industrial espionage, greatly assisted the Handelsvertretung's clandestine spying into the industrial secrets of Germany.

Yet another factor which greatly helped the functioning of industrial espionage in Germany was the willingness of the German Communist Party to co-operate. Unlike the French counterpart, the German Party was prepared and even eager to provide personnel for the Soviet espionage services operating in their country. And the agents they did produce were the products of German traditional efficiency, capable of conducting secret operations with great success. Outstanding among the foremost German operatives of this period were Hans Kippenburger, a former leader of the Communist Student Organization, Leo Flieg, Wilhelm Zaisser, for several years since the war police chief of East Germany, Arthur Illner, who gained infamy as a kidnaper and liquidator, and Ernst Wollweber, East Germany's Minister for State Security.

It is estimated that about half the local Berlin Party secretaries were members of the Handelsvertretung's clandestine organization, while the Communist Student Organization and Communist members of trade unions were also extensively drawn upon. There was certainly no lack of agent potential, and so important was this type of espionage considered by the Center that some of the very best and most experienced Russian professionals were assigned to cover jobs in the Handelsvertretung to direct operations. The German contribution to Soviet espionage between 1922 and 1933 was enormous, and the amount of information gathered was even greater, so great it is quite impossible to estimate its extent and its significance.

Based on local Communist networks, led by local Communists and controlled by first-class Russian professionals, Soviet industrial espionage increased in activity and volume as each year passed. It would have been impossible for German counterespionage not to be aware of what was going on; it was equally impossible, even when a constant alert was maintained, for the security forces to do little more than scratch the surface of the drill that was relentlessly being turned deeper and deeper into the lodes of their industrial achievement. Some of the mammoth undertakings, like I. G. Farben, to relieve the pressure on the State's resources and to give themselves some of the protection which the official agencies were physically unable to give them, set up their own security services. They helped, but the impression they made on the Soviet effort and achievement was scarcely visible.

Between 1924 and 1929 there was an almost constant flow of

cases of industrial spying—the theft and handing over to a foreign power of some industrial secret or other—through the German courts. The lenient official attitude toward this type of spying coupled with the official policy of collaboration produced such derisively lenient sentences that the Soviet Union and the German Communist Party were encouraged to spy. In 1928, however, an even more intensive effort was launched, which was to continue until the inauguration of the Nazi era in 1933, and it reached such proportions that the German government had to take a more severe attitude.

Under the tsarist régime, the great German chemical concern of Solvay, at Bernburg near Dessau, had maintained a branch in Moscow. With the accession of the Bolshevists this branch had been seized and nationalized, and in 1928 was scheduled for reconstruction under the first Five Year Plan. As the Soviet Government had refused to entertain the firm's claims for compensation, the only way to acquire the know-how to bring the Russian plant up to date was for the Russians to try to seduce a high executive of the German plant to come to Moscow to advise them.

With this in mind they instructed one of their agents, a Russian called Luri, to approach Meyer, an experienced chemist, who knew all the new secrets of Solvay, with the offer of the post of general manager of the Moscow plant at an exceptionally high salary. Meyer accepted the offer, but he needed more information than he possessed himself, and before he set out for Russia he tried to obtain this from former colleagues. One of these realized what the old man was doing and denounced him. He was arrested, tried and sentenced to four months' imprisonment.

Toward the end of 1930, a security officer at Krupp's works at Magdeburg stopped one of the chief designers, a man named Kallenbach, as he was leaving the plant one day, and asked him to allow his briefcase to be inspected. In the briefcase were found the details of secret patents and the designs of new machines, and the subsequent investigation revealed that Kallenbach and two others were acting on behalf of their former chief, an engineer called Russki, who had also engaged to go and work in Russia and was on the point of leaving. Kallenbach received four months, Russki and the two others a few weeks.

A few weeks later a Russian engineer, Feodor Volodichev, employed by Siemens, with the help of two young German assistants, was discovered sending to the Handelsvertretung the specifications of the latest telegraphic inventions, microphones and teletype machines. He was sentenced to forty days.

So it went on, until in 1931 the German authorities decided they could no longer smile with leniency on the clandestine activities of the Handelsvertretung, and openly accused the delegation of illegal acts.

The case which provoked public opinion to a degree that the government was compelled to take notice involved an Austrian engineer named Lippner. Lippner had been quite legally engaged by the Handelsvertretung as an adviser on gasoline, on which he was an expert. He had not long been in the employ of the delegation when he was approached by a man called Glebov from the Center, who asked him to procure from I. G. Farben at Friedrichshafen certain secret information relating to gasoline. Lippner refused, at once resigned from the delegation's employ and then sued for the sum which had been contracted for his services, nine thousand marks. The Handelsvertretung deposed in court that Glebov was quite unknown to the delegation, and argued that any document signed by him was not valid. Glebov was not found. The German press reacted with some violence, and the government could not allow itself any longer the luxury of shrugging off such cases.

Then in the spring of 1931 there came up a case which gave the German government the opportunity of showing that it could no longer tolerate this outrageous, almost open, espionage. The network involved was a comparatively large one. Led by Erich Steffen, chief of the Revolutionary Trade Union Opposition—an extensive Communist organization—it contained some two dozen agents, all German Communists. Both Steffen and Frau Steffen were employees of the Handelsvertretung. Their objective was the latest chemical developments of I. G. Farben, and most of the network members were engineers, chemists and workers employed by this great combine.

The leader of the cell at Ludwigshafen was a man called Karl Dienstbach, who had formerly been employed by the Farben works there. He had been dismissed by Farben, but had been able to maintain all the contacts he had made in the various plants situated in most of the great industrial centers.

Heedful of the lessons which had been learned in France, instead of presenting the contacts with copious questionnaires, the information was extracted little by little. Nevertheless, the large number of agents in the network constituted a danger, for each was seeking information from several contacts, so that the number actually involved was far higher than espionage prudence dictates.

Once again the downfall of the network had its roots in the lack of judgment of character displayed by one of the agents. Karl Kraft was asked to supply certain secret formulas relating to ammonia and carbolic acid, and immediately told his superiors of the approach which had been made to him. They instructed him to maintain his contact with the agent, Heinrich Schmid, while investigations were carried out. These lasted roughly ten weeks, and revealed (a), that the network's ramifications were extensive and (b), enough evidence for counterespionage to arrest Steffen, Dienstbach and a very large proportion of the network. Copies of formulas and lists of the names of his agents and their addresses were found in a search of Steffen's home, with the result that very few members of the network escaped.

When the official announcement was made, it was frankly stated that the German government had been aware for some time past that the German Communist Party had been engaged in obtaining industrial secrets through making contacts with German experts with the offer of more lucrative work in Russia. Though the statement did not refer openly to the role played by the Russians in this, it was nevertheless implicit in it that the German authorities were aware of this role also.

A short time after his arrest Dienstbach confessed all he knew, but this did not include any information about the Russian involvement, and in an attempt to discover who had been directing Steffen, it was decided to raid the Handelsvertretung. The German Foreign Office, however, refused to give permission for the search to be carried out, for the Handelsvertretung enjoyed extraterritorial advantages. The Handelsvertretung naturally denied all involvement.

The Russian responsible for the network was a man known only as Alexander, a high-ranking officer of the espionage organization, though ostensibly employed as a clerk in the Russian Embassy. Through the International Labor Defense, Alexander organized the defense of the arrested men. The attorney selected by Alexander not only had the task of representing the prisoners, but of visiting all the contacts who were still at large, to make sure that they did not talk.

This task he carried out successfully, but his task in the courts was beyond him in face of the overwhelming evidence which had been collected. Under the laws relating to industrial espionage, however, the sentences had to be light. Steffen, Schmid and Dienstbach received ten months, the remainder four months.

These sentences had the effect of raising such a public clamor that in March 1932 a presidential decree was published which raised the penalties for disclosing industrial secrets to three years' imprisonment if they were betrayed to a rival firm, or to five years if betrayed to a representative of a foreign firm or power.

By March 1932, there were signs of a coming change in the German political scene. As each week passed, the Nazis were becoming more and more active, and increasing support was being given to them. If the Western powers did not read the signs, the Russians did, and made preparations. Instructions were given, through the Comintern, to all prominent German Communists to make ready for a dive underground and a fairly long stay there, while Soviet agencies were similarly put in a state of readiness to destroy every paper that could be dispensed with, and to send to Moscow those which could not.

These preparations had scarcely been completed when in January 1933 the Nazis swept into power. One of their first targets was the German Communist Party, which was suppressed with a swiftness and a ruthlessness rarely experienced before in history. Though the leaders were safe for the time being in their hideouts and under the cover of their false identities, the rank and file of the Party practically ceased to exist within a few months. Though many of the espionage collaborators with the Russians might still be out of prison, it was too dangerous for them to undertake their former activities, and in any case anything they might have done would have been hampered by the lack of helpers and contacts. At the same time, though the preparations saved most of the Russian agencies from exposure, they too were hamstrung by the fierce activity of a new security force, the Geheimestaatspolizei, the Gestapo. Nor were the Underground leaders safe for long; under torture and threat of death, many of those who knew where and how they were hiding revealed what they knew, and those who escaped arrest were compelled to save their lives by flight.

Some of the Russian agencies did receive Gestapo visitations, but nothing was found to implicate them in espionage. These brought loud protests from the Russians and the threat of trade reprisals, but the Gestapo was not disturbed by either. They were feeling their way. New to espionage activity, they applied themselves to learning the ropes. They were good pupils, and soon Gestapo agents were being infiltrated into all Soviet agencies.

Under these conditions, the Soviet organization—which had relied to a very large extent always on the co-operation of the German Communist Party; indeed, Soviet espionage has everywhere always been at a loss if there was no local Party to collaborate with it—decided that it must withdraw from widespread activity in Germany. The reorganization, as it was called, left but a very small network in Germany, and this, too, was further whittled away when the Stalin purges of 1936 and 1937 removed many of the most successful professional operators in the Russian espionage organization as a whole. The espionage carried out in Germany between 1933 and 1939 was but a fraction of that carried out in the preceding decade. The agents operating within the boundaries were directed from outside the country. They had no contact at all with what remnant Communists still existed; and this introduced a new concept of espionage activity into the Russian operation.

Outstanding among the leaders of this new-look Underground activity in Germany was Ernst Wollweber, who had greatly enhanced his reputation in Moscow by his skill and cunning as an Underground leader since the advent of the Nazis. Under the cover of membership of the West European Bureau of the Comintern, based in Copenhagen, he was given the task of organizing a network which was to be recruited mainly from the Seamen's Unions. He chose between thirty and forty men, mostly of Scandinavian nationality, though a few German Communists were included. Their assignments were not so much espionage as sabotage—in the Russian vocabulary "diversion"—the targets being ships and any plant in any country outside Germany which was helping the Nazis to rearm—for example, the power stations which operated in the Swedish iron-ore fields.

Wollweber's network survived despite several inroads made into its personnel by counterespionage activity, until 1941 when Wollweber and his Swedish branch were arrested, and he received three years' imprisonment. But by this time the war had produced other active networks as well as one or two individual agents who were to achieve reputations that placed them among the brightest stars in the international espionage firmament.

☐ Great Britain

It was probably just as well for Great Britain that, in Soviet eyes and in her own estimation, France should be regarded as the leading European power in the immediate postwar era of the 1920's. We have seen the espionage activity to which France was subjected by the Russians, and there is little doubt that had Moscow considered that espionage on a similar scale was necessitated by the industrial achievements of Great Britain, it, too, would have been subjected to a like activity. Though this did not happen, it was not to be free of Russian interest altogether.

By 1924 the enmity shown toward Communist Russia by capitalist England had been mitigated by the passage of time, and when Lenin announced that he wished to co-operate with the Western countries in the industrial sphere in order to reorganize Russia's own industry, Great Britain was the first to hold out a welcoming hand. In 1924, on February 2, diplomatic relations between the two countries were established.*

The industrial co-operation of the two countries inevitably meant the setting up of a trade delegation in London. Here

*France followed suit two days later, and in the train of France came Italy, Scandinavia, Austria, Hungary and Greece.

known as Arcos Ltd, it leased two sizable blocks of offices in Moorgate, in the City of London; and from here it engaged in both its legal (trading) activities and in its illegal undercover ventures.

In England, Soviet espionage stood at a disadvantage. As we have seen, in this early period of spying activity, the Soviet organization relied on the national Communist Party to such an extent that its effort was entirely influenced by the size of this Party. The British Communist Party, when compared with the French or German, represented only a microcosm of the International. The British Socialists had made such headway since the end of the war, and their views were, in a Conservative Britain, so left-wing, that they seemed to satisfy the political aspirations of the workingman. From the beginning, therefore, Britain was protected from any really intensive espionage activity which the Soviets might have wished to launch. Nevertheless, it was not to escape entirely.

For a couple of years, Arcos operated in both its spheres quite undisturbed by any opposition which it could have expected from the British authorities, in view of what was happening in France at this time. In fact, it would appear that the simple-minded, trusting British had no suspicion that Arcos was not all it purported to be, and this state of affairs might have continued had not the Soviet government, or rather the Russian Communist Party, made a serious blunder in 1926.

During the General Strike of this year, the Russian Party sent more than a quarter of a million pounds to the English miners to support their strike effort. This was met with fierce resentment by the government of the day as an unwarrantable intrusion into the internal affairs of the country. The Trades Union Congress felt the same way, and returned the money; but Mr. Winston Churchill, Chancellor of the Exchequer, and chief strikebreaker, threatened to break off all trade relations with Russia.

The incident seemed to focus keen interest on Arcos, for it now occurred to people that the small amount of trade which was being done with the Soviet Union surely did not warrant the maintenance of the staff of more than three hundred in the

Moorgate offices of Arcos. It was also discovered by MI5 that at least one of the leaders of the trade delegation, N. K. Jilinsky, was a member of Russian espionage, and that the Commercial Counsellor at the Embassy, Igor Khopliakin, was a colleague in that organization. The effect of this was to make the British government withhold from Khopliakin's successor, L. B. Khinchuk, the diplomatic immunity which his predecessors had enjoyed, and this seems to have disturbed the Soviet agencies' chiefs in England somewhat, for a dispatch, which later came into the possession of MI5, from the chargé d'affaires to the Soviet Deputy Commissar for Foreign Affairs, Litvinov, asked the latter to agree to the temporary suspension of the forwarding to Moscow of all documents relating to espionage.

There had been another incident which, besides the investigation of MI5 into the workings of Arcos, had prompted this demand. A young Royal Air Force technician had been caught stealing secret drawings and calculations, and it was revealed that he had been intending to send them, as he had sent others previously, to Arcos.

Not long after this disquieting incident, yet another occurred, again involving British aircraft and weapons, particularly a new British monoplane, still on the secret list, and machine guns manufactured by Vickers. The man involved was an Englishman who had apparently become a professional mercenary spy, willing to sell his information to the highest bidder, until taken into the ranks of the Soviet organization in Germany.

This happened in 1926. Early in 1927 a secret government document, dealing with strategic plans for aerial bombardment, was found to be missing. The Special Branch and MI5 informed the government that they were convinced that this document had also found its way to Arcos, and recommended that the Moorgate offices should be raided. After a long consideration of the political implications of such an act, the Prime Minister, Stanley Baldwin, eventually gave instructions for a raid to be carried out.

At dawn on May 12, City of London and Metropolitan police surrounded the Moorgate offices, and their officers demanded entrance under warrant. They made their way to the basement of the building, where, after forcing a door, they found two men and a woman burning papers. One of the men was the chief cipher clerk at the Soviet Embassy, Anton Miller; the other was an Arcos man, Robert Kopling.

Miller fought to evade arrest, but was overpowered, and on his being searched, a list of the cover addresses of agents and of "letterboxes" relating not only to Europe, but to North and South America and a number of Commonwealth countries, were found, as well. The paper seemed to justify the Special Branch and counterespionage authorities in seizing all the papers found in Soviet House, and a vast haul was taken away for examination.

These documents proved beyond any doubt that Arcos had been used as cover for espionage activities, for among them were found copies of several vital British government documents and a list of some of the Russian agents who had been active in Great Britain. The document, however, which had precipitated the raid was not found. It was believed that a member of the organization had escaped with it by means of a secret shaft which had been built by Arcos, and which was not discovered until later.

The British government was not prepared to be so lenient as the German had been; indeed, the revelation that "all our military and naval centers, Aldershot and Plymouth in particular," had been penetrated by Soviet agents gave them much more encouragement to be strong minded. Diplomatic relations with the Soviet Union were broken off, and the trade delegation sent packing. For two years no Russian was allowed to enter the country.

The three-year period of Arcos activity represents the only serious attempt by the Russians to spy in England in the pre-Second World War era. Perhaps they decided that England had not much really valuable information after all.

☐ The United States

Diplomatic recognition of the Soviet Union was not granted by the United States until after the first Roosevelt Administration had come to office in 1933. This, however, did not prevent Russia from setting up in America two trading organizations which were amalgamated in the Amtorg Trading Corporation in 1924.

The Amtorg was the counterpart of Arcos and the Handelsvertretung, and acted as a blind for undercover activity in the United States as its two sister organizations had in England and Germany. Espionage in the United States, however, was slow in making a start on a wide front, chiefly because, even more so than in Britain, the national Communist Party was too small to provide the numerous contacts to make the effort sizable. Indeed, there was an added reason here; for several years the American Communists were highly suspect in Moscow, since the Depression years in the States attracted to the Party a large number of intellectuals, which gave it a kind of nonworkers gloss instead of the more desirable proletarian, truly revolutionary glow.

These factors did not, nevertheless, prevent some espionage, chiefly in the industrial, though also in the military, field, from being carried out, and the relationship with the Party in this early period was the conventional Party-espionage one.

Among the pioneers of espionage in America were Lydia Stahl, whom we have already met in France, and Alfred Tilton. Lydia Stahl was a photographer, whose assignment was the photographing of documents obtained by the efforts of Tilton. Tilton's assignment was the organization of a courier service to dispose of the documents photographed by Stahl, for which he recruited Communist seamen. Tilton returned to Moscow in 1930; Stahl was assigned to France in 1932.

Tilton was succeeded by Nicholas Dozenberg, like Tilton a Latvian immigrant, who had joined the American Communist Party in its early days, and left it on being recruited into espionage in 1927. Dozenberg's major task was to set up an American-Romanian Film Company, a branch of which in Bucharest was to be cover for espionage in that country.

Unhappily for Soviet espionage, they ran into trouble over this country. A hundred thousand dollars was required to back the Bucharest branch; the Soviet Union at this time could not lay hands on this amount of American currency, so decided to make some. Dozenberg was put in charge of the operation; an initial run of counterfeit hundred-dollar bills was made in Cuba and Brazil, where they passed muster. On the strength of this, Dozenberg was instructed to arrange for a hundred thousand dollars of counterfeit money to be put into circulation in New York.

To help him in this somewhat risky business, Dozenberg sought the co-operation of a Russian-born doctor, Valentin Burtan, who, though a member of the anti-Stalin Communist Opposition, was also the friend of the leader of the Stalin Communists, Jack Stachel. Burtan became vice-president of the American-Romanian Film Company.

Burtan had among his patients a certain non-Communist German, E. Dachow von Bülow, a former German officer, who tried to make a living gunrunning to South America. Burtan had a certain hold on von Bülow, for he had from time to time rescued him from financial difficulties, and now he sought his aid in distributing the counterfeit money.

Von Bülow had a plan which should have been as foolproof as it was easy to operate. Among his many doubtful friends he

counted the Guatemalan Minister of Finance. If suitably re-
warded, he was sure that this gentleman would be able to switch
the counterfeit dollars for the real thing, from the reserves of the
National Bank of Guatemala.

The negotiations between New York and Guatemala City began auspiciously; but something clearly went wrong, for suddenly Guatemala City fell silent, and could not be persuaded to
become vocal again. This did not deflect von Bülow, however,
who now recalled the existence of another friend, a Chicago
private detective, named Smiley. Smiley agreed to co-operate,
and had soon enlisted a band of distributors.

The matter was proceeding smoothly when one of the distributors was caught red-handed by the Chicago police trying to
pass a counterfeit hundred-dollar bill. He sang, and so did
Smiley. Only Dr. Burtan remained silent.

Ever since the days of the scandal of 1865, which led to the
disbandment of the secret service of which Lafayette Baker had
been the chief, the Administration had maintained a small secret
force in the Treasury Department purely to keep a strict eye on
possible counterfeiters, for since the beginning of the existence
of America as an independent state, counterfeiting had always
been regarded as an extremely serious crime. This was still so in
1934 when Dr. Burtan was brought to trial, with the consequence that the doctor was sent to prison for fifteen years and
fined ten thousand dollars.

Dozenberg escaped abroad, and was assigned to Romania. By
1939 he defected, returned to America, served a short term in
prison for making false statements to obtain a passport, changed
his name and vanished into obscurity.

As long ago as 1925-26, a Resident Director had been appointed for America. His name was Tschatzky and he served as
a member of the Amtorg staff. He was recalled to Moscow in
1928 and no successor was appointed—because no suitable man
could be found—until 1931. The man then chosen was Mark
Zilbert, one of the foremost leaders of Soviet espionage.

Among Zilbert's assignments was the gathering of naval secrets. His contact in this work was a Communist, Solomon

Kantor, who had formerly been employed as a draftsman by the Arma Engineering Corporation, engaged on secret orders for the U.S. Navy. Though no longer in a position personally to get the material Zilbert needed, Kantor had a contact still working for Arma, a man called William Disch, who, on expressing willingness to co-operate, was met by Zilbert. Afterward they met regularly every week for the next six months, and at each meeting Disch handed over the secret documents Zilbert wanted, and in return received between one and two hundred dollars.

Unknown to Zilbert, however, after his meeting with the agent, Disch had gone to his employers and told them what had happened; they in turn had contacted the Office of Naval Intelligence.

Now, although the ONI at this time comprised perhaps a dozen agents who were expected to protect the U.S. Navy from the maneuvers of all foreign spies, it was a very keen and a highly intelligent and dedicated body of men. Since the disbandment of Lafayette Baker's secret service in 1865, after the scandal, the ONI had constituted the only American secret service besides the Treasury Service, and it had not been formed until America had entered the Kaiser's War. In the twenties and thirties it carried out its role superbly in a running battle with almost overwhelming Japanese espionage, and Soviet espionage. When the FBI, having dealt with the menace of the Chicago and lesser gangsters, were instructed to undertake counterespionage duties, between them these two agencies represented a formidable opponent to anyone wishing secretly to harm the United States.

The ONI instructed Disch to maintain his contact with Zilbert and detailed the documents he should hand over. Whenever he went to his assignation with Zilbert, he was followed and the meeting was watched, though the attempts to discover for whom Zilbert was working failed.

After some weeks the ONI's attention was distracted by a Japanese attempt to penetrate the naval base at San Diego, so they turned the Zilbert-Disch case over to the FBI. The latter had an inspiration for discovering who Zilbert's superiors were.

On the next occasion that Disch handed over his batch of papers, he was instructed to tell Zilbert that he must have them back within a couple of hours. Zilbert agreed, and FBI agents following him saw him enter the Amtorg offices, and knew then that he was a Russian agent.

Why they did not pounce then has never been explained, but for some reason the FBI apparently wished to obtain more tangible evidence. What they did not appreciate, however, was that the spuriousness of the information which Disch was handing over would sooner or later become plain to the espionage experts in Moscow. The inevitable happened; Zilbert cut off his contact with Disch. Though he did not leave the country yet, he was not arrested.

Another of Zilbert's agents was the young American Robert Switz, whom we have also met in France. Though he was trained to take over the photographic work of Lydia Stahl, he qualified as a pilot, and before going to France was assigned to gathering information about the U.S. bases in Panama. A cell produced the information for him, and the documents were retyped by a clerk in the U.S. Army offices, Robert Osman, who was the lover of one of Switz's agents, a Russian girl called Frema Karry.

All went well until one day a letter addressed to Herman Meyers in New York could not be delivered, and was returned to Panama. There it was opened, and, as it contained copies of secret documents relating to the installations and fortifications in the Canal Zone, an investigation was begun, and presently the retyped documents were traced to Osman's typewriter. Osman was arrested, sentenced by court martial to twenty years, a fine of ten thousand dollars and dishonorable discharge. The sentence was set aside, however, by a retrial in the United States. By this time, Switz had left for France.

By the beginning of the thirties, Amtorg had grown to an immense undertaking, employing between seven and eight hundred people, the majority of whom were American Communists. Its espionage ramifications were extensive. One of its staff was an American Communist, Robert Pitcoff. He left the Party in 1934, and in 1939 he gave evidence before the House Committee on Un-American Activities, Investigation of Communist Propaganda Activities, in which he said, "There were commissions that were studying glass; there were commissions that were studying aviation; there was another commission that was here to study the chemical industry, and other industries; the manufacture of paper and such things as that. Almost every industry was studied by these commissions."

These were, in fact, the days of the first major effort in industrial espionage in America, and despite the constant watchfulness of the FBI, which was aware of much that was going on, and which frequently made arrests, the results must have been extremely successful. On the other hand, between 1930 and 1933, military espionage was practically nonexistent.

The reason for this was the great desire of the Soviet leaders to secure diplomatic recognition by the United States. Though the Amtorg contretemps could be shrugged off, because American public opinion was singularly unimpressed by the loss of secret formulas or designs, the Russians had learned by this time that a scandal involving some military objective had every likelihood of having a very different reception. This had certainly been the experience in other countries. The effect of the counterfeit money scandal and the Osman case showed that the American reaction might be very like that of the British and the French when their military secrets had been threatened.

So the professional leaders were withdrawn from the United States and assigned elsewhere, and although the cells and networks were maintained, between 1933 and 1935 no military espionage was carried out. When they started up again, however, it seems that orders had been given to make up for lost time, for by 1936 activity reached a new high level, and this despite the many "liquidations" and defections which followed the general pattern of the first great Stalin Purge in Russia. Indeed, the defections and the liquidations during the period 1936 to 1939 provide a very illuminating picture of cause and effect as it periodically seems to affect Soviet espionage.

At this point it is necessary to refer to one final difference between the Soviet organization and any other. This is the existence of the Ninth Section of the Special Division of the Second Directorate, which is known as the Section for Terror and Diversion.

On the face of it, the Ninth Section appears to have been inspired by James Bond-like fiction, so alien is its concept to Western thought and behavior. In reality, however, it is no figment of the spy novelist's imagination, but a very active and potent force in the over-all espionage effort.

Established at a time when the creator of Bond was a mere boy, it originally functioned as the office of the executioner during the Terror years of 1918 to 1920. As such it was one of the main departments of Dzershinsky's Extraordinary Commission for the Combat of Counterrevolution and Sabotage, but it later became a separate section attached to the Central Executive Committee. Its functions during these earlier periods were almost totally restricted to the commission of executions within Russia, but later, round about 1932, that is, after the removal of Zinoviev, Rykov and Bukharin from the seats of power, it became the personal agent of Stalin, and when the reorganization of the espionage agencies was carried out in 1934, it became incorporated into the new NKVD.

But long before this, the Ninth Section, in whatever form it existed, had been employed outside Russia to remove agents thought or proved to be unreliable, and defecting leading Communists, whether they had been involved in espionage activities or not. The method was of either kidnaping and removal to Russia, where execution followed a secret trial, or by assassination on the spot. Its function was also twofold: to permanently silence agents who might be able to betray important espionage secrets to the enemies of Communism, and, by terror, to dissuade agents and prominent Communists from defecting.

Since the middle thirties, kidnapings and liquidations have become so frequent and commonplace that little notice is taken of them nowadays. But the first kidnaping which came to the public notice—that of General Kutyepov from outside his flat in Paris on January 26, 1930—was a nine-day wonder. Soon it was forgotten, however, and though the kidnapings and assassinations continued throughout the next seven years, it was not until the disappearance of Juliet Poyntz in New York and the killing of Ignace Reiss, a former outstanding professional agent and Resident Director in France at one time, in Switzerland, both in 1937, together with the murder of Trotsky in Mexico in May 1940, that public interest was stirred again, and again as quickly went back to sleep. But if the public was not really concerned with these illegal acts of terror committed within the sovereignty of its own country, would-be defectors were impressed; though even here, several had the courage to defy the Ninth Section.

This was certainly true of a number of American Communists of the middle thirties who had at one time or another operated as agents for Soviet espionage.

Juliet Poyntz, for example, had been a really outstanding member of the American Communist Party before she agreed to spy for Russia in 1934. After a period of training in Moscow, she returned to New York with the assignment of finding new agents for the American networks. But something had happened to her while she had been in Russia, and already when she returned to the United States, she was not the one hundred per cent committed Communist that she had been for the twelve preceding years. Nevertheless, she appears to have attempted to carry out her assignment to the best of her ability, until the Moscow purge trials of 1936 finally crystallized her doubts. She resigned from espionage—on becoming an agent she had followed the traditional pattern and had resigned from the Party—and settled down to write her memoirs. With the very first word she wrote, she signed her own death warrant.

One day in the spring of 1937 she left her apartment, and was never seen again. Carlo Tresca, the American labor leader, openly accused the NKVD of her murder, and five years later he, too, met his death by apparent accident on the corner of Fifth Avenue and Fifteenth Street.

Juliet Poyntz had been only one of the outstanding agents in the America of the middle thirties who had become disillusioned. Another was Whittaker Chambers.

Chambers, like Juliet Poyntz, had joined the Party in the mid-twenties, and had been taken into espionage work by the OGPU. He had first worked on the *Daily Worker* staff, and was then editor of the *New Masses*. He joined the Underground in 1932, and two years later was given the task of reorganizing certain Communists employed in government positions in Washington, into a new network.

Among his contacts, he stated later, were Harry Dexter White, assistant to the Secretary of the Treasury; Abraham George Silverman of the Railroad Retirement Board; Dr. Gregory Silvermaster of the Department of Agriculture; and Alger Hiss of the State Department. As another part of his activities Chambers later told of forming with two others, John Sherman and Max Lieber, the American Writers' Syndicate, the real purpose of which was, Chambers testified, to provide legal cover for certain Soviet undercover operations overseas.

Chambers saw the light in 1938, and could not make up his mind which course to take in the problem of survival which now faced him. Deviators of this kind had two possible avenues of escape from the attentions of the Ninth Section; either they could seek the protection of the U.S. authorities after having told all, or they could try to buy their lives from the NKVD by going into hiding, thus hoping to impress upon the NKVD their intention of remaining silent.

To grapple with his problem, Chambers went into hiding for a year, and then decided on a compromise. He went to Washington to see President Roosevelt, but the highest he got was to Adolf Berle, Jr., Assistant Secretary of State, who was in charge of security. Chambers did not reveal his story in full to Berle. He stressed the Communist connections and sympathies of certain officials, but said nothing about their being agents of Soviet espionage. Nor did he name Harry Dexter White and Silverman, who were among the most important and active.

Roosevelt was not impressed when Berle passed on to him what Chambers had revealed, for the men Chambers had named were highly regarded in their departments and had excellent records in the government service. So no action was taken.

Two years later, Chambers made another attempt. This time

he saw the FBI, but once more held back the full story. In fact, ten years were to pass from Chambers' ceasing to be an agent until he finally plucked up courage to reveal every detail. Many of the men he named were still members of the Administration and still had contacts with Soviet espionage, and the results of his revelations led to one of the most sensational espionage *causes célèbres* of all time.

This brief outline of Chambers' record makes very clear how successful military espionage had been in establishing itself in America during the middle and late thirties. By 1938 it had penetrated the U.S. Administration to a really formidable extent. There can be no doubt that it was greatly helped by the official attitude which Chambers had experienced. This seems to have stemmed from the very top, perhaps because Roosevelt, who believed implicitly in his ability to "handle Stalin," was unwilling to do anything which might be construed as anti-Soviet lest it should harm his chances of successfully negotiating with Stalin.

If American counterespionage came upon any case of spying that was, of course, another matter. There was, for instance, the case of Mikhail Gorin.

Gorin was a professional Russian agent. He had arrived in the United States as an employee of Amtorg, from where he was transferred to Los Angeles as manager of Intourist, the Soviet State Travel Bureau. In Los Angeles he made contact with an American Naval Intelligence officer, Hafis Salich, who, in the course of his official duties, had access to secret information about Japan.

At the first approach, Salich, who was Russian-born and still had relatives living in Russia, refused to have anything to do with Gorin's suggestions. Then Gorin, in the traditional pattern, referred to these relatives, and achieved the results he desired. Salich thereafter handed over to him secret Navy documents, many of which referred to Japanese espionage.

Altogether, Salich handed over sixty-two Intelligence documents, and might have gone on supplying Gorin for some time longer than he did, had not Gorin committed the most extraordi-

nary blunder, one quite inexplicable for an agent of his experience to make. He left some of Salich's documents in a suit which
he sent to the cleaners, who at once got in touch with Naval
Intelligence. Both men were arrested.

Now, in the normal course of events, discovery is an occupational risk of spying, and spy masters are conditioned to brazen
out such embarrassing situations. But in the climate of 1938,
and taking into account Gorin's proved professional skill as a
spy, doubts were now planted in the minds of the Soviet directors of
espionage in America about his trustworthiness. Could it be that
he was really planning to defect?

In FBI custody, Gorin broke yet another rule of espionage
which was vigorously impressed on all Soviet agents. (The
Gorin affair illustrates very well how overtrained Russian agents
can tend to go to pieces when faced with disturbing situations.)
He asked permission to telephone the Russian Embassy in Washington. This was granted and he asked to be put through to the
Ambassador, Constantin Oumansky, whom he asked for instructions.

Oumansky, even more perturbed now, decided to send the
Soviet vice-consul, who was actually an NKVD agent in New
York, to see Gorin in Los Angeles Jail, while he himself called
on Sumner Welles, then Acting Secretary of State. To Welles, the
ambassador protested strongly about the arrest of Gorin, and
accused the Department of Justice of behaving in a way that was
not strictly legal; though what the basis for this argument was
Welles was at a loss to apprehend.

Having registered his protest, Oumansky then visited Loy
Henderson of the European Affairs Division of the State Department, to request permission for Gorin to be visited by the vice-
consul, Ivanushkin. Despite the fact that as long ago as 1933
Roosevelt and Stalin had signed an agreement that American
citizens arrested in Russia could be held incommunicado for the
first three days of their arrest, and this agreement had been
taken to have reciprocal reactions, Henderson gave the permission asked.

When Gorin and Ivanushkin met, the latter said quite openly,

"We admit nothing; we will ignore the papers found in the suit."
This the FBI took to be an official warning to Gorin not to
talk.

During the days that followed, the ambassador made several
attempts to bail Gorin out, but the State Department refused to
intervene. Gorin had no diplomatic immunity, and it was therefore purely a matter for the civil courts to handle without inter-
ference from the Administration.

In May 1939, Gorin and Salich were brought to trial and
found guilty of espionage. Gorin was sentenced to six years' and
Salich to four years' imprisonment. Immediately the Soviet
entered an appeal on Gorin's behalf, and for the next two years
the case made its slow way through all the appeal machinery,
until in January 1941 the Supreme Court upheld the verdict of
the court of first instance.

As the war years approached, Soviet espionage in the United
States gained momentum, until the peak of activity was reached.
A few figures will show how the tug of war between the networks and the counterespionage agencies progressed. Between
1933 and 1937, the FBI investigated an average of 35 espionage
cases a year; in 1939, the figure was 250 for the preceding
twelve months, from June 1938 to June 1939, while in the last
six months of 1939, a further 1400 were dealt with. Only in a
very few, of course, were arrests made and proceedings brought;
but the extent of espionage activity is accurately mirrored in
these statistics.

But the efforts made and the results achieved during this
period were to be almost puny as compared with the efforts of
the decade to come.

PART III

The Second World War

☐ To Meet
the Changing Times

After the Arcos affair in Great Britain, the Russians did not attempt any more widespread espionage there before the outbreak of the war. In France, also, by the end of 1934, the effort was greatly relaxed after the exposure of the Switz network. The effort in Nazi Germany had been forced out of activity by the suppression of the German Communist Party and by the increasing efficiency in counterespionage by the Gestapo, the Sicherheitsdienst, and the re-established military counterespionage agency, the Abwehr.

The middle and latter part of the decade of the thirties was a period of doldrums for the Russian organization, a period which was extended by the Stalin purges which hit the ranks of the NKVD as viciously as it hit the Army and the Party. But of the three organisms, it was the NKVD which recovered most rapidly.

The effect here was the same as that seen in the Army toward the end of the first six months of the German-Russian war, when a new cadre of young officers divorced from the outmoded military techniques of the Voroshilovs and the Budennys developed. Under the drive of the newly appointed chief of the security services, Lavrenti Beria, a new generation of agents was quickly incubated.

It was an ill wind which had swept through the NKVD for those who fell victim to its pulverizing forces; but it was followed by a benign wind of change which brought with its new techniques the possiblity of an achievement so far not experienced by any Soviet agency dedicated to clandestine activity.

The main target was Germany, since it was evident that before long Hitler intended provoking the Western powers into war; and despite the peculiarly mystifying behavior of Stalin in the few weeks before the launching of Operation Barbarossa, everyone in the Soviet hierarchy was convinced that sooner or later Hitler would turn his attention to the East. On the other hand, there was no sense in attracting that attention, since there was too much to be done to put the country on a potential war footing if the trial of strength were to swing at all in favor of Russia.

Since the establishment of networks on German soil would certainly be deemed sufficient provocation to the Führer to launch a defensive war on the country to which those networks belonged, the Center decided to establish a number of networks whose agents would operate individually inside Germany from a base either in Belgium, Holland, Denmark or Switzerland, from which bases the networks would also be controlled.

In the nine months of 1939 preceding the outbreak of the Second World War, therefore, quietly but with great efficiency, the bases were set up in the countries mentioned, the chiefs and the operatives arrived, and the organization of each was poised to go into action at the signal, which was to be the outbreak of hostilities.

Each base was self-contained. It was equipped with short-wave radio, with radio operators, with expert coders, with couriers, and go-betweens, with agents who were to operate within Germany, with "letter boxes"—in fact, with every facility to make the gathering of intelligence and its transmission to Moscow as simple as possible.

At the head of each network there were old and tried hands

who had somehow escaped the holocaust of Stalin's ruthless removal of all opposition. But the men they controlled were new stock for the most part, men trained to get the information themselves, or to seek out sources of information, working along broad instructions from the Center.

The Center still controlled all activities. It still arranged the assignments; it still had to approve all those engaged to help; it still very largely hamstrung the Resident Directors by denying them independent action; it still tended to frustrate initiative. But one great innovation had been introduced: no longer were there three agencies—the NKVD, the GRU and the Comintern—which in the past had maintained separate organizations, even though the Center had the last word; now there was to all intents and purposes only one agency, for no matter to which agency a man might belong, if he was sent abroad he gave his effort and his allegiance to the network of the agency already established there, and could do so inspired by the knowledge that in the end it would be the Center which would receive and assess his results.

The networks went into action as soon as the German-Polish war could be seen to be certain to end in a German victory, and throughout the period of the "phony war," they operated with great keenness and skill. With the network's base outside Germany and only the field agents operating within the Reich, if an agent fell foul of German counterespionage at least the main apparatus was safe, the lost agent could be replaced and the work go on without a break.

All went well. The results, however, scarcely justified the effort, but that did not seem to worry the Director, the Center's chief. The networks would really come into their own when war broke out between Russia and Germany.

But before that happened, Belgium, Denmark and Holland ceased to be neutral countries and France was divided into two parts. The very foundations of the plan were knocked away, as the chocks are knocked from under the dry hull of a ship about to be launched. German counterespionage agents swarmed everywhere, and as Jews were among the leading members of the net-

works they constituted a new and an unforeseen danger. Nevertheless, the networks had to hold on, since they were the only networks
capable of penetrating German secrets; and until one of the most
shameful chapters in the history of all Russian espionage opened,
they worked with courage, determination and a fair measure of
success.

☐ The Networks
in
Belgium and Holland

The network in Holland, which was of secondary importance to the one in Belgium, was organized by Johann Wenzel, a German of long-standing membership in the German Communist Party. His second-in-command was a Dutch Communist, Anton Winterink. Winterink had been formerly on the staff of the Comintern's agency for helping Communists in prison, but when the reorganization took place and he was ordered by the Center to join the Dutch network he followed the traditional pattern, and withdrew from all active participation in Party affairs.

The Dutch network had its own radio, which was operated by a Wilhelm Vogeler, while four of its active agents were three men—Lutterman, Nagel, Gouloose—and a woman, Hendrika Smit. Though independent of it, the Dutch network was required to maintain close liaison with the Belgian network, and three couriers were attached for these duties. They were Maurice Peper, and Jacob and Hendrika Hilboling.

During the "phony war," the Dutch network remained inactive on instructions from the Center, but when the German invasion of Holland took place, their assignment was to report on German troop movements inside the country. As will be described shortly, this network was short-lived.

The Belgian network was much more extensive in organization and in the scope of its assignments; an altogether more significant setup than the network to the north of it. This was deliberate policy of the Center, as may be judged by the fact that the man designated to lead it was a Polish Jew of outstanding espionage experience, named Leopold Trepper, who was eventually to be appointed Resident Director for all the networks in the West.

Besides being a very experienced professional, Trepper was also somewhat of a rarity in Soviet espionage. He had a talent for making swift and true judgments, was prepared to act on his own initiative, and was remarkably daring. He had escaped the Purge by being able to convince Stalin of his loyalty, and the fact that he was one of the few of the more experienced agents to remain alive after the second Purge of 1938 automatically made him a candidate for a high post.

Trepper's second-in-command was a Latvian, a former officer in the Red Army, Victor Sukulov. It is said that while still in his teens he had read a book, *Diary of a Spy*, an account of the fictional exploits of a British agent called Edward Kent by the Russian writer N. G. Smirnov, and had been so deeply impressed by the ruthless character which Smirnov had given Kent that he decided to model himself on him. There appears to be some basis for this story, for one of the cover names which Sukulov adopted was Edward Kent.

He had originally been selected to organize the network in Copenhagen, but on his way to the Danish capital from Paris he stayed a few days in Brussels, and while he was there, war broke out. Whereupon the Center instructed him to remain in Belgium as assistant to Trepper.

Besides these two men, the members of the network were a nephew of Molotov, Mikhail Makarov, a lieutenant in the Red Air Force, who acted as coding expert and radio operator; Anton Danilov, a Red Army officer, who was the chief go-between; Rita Arnould, a German, who acted as "manager" of the network headquarters; and Sophie Poznanska, a Polish Jew, a cipher expert and "keeper" of the false document section for the network.

Among a host of lesser agents, mention must be made of Leo Grossvogel, a German, who organized the cover businesses; Grossvogel's mistress, Simone Phelter, who was on the staff of the Franco-Belgian Chamber of Commerce, and who acted as courier between Brussels and Paris; August Sesee, an outstanding radio operator and technician, and Abraham Raichmann, a Pole, who was an expert forger of identity documents.

Added to this already formidable list must be Colonel Konstantin Yefremov, a military engineer and expert in poison gas. He took for his cover the role of a Finnish student, and was so thorough in establishing his new identity that, according to a later Gestapo report, "even the buttons on his underclothes were of Finnish manufacture."

The headquarters of the network was in part of a villa at 101, rue des Attrebates, in the Etterbeck suburb of Brussels. In the other half lived the elderly Belgian widow who owned the villa, and who was so innocent that she had no suspicion of the true role of her tenants.

It was an extensive organization, and took some time to establish, but by the time the war in the West broke out, it was ready to go into action. The Center's original plan had been to use this network only in the event of war between Germany and Russia. With the exception that orders were given for the German agencies, and the Organization Todt in particular, to be penetrated after the invasion of Belgium, this plan was adhered to. To carry out this assignment, Trepper founded the firm of Simexco, whose object was to supply building materials to the Organization Todt, and thereby win the confidence of the German officers of that organization and gain access to the secrets of the German offenses. In the very short time it existed, its achievements were of a very high order.

When Germany did at last attack Russia in June 1941, the Belgian network immediately went into full action. An idea of the activity in which it, the Dutch and the French networks engaged in these early days may be obtained from the later Gestapo and Abwehr admissions that in 1941 the radio listening posts of these two counterespionage agencies monitored no less than five hundred messages sent from the West to the Center. The radio techniques used were so good that the attempts by German counterespionage to discover the posts from which the sets were operated were all in vain, though it must be pointed out that at this time direction-finding techniques were in a somewhat primitive stage of development. Nor was this all; the codes used resisted all attempts of German codeographers to break them.

The authorities in Berlin were thwarted and angry, and both Himmler and Canaris, chiefs of the Gestapo and Abwehr respectively, issued urgent orders that the Russian posts must be discovered at all costs as quickly as possible. As a result of an intensified effort, in the autumn of 1941 the main post was tracked down to "somewhere in Belgium," and the Russians, in their ignorance of the advances that the Germans were making in direction-finding techniques, eventually betrayed themselves by operating transmitting schedules far too frequently, at far too regular set times and for much too long—five hours at a time.

In consequence, on the night of December 13, 1941, German troops, under the direction of the Abwehr, raided 101, rue des Attrebates. They found the transmitter, a number of false documents, supplies of invisible ink, and Mikhail Makarov, Sophie Poznanska and Rita Arnould. Greatly to their disappointment they found no details of codes.

While the raid was in progress, Trepper arrived at the house unaware of what was happening. Thinking quickly, however, he insisted to the Germans that he was a door-to-door rabbit salesman, and was allowed to go.

Sophie Poznanska was able to take her cyanide tablet before the excited Germans realized what she was doing. Makarov died under torture without having betrayed a single detail, but Rita Arnould not only told all she knew, she also voluntarily handed over to the Abwehr a photograph of Trepper, which she ought never to have had. When her usefulness was at an end, she was beheaded. Trepper, known as the Grand Chef, and Sukulov, known as the Petit Chef, both made their way successfully to France, where the French network, under Trepper's over-all direction, was functioning in the Unoccupied Zone, while Yefremov, who had not been compromised by Rita Arnould, assumed the direction of the remains of the Belgian network, and Johann Wenzel was brought from Holland to assist him.

This latter was a most unfortunate move by the Center, for Rita Arnould had betrayed Wenzel. He had made frequent visits to Brussels and visited the rue des Attrebates villa. However, Wenzel continued to operate successfully for six months, until in June 1942, when his transmitter was located by the Abwehr and he was arrested.

By this time the Abwehr had had the idea which was later to develop into the *Spiel*. Though they had failed to find the details of the codes being used at the villa, later, when a more thorough search was made, torn scraps of paper bearing groups of letters were found. From these, by careful and persistent patience, the German cipher experts were able to reconstitute, and it occurred to Canaris that not only would this be useful in discovering what information the Russians had gathered, but that a good deal of havoc could be caused if false messages were transmitted to the Center in the code. By the time they were ready to do this, however, Makarov, who could have been used for this purpose —in fact must be used*—was dead, and the Center had changed the codes.

Now, however, they had another operator in Wenzel, and one moreover who knew the new codes. At first Wenzel refused to co-operate, but when confronted with the German dossier on him, and given the alternative of death or collaboration, he surren-

*The individual transmitting technique of a radio operator is as distinctive as his handwriting. Though messages containing all the necessary identity checks might be transmitted, unless the agent who had been assigned to a particular post operated, those receiving the transmission would know at once that a false agent was operating this set. It was therefore essential to the Germans that captured agents should transmit the false messages for them, though, over a period of eighteen months in Holland, in the course of what has now become notorious as the *England Spiel*, German operators did transmit and the communications headquarters of Special Operations Executive did not recognize that the "handwriting" was not that of their Dutch agents.

dered. As an agent of long standing and a former Resident Director, the information he had available to give the Abwehr was extensive.

Nevertheless, it would appear that he did not betray Yefremov, for the latter was arrested in July 1942, when Raichmann, the false-documents expert, took a photograph of him to a Belgian police inspector called Mathieu, whom he trusted, but who was, in fact, now collaborating with the Germans. (Raichmann, owing to the slight disorganization into which the false-document department had fallen with the seizure of his rubber stamps at the villa, required Mathieu to put an official stamp on the photograph of Yefremov, which was needed for a new passport, as Yefremov had decided to change his nationality from Finnish to Belgian.) Mathieu agreed to deliver the passport to Yefremov himself when he had been able to stamp it, and when the two men met, Yefremov was arrested.

At first he refused to give any information whatsoever to the Abwehr, but somehow or other the Abwehr discovered that their prisoner had a very great attachment for his family back in Russia. They threatened, therefore, to send a message to the Center saying that he had betrayed Wenzel, knowing that the Russians would arrest and probably execute Yefremov's family in revenge. Under this threat Yefremov weakened, and once he had begun to talk he quickly became a two hundred per cent collaborator.

As a result of Yefremov's talking, Maurice Peper and Hendrika Hilboling—the couriers between the Belgian and Dutch groups—were arrested. Mme. Hilboling refused to collaborate and was executed, but Peper betrayed Winterink, who had led the Dutch network since the departure of Wenzel for Brussels. Winterink also initially refused to talk, but was eventually broken and in turn betrayed the rest of the network.

Thus, at almost one blow, the Dutch and Belgian networks were entirely smashed; the Danish had never been established; and only the French and Swiss, of the great Soviet *apparat* in the West, remained.

☐ The Network in France

When Trepper took over the leadership of the *apparat* in France, there were already in that country two or three separate networks—all, as far as it is possible to discover, working independently of each other and in direct contact with the Center. Of all the Western networks, the French had become the most important to the Soviet Union, especially during the period of the Nazi-Soviet Pact, which corresponded very largely with the "phony war." Even when the Germans overran France in June 1940 the French network did not find itself in the same situation as that in which the Dutch and Belgian were involved, and after the partition of the country it was able for some months to supply a good deal of the information demanded by the Center on such subjects as the strategical plans of the German armies, relations between the Nazi leaders and the High Command, the whereabouts of Hitler and his headquarters, the strength of the Luftwaffe, and the fuel situation in Germany and troop movements on the Belgian and French coasts.

Among the networks established in France before the Trepper era, the most outstanding were the Comintern group led by a man with an English name—Henry Robinson, who was actually the son of a wealthy Frankfurt merchant—and that led by an aristocratic Russian turned Communist, Vasili Maximovich. These two groups were to provide Trepper with much of the most important information gathered from French bases.

Despite his well-off middle-class background, Henry Robinson had been a Communist from the foundation of the German Party. In fact, he had been a Spartakist, which was really a forerunner of the GCP, and to which his mistress, Clara Schabbel, had also belonged. During the 1930's he had served as chief of the secret section of the Comintern, and had acquired an extensive circle of friends and acquaintances among French politicians and government officials. He had taken out French citizenship, and at the beginning of the war, having separated from Clara Schabbel, he lived in a second-rate hotel, regarded as a rather eccentric intellectual.

Included in his group were a number of outstanding agents. There was Maurice Aenis-Hanslin, an engineer, who acted as courier between the group and the Swiss network; Louis Mourier, who fulfilled the vital functions of a "letter box"; and Medardo Griotto, an engraver, whose arts and skills were greatly valued by the group.

Vasili and his sister Anna Maximovicha were the children of a Russian nobleman who had emigrated to Paris after the defeat of the White forces in 1922, and there he had died, wifeless and in poverty. The upbringing and upkeep of the two children he left behind was undertaken by the Bishop of Paris, Monseigneur Chapital, who had funds at his disposal for the care of destitute foreigners. Vasili became an engineer, Anna a doctor, specializing in psychiatry and neurology.

Strangely, in view of their antecedents, the Maximoviches became attracted to Communism, and though they never joined the Party and never publicized their sympathies, they did frequent those White circles which were being discreetly courted by the Soviet Embassy in the late 1920's and early 1930's.

On the outbreak of war, Anna, who had established a home for mental patients from the profits of which she financed the fellow-traveling Union of Defenders, was arrested; but, being able to produce her bona fide patients, was soon set free. Vasili was not troubled by the authorities for a time, but about the beginning of October 1939 he was interned in the camp at Bernet, near Toulouse, which had been primarily established to house Spanish Communist refugees from Franco, and had now become a Russian detention center.

Here he stayed until the Germans overran France, when he was released by the Germans on his undertaking to act as interpreter to a German general of anti-Hitler leanings.

By this time, indeed for some months previously, Trepper had been organizing his own group in France, and had also by now become the Resident Director. With the assistance of Leo Grossvogel in 1939 he had founded a textile firm very like that which they had set up in Brussels and Ostend, as can be seen from the similarity in their names—Simexco in Belgium and Simex in France—as cover for their operations. Operating from offices on the Champs-Elysées, Simex also maintained a branch office in the Boulevard Haussmann, with yet another in Marseilles, and after the fall of France yet another in the Unoccupied Zone.

Among the outstanding members of Trepper's French group were his assistant and secretary, Hillel Katz, and his private secretary, Suzanne Cointe. The front members of Simex were Alfred Corbin, who was the ostensible managing director, and Robert Breyer, both of whom, while carrying out the legal operations of the firm—supplying the German organizations with building materials—also operated in the espionage field, though not on any wide scale. The Simex cover gave Trepper and his assistants the official German entrée to all building sites, including some of the work on the fortifications, and it was in this way that much of the information was gathered.

Trepper and Robinson did not begin to co-operate until after the fall of France, but during their short contact Robinson supplied much valuable information. But most successful of all was Vasili Maximovich. Trepper had got in touch with Vasili very soon after the latter had taken up his post as interpreter, and when Maximovich had expressed a willingness to work with Trepper, and the Center had given the Russian clearance, though with the warning to Trepper to proceed with caution, soon a constant flow of high-grade material was reaching the Grand Chef.

Maximovich increased his own personal sources by offering marriage to a forty-four-year-old maiden lady, Anna Margarete Hoffman-Scholtz, who was one of the confidential secretaries in the German Military Administration in Paris. Though Vasili could not be called a handsome figure of a man at the prime of thirty-eight—indeed, he was stocky, paunchy and suffered from swollen legs—to Fraulein Hoffman-Scholtz he represented the finest acquisition a middle-aged maiden lady could hope for—a husband.

The engagement, approved by the Center, was celebrated by a brilliant party at which, except for the bridegroom-to-be, every member was violently anti-Communist. His German chiefs also regarded the liaison with approval, and Maximovich was given special permission to visit Military Administration headquarters as often as and whenever he wished. Few Soviet agents, with perhaps only two notable exceptions—Rudolf Rössler, operating with the Geneva network, and Richard Sorge, in Tokyo—ever had better facilities for their espionage activities than Vasili now possessed. For not only had he access personally to practically everything that went on in Military Administration headquarters, but his betrothed also proved quite willing to help him, and reported to him all that her gossiping girl colleagues related.

The information which Maximovich forwarded to the Center through Trepper included reports on the French attitudes to their uninvited guests, the whole layout of the German military economy both in France and the other occupied countries, the seriousness of the manpower situation, and the details of concentration camps and the identities of their inmates. Secret documents were "borrowed" for a few hours, copied and returned before they were missed, and blanks of practically every form used by the bureaucratic Germans were to be had for the taking.

Maximovich's espionage effort was neither a solo nor a double act. Among his agents were included two of the interpreters on the staff of the German commandant in Paris, through whom he received exact details of German forces in and around the French capital, their supplies and equipment, and their movements, the latter also giving him a picture of the general military build-up in France. Kathe Völkner, the secretary to the chief of the Arbeitseinsatz, the forced-labor department, supplied him with information of equal importance. Kathe, who had formerly been an acrobat of some reputation and had traveled throughout the length and breadth of Europe, including European Russia, with her lover, Johann Podsiadlo, had been saved from French internment at the beginning of the war through the good offices of the Soviet organization. Both learned shorthand and typing, and when the Germans came to Paris, Kathe procured her present job, while Johann was taken on as an interpreter in another labor recruitment organization.

Anna Maximovicha, Vasili's sister, was also included in the group. With Trepper's aid, she established a new clinic on the line of demarcation between the Occupied and Unoccupied Zones. This not only made it an extremely useful rendezvous for clandestine workers, but a well-run and productive farm was able to supply food for many who were without ration cards.

Here she tended her legitimate patients assisted by Dr. Jean Darquier, whose brother was Commissar-General for Jewish Questions in the Pétain Government. As Jean Darquier was in her confidence, this relationship opened up a source of information not only relating to Jewish questions but to a wide variety of general subjects, all of them of great interest in Moscow. Since the marriage of her brother to Fraulein Hoffman-Scholtz greatly enhanced Maximovich's position with the Germans, it was not long before German officers sought treatment from Anna for the nervous ills brought on by the strain of subduing a proud and restless people. These officers, too, provided yet another source of information. So, taken all in all, Maximovich's network assumed considerable importance in the supply of intelligence to the Center.

All went well until the arrest and breakup of the networks in Belgium, consequent upon which German attention was focused on France. Once more, it was the radio operators who fell first.

In June 1942, Abwehr direction-finders led the Germans to Dr. Herz Sokol and his wife Miriam. These arrests placed Trepper personally in great jeopardy, for he had used them as his chief channel of communication with Moscow. Fortunately, Dr. and Mme. Sokol, both Poles, were veteran Communists and refused to talk for some time. Only when the Germans threatened to shoot the doctor before Mme. Sokol's eyes did she give in. She told all she knew about Trepper, but she did not know enough to compromise him. Frustrated and angry, the Abwehr executed both the Sokols without further ado.

The greatest threat to the French networks came from those members of the Belgian network who had decided to collaborate, a fact which revealed the lack of wisdom of having one chief concerned with, if not actually leading, two organizations in two separate countries. In October 1942 the Abwehr officers who had been responsible for seizing the Belgian network arrived in Paris, bringing with them some of these collaborator-agents, and within a short time of their arrival a couple of score of Soviet agents, or persons suspected of being agents, had been arrested.

Their chief objective was naturally Trepper, the Grand Chef, about whom they knew a good deal; they had his photograph, provided by Rita Arnould, they knew his role in the Brussels network, and they were also aware that he was in France. They did not know, however, where he was living.

In an attempt to draw him out, they brought Raichmann to Paris, and promised him that if he would get in touch with Trepper, he could save his own life. Raichmann undertook to do what he could, and though he was able to betray several agents to the Germans in the course of his "investigations," he could not tempt Trepper to reveal himself.

But if Raichmann failed, it looked very much as though Trepper's days were numbered when an interpreter at Simex, his cover firm, a former White Russian, Maria Kalinina, and her son Evgeni, who was a driver for the firm, betrayed Simex's true role. Forewarned, however, Trepper went underground, and though many tempting baits were laid out for him, he did not bite.

He finally fell into German hands through his own carelessness. In a diary which he left on his desk at Simex, he had noted appointments with his dentist. For an agent of his experience it was an incredible thing to do; but it was even more incredible that he should keep his next dental appointment after the defection of the Kalinins. He was arrested in the dentist's chair on November 16, 1942.

At first Trepper refused to talk, but when he learned that if he did not he would be handed over to the Gestapo for more persuasive treatment than the Abwehr had either the means or the taste to administer, he agreed to give certain information which would not conflict too much with his conscience. Once again, it is surprising that an agent of Trepper's long experience did not realize that once a man in his situation begins to talk there can, in fact, be no limit to what he reveals. The more information he gave, the tighter the screw was turned, and in the end he found himself collaborating one hundred per cent.

The first assistant he betrayed was his secretary, Hillel Katz, whom he asked to meet him at the Madeleine métro. When Katz was confronted with Trepper, the latter ordered him to reveal all he knew. Katz obeyed, and when he had told the Germans everything, he was executed.

Between them, Trepper and Katz also betrayed Henry Robinson, the leader of the network that, after Maximovich's, operated most successfully. Robinson was arrested on December 21, 1942.

But Trepper's greatest treachery was his betrayal of Vasili and Anna Maximovich and all their network. Their arrests destroyed all the networks based in Paris, networks that had so skillfully been established and had proved highly successful.

This, however, was not the end of Soviet espionage in France. Victor Sukulov, the Petit Chef who had escaped from the Abwehr's clutches in the Brussels roundup, moved to Marseilles, where he was directing a very successful *apparat*. There was yet another operating in Lyons, one of the centers of French Resistance, led by Jezekiel Schreiber. Within a few months these two networks had also fallen, and the same wretched story of treachery was repeated.

It is difficult to comprehend the complete collapse of the leading Russian agents, the men of records of great bravery and long service in Soviet espionage. Unfortunately there is not sufficient space here to attempt a detailed analysis of the breakdown of morale and loyalty from which one might reasonably have expected men like Trepper, Sukulov, Katz, Raichmann, the Kalinins, Maximovich, Henry Robinson and others to be totally exempt. They were veteran Communists, so one would have thought ideology would have prevented their collaborating with Fascists; they were highly trained agents, and this, too, would have conditioned them utterly to accept death before dishonor. While they had operated they had shown every kind of ingenuity, every range of courage, an utter devotion to the tasks assigned them. All this makes their treachery even more difficult to understand.

Trepper collaborated with the Abwehr in their "radio game" and for many months operated a radio station for them. As a result of his activities, the French Communist Resistance, one of the most powerful and active Resistance groups in all France, was rendered largely ineffectual.

Permitted to live in a private house in the avenue Foch with his mistress Georgia de Winter, he managed to escape from his guards in June 1943, and was never seen by the Germans again. Recalled to Moscow at the end of the war, obediently he went, though he must have known that his fate would be liquidation; a fact which makes his defection all the more puzzling.

But more damaging still were the activities of Sukulov, and his motives for treachery were simple and personal. On being arrested he had firmly and flatly refused to say a word. No threats or tortures would move him. He asked to be executed.

Then one day he was confronted with his mistress Margarete Barcza. According to Der Stern, which on June 17, 1951, published statements by the Gestapo agents involved relating to the breakup of the French networks and the "radio game": "On seeing Barcza, Sukulov went quite mad. He rushed to her, and embraced her with a passion of which only a Russian is capable. Then turning to the Commissar, he exclaimed, 'Set her free and I will tell you everything.' . . . He fell on his knees before the officer and wept like a child."

The Germans accepted the offer, and within a few weeks Sukulov, accompanied by Margarete Barcza, was back in Marseilles operating a transmitter for the "radio game," completely deceiving the Center, which continued to send him instructions and to whom he sent in return information prepared by the Germans. He even offered to try to make contact with the network operating in Switzerland, but the British agent was too wary for him, and the attempt failed. This attempt ended his usefulness to the Germans, for Foote's report to the Center caused the Director to institute inquiries, and at last it was discovered that Sukulov had been in German hands for the last four or five months.

Sukulov retreated with the Germans when France was liberated, while Barcza set up home for them in Brussels. Here he visited her from time to time, while living underground to escape both Russian and Allied attentions. Shortly after the war, he went to the Balkans, and there disappeared. The Section for Diversion and Terror, it seems, caught up with him at last.

☐ The Red Orchestra
   and Others

Though through no fault of his own, Victor Sukulov was also involved in the seizure and suppression of one of the most remarkable Soviet espionage organizations that operated during the war. Known as the Red Orchestra (*Die Rote Kapelle*),* it was outstanding both in its membership and in the importance of the information it was able to transmit to Moscow during the fourteen months of its existence.

During the period of Nazi-Soviet "co-operation," from the signing of the Ribbentrop-Molotov Pact until the outbreak of the Russo-German war in 1941, which coincided roughly with the elimination of the prewar Soviet networks in Germany, as in other countries of Western Europe there followed a dormant period. But as in those countries, if active espionage was not engaged in, so in Germany the time was used to set up an organization which could operate when war should break out between the leading Fascist and Communist powers.

*The Red Orchestra was the name given to the network by the Germans, who derived it from the espionage jargon terms given by the Russians to a radio transmitter—"music-box"—and to a radio operator—"Musician." The name covered all the German networks in Nazi-occupied Europe, but it was especially applied to the networks in Germany itself.

For some reason or other, however, the organization of this *apparat* was left to the professional agents attached to the Soviet Embassy in Berlin, who, for yet other reasons which cannot be discovered, either panicked or procrastinated until June 22, 1941 came upon them with their task only vaguely fulfilled. The result was that when the embassy packed up and left hurriedly on the day following the outbreak of the Soviet-German war, the intelligence staff accompanied it, and there was left behind only the barest of bare bones of a network, and nothing like a complete skeleton at that.

It must be remembered, of course, that by the breakup of the pre-Nazi networks and the almost complete suppression of the German Communist Party, local talent had been seriously curtailed both as to quality and availability. Nevertheless, on the evidence of the Red Orchestra, there can be little doubt that if the effort of the Soviet Agencies had been sustained during the 1939–1941 period, a network could have been organized that could have gone into immediate and effective action as soon as D-Day came. As it was, the small group who were collected were not only inexperienced in espionage techniques but so undertrained that in the best espionage circles they would have been considered a grave security risk. Despite this, they overcame most of their difficulties, and fell victim only to the Abwehr's direction-finders.

The leaders of the group were Harro Schulze-Boysen and Arvad Harnack, both of whom were quite outstanding men, and who were to gather around them a number of others who outstripped most ordinary members of Soviet espionage up to this time. Originally, their espionage circle was a small part of a larger anti-Nazi pro-Communist Resistance group, but though it is conventionally traditional for the Russian and German Communists to admit only to their Resistance role, they were far less successful and important in this role than they were in their espionage achievement.

Harro Schulze-Boysen was the son of an aristocratic German officer who had served in the Navy in the First World War and as Chief of Staff to General der Flieger Friedrich Christiansen,

German Commander-in-Chief in Holland during the Second World War. In his middle teens, Schulze had been attached to a right-wing anti-Nazi movement, but not for long, for he was soon moving to the other extreme, and in 1932, when he was twenty-two, he was the mouthpiece of a young progressive group. For these activities he was arrested and imprisoned by the Gestapo when the Nazis came to power, and these experiences pushed him over to the far left and Communism. This did not, however, prevent his becoming a member of the German Ministry for Air, in which, at the operative time, he was serving as an Intelligence officer.

When he was twenty-six, he married a granddaughter of Prince Philip von Eulenberg, Libertas Haas-Heye, who was to be a great help to him when he eventually took up his espionage activities in the same year as his marriage, 1936, when he passed information to the Spanish Reds relating to German Intelligence.

In this year he began to gather around him a group of men similarly politically orientated as himself. He was never, at any time, however, a truly orthodox Communist, and though his sympathies lay one hundred per cent with the Soviet, his character—he was too emotional and unstable—would never have permitted him to obey the dictates of Moscow in every particular.

Just before Hitler marched against Russia, Schulze-Boysen was introduced to a Soviet agent on the staff of the embassy, whose role was to assist Bogdan Kobulov, who had been provided with the cover of Counsellor to the Embassy in order to carry out the task of setting up the network that was to operate in Germany after the outbreak of war. This agent, who had successfully disguised his real identity under the cover name of Alexander Erdberg, at once recognized in Schulze-Boysen the type they were looking for, and within a short time Schulze had been selected by the Center to be one of the three men who were to lead the network. The other two were Arvad Harnack and Adam Kuckhoff.

Harnack was very different from Schulze-Boysen. Ten years

older, he was a member of a famous family of German philosophers. Like Schulze, however, Harnack had first become attached to extreme right-wing groups at the end of the First World War, and then had switched to Communism. But he was a true Communist, a Marxist.

When a group of young German Communist intellectuals founded, in 1931, a pro-Russian propaganda society called the Society for Study of Planned Economy, Harnack was prominent among them. Though the Society, which had the full backing of Moscow, was not primarily intended to carry out espionage, it was required to supply certain information to Moscow.

In 1932, a small number of the Society, among them Harnack, visited Russia on a study tour, and this appears to have played a large part in Harnack's future political development. His intellectual abilities were noted by the Soviet chiefs, and he was invited to undertake espionage for the Soviets. To this he agreed, and, with the possible exception of George Blake, Soviet espionage has probably had no other agent in its employ who was so altruistic in his motives, for Harnack was ideologically involved in espionage for the next ten years, and for no other consideration.

Shortly after his return from Moscow, Harnack applied for and obtained a post in the German Ministry of Economics. How he was able to conceal his visit to Russia still remains a mystery, but it was not discovered by the Nazis until the Red Orchestra was broken and his role in it revealed.

It is quite obvious that Harnack was one of those very rare creatures—a natural spy. Though he had received no training in espionage, throughout his long career he observed the principles of security consistently, and never once gave the slightest hint of his secret activities. So successful was he that in the Ministry of Economics he was soon regarded as the model of what an official should be—a conscientious, hard-working bureaucrat.

In the late twenties he had spent two years in the United States on a Rockefeller scholarship, and while there he had met and married Mildred Fish, a lecturer in literature. Mrs. Harnack needed little persuasion to adopt her husband's ideas, and when he returned from Moscow, she was equally enthusiastic about his new role. When the Red Orchestra was broken, she was arrested with him and tried, though it was never established that she had actually taken part in espionage.

The third member of the triumvirate, Adam Kuckhoff, was a prominent writer and theater producer. He was in his middle fifties when the Red Orchestra's foundations were laid. Like the other two, he had started out as a right-wing nationalist and then, with the advent of the Nazis, had swung over to Communism as the most effective means of overthrowing the dictatorship. His wife, Margarete, who helped him in all his anti-Nazi activities, was employed by the Nazi Party in Alfred Rosenberg's race policy department. Kuckhoff played the least important part of the three.

About them these three gathered a motley of roughly one hundred. Of these, members of the old German Communist Party were predominant, though they were not very influential. The remainder was made up of young Communists, ideologically unsound, but fanatical in their hatred of Hitler and all he stood for; with a smattering of non-Communists, who did not know exactly what they stood for except that they were anti-Nazi.

The group which carried out active espionage were merely a very small fraction of the whole, and they kept their secret well, though this was not to save the others when the tragedy overtook them. The two main leaders, Schulze-Boysen and Harnack, the first in the Air Ministry Intelligence and the second in the Ministry of Economics, were, it will be appreciated, extremely well placed to gather information of the greatest importance. The remainder of the espionage group were similarly well placed. Horst Heilmann worked in the Wehrmacht communications in the decoding department; Johann Graudenz, a traveler for a brake manufacturer who supplied the Luftwaffe, kept check on Nazi aircraft production; Erwin Gehrts was working in another department in the Air Ministry; Herbert Gollnow had access to Wehrmacht counterespionage secrets; Gunther Weisenborn worked with the national radio service; while others were firmly entrenched in the Foreign Office, the Ministry of Propaganda, the Ministry of Labor, the Berlin City Administration, and other important departments.

The Red Orchestra was the only network operating in Germany, but there were in addition one or two single, independent agents also working. The most important of these were Hans Kummerow and Rudolf von Scheliha, whose early removal from the scene by counterespionage left the field open to the Red Orchestra. These two are so interesting, however, that they merit a particular mention.

Kummerow was a leading engineer and inventor. He had taken part in the industrial espionage high noon in the late twenties, when he had passed to Moscow the particulars of his inventions in primitive radar and chemical warfare. Considered a useful man still, when war broke out, the Russians tried to send him a radio operator of his own since he had no means of communicating with the Center. Unfortunately, the operator, who was dropped by parachute, was caught on landing, and talked. Kummerow and his wife were arrested and executed in 1943.

Von Scheliha was a far from pleasant type. He first came into the Center's orbit when he was Counsellor in the German Embassy in Warsaw. Coming from an aristocratic family, he was a career diplomat of the old type. He had married a wealthy wife, but he had extremely extravagant tastes, particularly in mistresses, and despite his own not inconsiderable private income and his wife's wealth, he eventually found himself deeply in debt. It was then that he thought of selling his government's secrets to the highest bidder. The British at one time did quite successful business with him, but when it was discovered that he was simultaneously supplying the Russians with the same material, they dropped him. The Russians were not so fastidious, and he continued to work with them, and might have continued to do so without discovery but for the shortage of radio operators. The departure of the Soviet Embassy from Berlin in June 1941 had left Scheliha without a channel of communication with Moscow, and a radio specialist, Kurt Schulze, was assigned to the diplomat and his assistant Ilse Stöbe. But by the time this happened, it seems that Scheliha had reconsidered the risks he was running, and became very reluctant to continue his co-operation with Moscow. The Center was equally reluctant to lose his services, and arranged to send a courier by parachute to blackmail Scheliha.

The man who had been ordered to investigate Scheliha's reluctance in the first place had been Victor Sukulov. This was before Sukulov had been arrested and begun to collaborate with the Abwehr, indeed, before the breakup of the Belgian network. Having seen Scheliha and arranged for Kurt Schulze to be the radio link with Moscow for him, Sukulov submitted a report in code to the Center. The Abwehr came into possession of this report and their experts were able to decipher it with the help of the Belgian traitor Wenzel. The Center was ignorant of this, and they were ignorant also of the fact that Ilse Stöbe had been arrested before the decision had been taken to send their blackmailer to Berlin.

The result was that a woman Gestapo agent, posing as Ilse Stöbe, was waiting in Scheliha's flat when the blackmailer, Heinrich Koenen, arrived. They had a revealing conversation before Gestapo officers arrested him. Ilse had refused to talk, but Koenen agreed to collaborate, with the result that Scheliha was arrested, and he and Stöbe were executed on December 22, 1942.

With the removal of the Kummerows and Scheliha, the importance of the Red Orchestra proportionately increased, and for fourteen months the group more than made up for the loss. They were able to send Moscow information regarding the strategic plans of the German High Command, troop movements and the disposition of Goering's air squadrons, the plans for attacks on British convoys to Russia, monthly aircraft production figures, the fuel situation of the armies in Russia and much more information of lesser importance, though nevertheless well worth having.

Ever since it had begun its operations, however, the Abwehr and the Gestapo radio monitoring stations had been noting the activities of clandestine transmitters within the German boundaries and had instituted an intensive search for them. As we have seen, they had their first break with the Belgian network, and when the second network, of which "Hermann" Wenzel was the operator, was also seized and Wenzel turned traitor and revealed his codes, many of the previously monitored messages were able to be deciphered.

Now, at the same time that Victor Sukulov had been sent to find out what was happening with Scheliha, he had also been instructed to see what help he could give to the Red Orchestra of Schulze-Boysen and Harnack, and he had met the two leaders in Berlin. He had found that their greatest difficulty was also related to the lack of first-rate radio facilities. Sukulov had removed these difficulties for them, and returned to Belgium, only shortly afterward to escape arrest in Belgium and to flee to France.

Among the monitored messages was that which had been sent him instructing him to go to Germany to see Schulze-Boysen and his companions. In it Adam Kuckhoff's address had been given together with brief particulars about the other two but quite sufficient to identify them to the Abwehr. It was on the basis of this information that all three were arrested, Schulze-Boysen on August 30, 1942, his wife a few days later, and the Harnacks on September 3.

Before arresting Schulze-Boysen, the Gestapo had tapped his telephone, and as a result, they were led to nearly one hundred other members of the larger group. Not all of these were trapped as a result of the tapping, but a few members, among them Libertas Schulze-Boysen, agreed to co-operate. Within a few days the Red Orchestra in Germany ceased to exist.

The trial of the chief defendants began on December 15, 1942. The Schulze-Boysens, the Harnacks and the Schumachers, Hans Copp, the radio operator, Heilmann, Gehrts, Kurt Schulze, the operator for Scheliha, Graudenz, Gollnow and Erika von Brockdorf were in the dock. Of these fourteen, eleven received the death sentence, but Mildred Harnack and Erika von Brockdorf were given prison sentences. The death sentences were carried out within a few days of their being pronounced, the victims

being hanged from meathooks. True to his often repeated principle that "those who have come within the shadow of treason
have forfeited their lives," Hitler ordered new trials for the two
women, and they too were sentenced to death and were guil-
lotined.

Of the remainder, the Kuckhoffs were tried on February 3,
1943, together with others. All were sentenced to death, but,
somewhat curiously, Frau Kuckhoff was reprieved. Taken all
in all, just over fifty of those arrested were executed.

The whole business of the Red Orchestra was surrounded
with such secrecy by the Nazi authorities that only after the war
was over was the story of their trials and executions revealed. It
is said that the Minister of Economics, Walther Funk, had no
idea that Harnack had been arrested until the eve of his execution.

The Red Orchestra and the single agents were not the only
espionage effort in Germany by the Soviet Union. The Russian
authorities were impressed by the British organization, Special
Operations Executive, and decided to have a similar organization of their own. So before the Americans came to England to
see what the British could teach them for their projected organization, the Office of Strategic Services (OSS), the Russians sent
experts to London also to pick the brains of the SOE. This writer
was undergoing training by SOE for a subsequent mission to
eastern Europe when the Russians arrived, and recalls very well
the unease felt by his instructors about the wisdom of letting the
Russians into the organization's secrets.

That they were justified in these fears seems to be apparent
from the subsequent Russian record in this field. The man responsible for the setting up of this organzation in Russia was the
mysterious Alexander Erdberg, formerly of the Russian Embassy in Berlin. These agents were chosen for the greater part
from among those of the many thousands who had fled from the
advancing German armies who were young enough and strong
enough to undergo the rigorous course in weapon and parachute
training; while those selected for Germany were young Communist émigrés.

It would seem that the Russians did not comprehend exactly what the difficulties were in fitting out missions of this kind. The need for such agents was urgent, and their training was therefore hurried. The vast majority of them were, in fact, security risks of the first class the moment they touched the ground, so cursory had been their instruction in every aspect relating to their role as secret agents. Radio operators were sent into the field with instructions which would precipitate them into the arms of the ever growing efficiency of the radio direction-finding units. Their codes, necessarily simple, were so rudimentary that the messages sent in them might as well have been transmitted *en clair*. Then no attempt was made, or so it would seem, to build up the kind of "reception" organization in the field which meant so much to this type of agent, and which the British, using the same kind of personnel, and the same kind of clandestine Resistance organization, had so successfully built up.

It would appear, too, that the men in Moscow responsible for this organization were endowed with and viewed their task with a cynicism rare even among the Russians. Perhaps they did have vast human resources on which to draw, but whether this was true or not, they used their men and their women with a prodigality which almost eludes belief.

This writer himself fell a victim to the Abwehr, but this was due to no fault of SOE or himself. During his early stay with the Abwehr three events were to disclose the actuality of all the points he has referred to above.

First, he spent his first night in prison in a cell already occupied by a young Russian agent who was going to be shot the following morning. They found a common language, and the writer, in conversations which continued through a great part of the night, learned that his companion was not quite nineteen, that he had received five weeks' training before being dropped only just behind the German lines, that he had been caught operating his radio two days after landing. He was no traitor, however. He had been severely tortured, and the results showed clearly on his body; but he was loyal to his country, to his rulers and to his ideology.

Second, a young girl agent, aged eighteen, was brought to the writer's cell, with the suggestion that they should enjoy themselves in the short time left to them. Though each was suspicious of the other, suspecting a trick, and though he objected strongly that he preferred his solitude they were left together for some hours, during which time they overcame their mutual suspicions, and talked a little.

The girl was not a Russian, but was from one of the eastern states overrun by the Germans. She had been trained as a radio operator for six weeks—SOE's radio course was a minimum of three months—and dropped with a party of five men. She was caught within a week through her radio. She was disillusioned, because she felt that she had not been properly trained, and she later saved her life for a short time by joining the "radio game."

Third, the writer was in a block of twenty cells, designed for solitary confinement. Every cell but his own was occupied by four or five Russian agents—a guard told him that they were falling out of the skies like leaves in autumn; two or three mornings a week the cells were cleared and their inmates, shackled together, were taken down to the courtyard below his window in batches of a dozen or more, and executed by machine-gun fire.

In Germany there were possibilities for organizing "reception committees," but little or no attempt was made to organize and train them. Because of the suspicions of their masters, the agents were never sent in less than twos—except in exceptionally rare cases—lest they should hurry to the nearest German and give themselves up. This is an extremely bad basis on which to build such a force, for unless the masters have faith in their agents, the latter can have little faith in those they are serving. If an analysis could be made of the number of those who did collaborate and the reasons why they did stated frankly, it would be very surprising if this lack of confidence were not found to be at the very root of the majority of the defections.

Since Germany was out of range of the long-range Soviet

aircraft—and even if they had aircraft capable of flying the distances involved, the greater part of the flight would have been over enemy-held territory well provided with flak—the Russians asked the British to co-operate in delivering their agents for them. The British agreed, and though no figures have ever been made available for the number actually dropped, they could not have been many, since the number put into Germany proper was not great. Nearly all those who were dropped were caught within a short time, and a good proportion of those who were not caught gave themselves up.

The longest period of freedom for the early agents was five months. This was enjoyed by Wilhelm Fellendorf and his partner, Erna Eifler, who arrived in Hamburg in May 1942, and were arrested in October. Their successors, Albert Hössler and Robert Barth, were dropped in August 1942, and were arrested two months later. The third, Heinrich Koenen, who was sent to blackmail Scheliha, arrived at the latter's flat six days after landing and was arrested immediately. The next pair followed in February 1943 near Freiburg, in the Black Forest, and found the Abwehr waiting for them. They managed to escape, however, by abandoning their equipment, and were able to contact a veteran German Communist, Heinrich Müller. They were traced within a short time, and were executed along with Müller and his wife.

As the Russians began to push the German armies back, and their front came nearer to Germany proper and within range of Soviet aircraft, co-operation with the British ceased. This was from about the middle of 1943, and after this time large numbers of agents were put into Germany by the Russians themselves. None of them fared any better than their predecessors. Since, by this time, the Russians had begun to use professed anti-Nazi prisoners of war, the collaboration rate became higher than ever. It would seem that Erdberg was aware of this, but he nevertheless stepped up his deliveries, probably on the principle that by putting in large numbers there might be a very few who would not defect as soon as they landed. They were even less

well equipped, especially as to documentation and security techniques, than the earlier agents had been. Erdberg's cynicism appears to have increased rather than abated.

Taken all in all, this chapter of Soviet espionage activity
represents possibly the least fruitful of all. It certainly played no
part in subsequent Russian victories, and it would have been
more humane to have abandoned the project after the first few
failures.

On the other hand, the saboteurs who were also trained and
dropped by the same organization did play a useful part. But
they had a less difficult task clandestinewise. They were sent in
fairly large groups in the rear of the German lines with a single
or a twofold task: they were either to cause as much havoc as
they could operating by themselves, or they were to join up with
the large bands of guerillas based in the forests and train and
lead them in sabotage exploits. German records show that these
bands were certainly worth the effort to put them in the field.

The war record of Soviet espionage, however, plainly indicates that there was still much to be learned about the choice of
agent and his training before its reputation could rank it among
the espionage agencies of the world. The lesson was taken to
heart, as present experience shows.

☐ The Great Swiss Networks

How Alexander Foote, the Englishman, was recruited into Soviet espionage has been described in Part I. There also was set out a brief biography of this truly remarkable man up to the moment that he entered the Swiss network. But before going on to a description of the work of this espionage group, it would be as well to take note of Foote's qualities as an individual, which more than made up for his lack of specialized training in espionage techniques.

First and foremost, he was a common-sense Englishman, who also possessed naturally the ability to sum up a situation accurately. Since common sense and sure judgment stand high in the list of qualities which a spy must have—and innately so, since they cannot be acquired—he was reasonable material, particularly when it is taken into account that at the time of his recruitment the Swiss network was one of the poor relations of Soviet espionage. In 1938, no one, not even the Director in his omniscient Center, could have foreseen that three years later Switzerland was to become the most important base in Russia's espionage war against Germany, and was ultimately to render to Russian war strategy a service probably unmatched by any other network.

Up to 1937, the small GRU network in Switzerland had had at its head a good-looking young woman known as Vera—her true identity has never been discovered. At the end of the Second World War she had been promoted to the Swiss Section in the Center, was involved in the Canadian Spy Case in some way through a woman called Rahel Dubendorfer, and liquidated.

Vera was succeeded by a number of good agents, outstanding among them being Sonia, Foote's contact outside the General Post Office in Geneva. Her real name was Ursula-Maria Hamburger, and she was the first Soviet agent ever to operate a radio transmitter in Switzerland. With her husband, Rudolf, she was a member of the German Communist Party, and together they had worked for many years as Soviet agents in the Far East and Poland, among other countries, until Rudolf was arrested in China. Maria had then been sent to Switzerland to reorganize the network after the great Russian purges of 1937–38, in which military Intelligence suffered very heavily. She was a good-looking, intelligent woman, completely devoted to Communism.

When Foote met her as Sonia, she was posing as a woman of independent means, living with her two children and a maid in a rented villa at Caux, near Montreux. From the Center she received a monthly salary of roughly $300. From her villa she transmitted to Moscow, which in those days of rudimentary direction-finding was quite safe, even if the Swiss had become interested in her.

On the outbreak of war Sonia was instructed by the Center to withdraw all her agents from Germany. (This was a good example of the Soviet technique of having the Resident Director of a network living outside the country in which his network was operating.) She was to remain in Switzerland herself and instruct Foote and another Englishman, William Phillips, in radio procedure. Her salary now began to arrive irregularly, causing her some difficulty, and when her information warranted only one schedule a month, she was transferred to England, where she arrived in December 1940. She worked in the Soviet Embassy until the end of the war, and was then transferred to the Russian Zone of Germany.

The Regional Director of the Swiss network was Alexander Rado. Brief biographical facts relating to him have also been given on page 41. As we have seen there, he had been appointed to this post in 1936, from Paris, his cover being a firm called Geopress. With the outbreak of the war, the Geopress achieved a high reputation, for its productions were exceptionally good.

Rado himself was greatly liked and esteemed by the circle of acquaintances in which he moved. He lived in Geneva with his German wife Helene, and their two sons, and was certainly never suspected of espionage, let alone of being a prominent Soviet agent.

As an agent, however, he had many faults. He was something of a sybarite, and this led him to indulge in activities of a private nature normally shunned by a first-class agent. In a crisis, too, like many of his fellow agents, he was prone to lose his nerve and become excited. Again and again he contravened the strict security rules imposed by the Center. He also broke regulations governing finance, and this eventually led to his liquidation.

Under Rado, at the peak of the Swiss network's operations, were about fifty agents of all categories. Most prominent, and certainly the most highly successful of them all, was the mysterious Rudolf Rössler, whose cover name was Lucy.

Rössler, who was the son of a Bavarian forester, for a time had been editor of an anti-Nazi newspaper in Augsburg. In 1933 he moved to Switzerland, where he became head of the publishing firm of Vita Nova, in Lucerne. Like Rado's Geopress, Vita Nova became well known, but for a different reason —its very strong anti-Nazi bias. His political credo was more anticapitalist than anti-Communist, and he was a member of *Die Entscheidung,* a leftist Catholic group.

Rössler was introduced to espionage by a young Swiss friend, Xavier Schnieper, who had met him in Berlin shortly before he moved to Switzerland. Schnieper was a journalist, and also a member of *Die Entscheidung.* In 1939 he was recruited into the Swiss Army Information Service, the *Nachrichtendienst,* and when asked to name others who might be useful, he recommended Rössler.

Rössler entered the service of the ND in the autumn of 1939, but it was not his intention to work for the ND; he was to be available to all those who were anti-Nazi. He had excellent contacts in Germany, and though, as will be seen presently, he supplied some of the most fantastic information ever to come the way of any espionage agency, to his death in 1962 he resolutely refused to reveal who his sources were. (Indeed, though twice convicted of spying by the Swiss, he also maintained that he was not guilty with equal firmness.) But whoever his sources were, they must have been in the highest circles of the Nazi High Command and Foreign Office, otherwise he could never have had access to his information.

From the beginning of the war, the Western Allies had exchanged intelligence, and after Hitler attacked Russia, that country was also included in the arrangement, though she was disinclined to reciprocate. Stalin should not have been surprised by the launching of Operation Barbarossa, for as early as March 1941, the American Undersecretary of State, Sumner Welles, had warned the Soviet Ambassador in Washington that Hitler was completing preparations for an attack on Russia; and this was confirmed by Richard Sorge, the Soviet spy master in Japan, by Sir Winston Churchill, and finally by Rössler.

With the permission of the ND, Rössler passed the information to Rado, by way of a friend, Christian Schneider, who himself contacted Rahel Dubendorfer, one of Rado's chief go-betweens. This was Rössler's first contribution to Soviet Intelligence, but from now on he worked regularly for Rado's network, it is presumed with the knowledge of his Swiss masters and of British Intelligence.

Rössler's information was not only fantastic in its accuracy and importance, but of equally incredible bulk. At first it seemed to the Russians to be too good to be true, and they suspected that the Nazis were playing with them. But Rössler was undeterred by their skepticism and continued to supply his information. As a result the Center began, little by little, to be won over, and eventually became so excited about this source of intelligence that they became un-Russian in their treatment of their star agent.

The Center would have been foolish indeed had they discarded his services, for after the Russo-German war began, he at once supplied regular, often daily, accurate information concerning Hitler's strategy, the strength, composition and location of all German armed forces, and a good idea of what German Intelligence knew about the Russians' positions, strength and plans. Without exaggeration, Russia owes her victory as much to Rössler as to any other factor. Certainly no agent working for any of the other Allied Intelligence agencies can claim to have had such a direct and personal influence on strategy and plans.

As soon as the Soviet espionage accepted Rössler, they could not do enough for him. He was paid more than any other agent had been paid up to that time—$1200 a month. When the physical difficulties of getting funds to the Swiss network became almost insurmountable, the anxiety shown by the Center lest Rössler should show himself so mercenary that he would adopt the principle of no pay, no results, was at times pathetic.

On December 9, 1943, the Director himself sent him this message:

> Tell Lucy he should not worry about payments; we will certainly pay our debts not later than January. We request him to continue giving us his most important information. Director.

and on January 8, 1944:

> Please tell Lucy that he and his group will receive large payment as soon as possible. He should wait patiently and should not waste time and effort at this important hour of the last battle against our common enemy. Director.

Besides Rahel Dubendorfer, whose cover name was Sissie, Rado's other main go-between was Otto Pünter, cover name Pakbo. Pünter had never been a member of the Communist Party, but from his youth had belonged to the Swiss Social Democratic Party. He was a journalist, and at the climax of the feud between Communists and Socialists in the thirties, was one of the leading Socialist protagonists. His eventual work for the Soviet network in Switzerland sprang from motives very like Foote's. He was bitterly anti-Fascist and gave his support to the

Communists because they seemed more bitterly opposed to Fascism than any other bloc.

Pünter's non-Communist-anti-Fascist career was an outstanding one. In the middle twenties he had allied himself to the Italian anti-Fascist Randolfo Pacciardi, and helped to organize the sensational flight which, on July 10, 1930, dropped anti-Mussolini leaflets over Milan. He had also joined the Spanish Republicans during the Civil War, and had undertaken espionage missions for them in Italy to discover information about Italian shipments of arms to Franco. It was this which had brought him to the attention of Soviet espionage.

In 1940 the GRU had approached him and the group of half a dozen friends he had gathered about him. The outcome of the negotiations which followed was that the Pakbo Group, as it was called, joined Rado's network. He enlarged his group, and throughout the entire time he worked for Soviet espionage—also with the acquiescence of Swiss Intelligence—he was able to supply information second in importance only to Rössler's.

The other two radio operators of the network, besides Foote, who operated in Lausanne, were the Hamels, husband and wife, in Geneva, and Margaret Bolli, cover name Rosie, also in Geneva. Edmond and Olga Hamel had been recruited on the recommendation of the Swiss Communist leader, Léon Nicole. Edmond had trained at a radio school in Paris, and in 1933 had started a successful radio business in Geneva. In 1940, at Rado's request, he had a short-wave transmitter installed in a room above the shop. Under Swiss law, radio transmitters were forbidden, and when Edmond's set was discovered by the Geneva police in 1941, he was so highly regarded by the Swiss Intelligence authorities that he received only a suspended sentence of ten days' imprisonment. Under the Center's strict rules, the Hamels' connection with the network ought to have been terminated forthwith. Instead, at Rado's suggestion, he built another transmitter, which he also installed in the room above the shop.

Margaret Bolli was yet another example of Rado's disregard of the rules. She was twenty-one in 1941 when Rado first made her acquaintance, also through Léon Nicole. Within a very short time they had become lovers, and Rado had persuaded her to become a radio operator.

Finally there was Christian Schneider, cover name Taylor. Schneider was a friend of Rössler and was employed by the International Labor Office, who, through Rahel Dubendorfer, also employed by the ILO, was brought into contact with Rado's network. Schneider's importance in the network was that, besides being an agent and talent-spotter, with Rahel Dubendorfer he served as Rado's go-between with Rössler. Foote says that only he, of the whole network, knew Rössler's identity, and it would seem that he collected Rössler's information and passed it to Dubendorfer, who, in turn, passed it to Rado. Neither Rado nor Foote nor anyone else in the network or in the Center ever knew who Lucy was until the war had finished.

When Foote had passed his preliminary tests, it had been the Center's intention to train him in Moscow, but by the time he was ready the situation was such that it was decided to keep him where he was, in Switzerland. This was in August 1939.

The Ribbentrop-Molotov Pact of this same month had a shattering effect on many Soviet agents. Sonia particularly took it badly. She could not understand how Stalin could come to terms with Nazism, let alone become an ally of Hitler. She had not recovered from the shock two days later when she was instructed to withdraw her agents from Germany and disband the network she had so patiently organized. Among these agents was William Phillips, who was holidaying on Titisee. Foote was able to speak to him on the telephone and warn him not to return to Germany. So Phillips joined Foote, and together they waited for new instructions.

During the waiting period, the two men taught themselves the intricacies of radio transmitting. They lived in a *pension* at Montreux, and at the beginning visited Sonia in her villa, and from her learned some of the technique. As the Center had nothing for them to do, they soon became proficient operators and learned a good deal about radio construction.

Sonia had had no idea that Rado's network was also operating

until it became essential for the Center to instruct the two organizations to get in touch with one another. The need for this was
the breakdown in communications arising out of the temporary
disorganization of the Trepper network in France. Up to this
time Rado had had no radio operator of his own. He had
recorded his information on microfilm and sent it to Trepper for
transmission to Moscow.

After contact had been made, Sonia used to collect Rado's
information and transmit it herself from her villa at Caux. In
August 1940, however, Foote was instructed by the Center to
leave Montreux and settle in Geneva, there to train an operator
for Rado's network. It was thus that Foote and Rado first met.

The operator selected by the Center was Edmond Hamel,
who, although a very proficient radio engineer, did not know the
Morse code or Russian wireless procedure. Sonia's transmitter
was moved to the room above Hamel's shop, and Foote began to
instruct Hamel, who, curiously, was not a very apt pupil.

In the autumn the Center acceded to Sonia's request that she
might go to England. Before she left she received a new transmitting schedule and codes which she handed over to Foote. At
the same time, Foote was ordered back to Lausanne to set up
another transmitter there, the set to be built by Hamel on the
pattern of the one supplied to Sonia. With it Foote left for Lausanne, leaving Phillips to continue Hamel's training.*

Foote moved to Lausanne on December 15, 1940, and after
some initial difficulties managed to establish himself in a private
flat with his transmitter. His cover was that of a wealthy Englishman caught in Switzerland by the war and unable to return
home, a role which the Swiss authorities accorded him without
question, since there were a number like him in their country.

Safely installed at last, with his line to Moscow established, he
now encountered another difficulty. His transmitting crystal
refused to oscillate. Being untrained in radio mechanics, he was
tempted to go to Geneva to seek Hamel's advice. Since this
would have been bad security, however, he resisted the tempta-

---

*Phillips remained in Switzerland until March 1941, when he returned to
England.

tion and suddenly, for no reason that was apparent to him, on March 12th, Moscow replied that they were receiving him loud and clear.

In the period March 12 to June 22, 1941, Foote found life as a Soviet spy leisurely and pleasant. He had two schedules a week only, and his supply of traffic was not great. He had already been appointed understudy to Rado—a most unusual occurrence in Soviet espionage—and on this account had to remain as much as possible in the background.

He employed his time, however, in establishing himself firmly in Lausanne. He himself says that this was not easy, for his fellow countrymen there varied from officers and civil servants who had settled in Switzerland on retirement, to the riffraff of the Riviera who had fled from the Germans and were living on their wits.

He plugged his reputation for wealth, and was so successful that he was soon said to be an eccentric millionaire escaping from a war-stricken England. Besides explaining his leisure it also had the effect of satisfying the police still further. Though regarded by many as a recluse, he did form a small circle of acquaintances who eased his loneliness.

The fall of France had also dealt Rado's finances a body blow. Switzerland was indeed an island of neutrality isolated in a sea of hostility, and communications of all kinds were extremely difficult.

To keep his network going, he borrowed funds from the Swiss Communist Party, but the Party was not so wealthy that it could make more than a short-term loan, and was soon pressing for the return of their money. The bulk of Rado's communications with the Center via Foote at this time was concerned with finance.

The Center itself seemed to be quite unable to propose any way of getting any funds to Rado. The suggestions they did make illustrate a complete ignorance of conditions and possibilities. Eventually Foote himself devised a plan.

The Center had said that they were able to place funds to Foote's credit in banks either in Great Britain, America or Sweden.

Foote therefore made very discreet inquiries among his Swiss friends and found one prepared to help him make contact with an American firm operating in Switzerland which, in the course of its business, had to send money to the United States. Normally this was done through the National Bank of Switzerland, but Foote now proposed that all the trouble of formalities could be avoided if he transferred funds which he had in America to their account there, while they paid him the equivalent in Swiss francs in Switzerland. As a further inducement, he said he was willing to accept black-market rates, which meant that the Americans would make a reasonable profit.

It was a simple and practically foolproof plan. The Center paid into an account in Foote's name in New York dollars which he in turn credited to the New York account of the American firm. As soon as this had been done, the New York bank credited the Swiss account of the Americans, who paid Foote the equivalent in Swiss francs. There were small hitches, but usually the transaction could be completed within ten days.

The plan worked well all the time Foote was working for the network. No one, neither the Swiss who introduced him nor the Americans who collaborated with him, ever suspected that they were financing Soviet espionage.

Rado and Foote at this time were meeting only about twice a month. It had originally been the Center's intention that the little group that Foote had gathered around him should remain quite separate from Rado's network. As the German invasion of Russia became more imminent, and the volume of traffic with which the Swiss groups had to cope increased, this was clearly going to be impossible, and early in June 1941, Foote received instructions that he must contact Rado at least twice a week so that he might relieve Rado's radio operators of some of their burden. As Foote had his own code and could cut down the time between receiving the information and passing it to Moscow to a few hours, compared with the twenty-four hours and more which it took Hamel and Bolli, for some unknown reason, the Center began to rely more and more on Foote for passing urgent information. It was this that brought Foote the vital information which Rössler, in June 1941, began to supply daily.

When Rössler sent word that the German attack was timed for June 22, Rado summoned Foote to meet him. Foote found him perplexed and undecided. He could not believe that such information would be genuine, and was inclined not to pass it on to Moscow, who had already let him know that they were skeptical of Rössler's sources. Foote argued, on the other hand, that the Center was in a much better position to assess its value than they were in Switzerland with their restricted horizon. If they held the information back and it turned out to be correct, the Center could, quite rightly, accuse them of criminal negligence. Rado saw the point, and the message was dispatched.

With the invasion of Russia the Swiss network immediately took on an entirely new significance. Along with an exhortatory injunction to fight "the Fascist beasts to the best of your ability," Foote was informed that henceforward the Center would maintain a twenty-four-hour watch on his wave lengths, and arranged a system of priorities.

Since Foote, to all intents and purposes, was a lone hand and was thus uncluttered by other considerations which the running of a network involves, he was able to devote all of his time to radio transmitting, which also further reduced the time he took to forward information, and this gave the Center so much confidence in him that he was given other tasks as well. Among these was an attempt to compose the rivalries which some time previously had begun to split the Swiss Communist Party. Another was to find and make contact with two agents, George and Joanna Wilmer, with whom the Center had lost touch. The Wilmers were agents of long standing, having worked in Japan before Richard Sorge took charge of the network there. They were experts in photography and microphotography. Before the war they had worked in Germany, and it was when the war broke out that they lost contact with the Center.

Foote found them in a well-appointed villa just above Lausanne. They claimed to be in touch with two sources in Germany and to have contacts with the French counterespionage. Foote arranged to visit them periodically to gather their information and pass it on to Moscow.

These and other matters on top of Foote's normal work, which was now of considerable bulk, made him a very busy spy and it became more and more difficult for him to maintain his pose of an English gentleman of leisure. He transmitted as a rule two hours every night, and anyone who has had experience in radio operating will appreciate the strain this must have been. But besides transmitting, he had to encode all his material in his own code. This, too, is a task which imposes a tremendous strain on the encoder. Added to this was receiving and deciphering long messages from the Center.

Besides the normal difficulties of reception conditions, with which all radio operators have to contend, Foote met with many other frustrations. Whenever the Luftwaffe raided Moscow, the Center would stop sending immediately. Then when the Soviet Government moved to Kuibishev, the Center broke off suddenly in the middle of a message, and though Foote and Rado tried to make contact with them, they did not come up again for six weeks. Then, without any explanation at all, the next group in the broken message was sent.

By the end of 1942, Rado was beginning to run into difficulties which continued into and throughout the first nine months of 1943. The Swiss network had two main opponents—the Swiss counterespionage, known by its initials, BUPO; and the Abwehr. The BUPO was prepared to take no notice of the network, on the principle that Rado, Foote and their friends were not engaged against Swiss interests. They were, however, ready to pounce if the network became too blatant and could be "seen" to infringe upon Swiss neutrality. The Abwehr, on the other hand, were naturally extremely anxious to destroy the network.

Foote has always maintained that George and Joanna Wilmer were largely responsible for the eventual breakup of the network. There were several things about the couple which roused his suspicions, but the Center, when he reported how he felt, replied that he was mistaken. Before the middle of 1943, however, it was discovered that the Wilmers were in fact collaborating with the Abwehr, having defected before leaving Germany, and that they had come to Switzerland expressly to find out what they could about the network so that they might betray it.

Because of his contact with the Wilmers, Foote was compromised as far as the Abwehr were concerned; and the breakup of the French network had compromised Rado, though neither he nor the Center knew this. Foote was instructed to have no further personal connection with Rado, and to employ go-betweens in his contacts with his own small group. His transmissions to Moscow were reduced to twice a week, and his messages dealt mainly with the liquidation of one group, and finance which by the end of June 1943 had reached new peaks of difficulty.

Foote's arrangement with the American firm had become very difficult, and the new channel which Foote hoped to establish demanded proof that the money really belonged to him. Before Foote could provide the proof many things were to happen.

The Wilmers anonymously denounced Foote to the Swiss police via the French Consulate General in July. Fortunately the police did not act, as the only identification was a photograph. At about the same time, the Center ordered Foote to move. This was more difficult to perform than to order, for not only was he once again in daily contact with the Center, but he would have to obtain police permission to move, and they would require very good reasons before granting his request.

Rado had been unable to cope with all the material through his own operators, and Foote had been ordered to make contact with him again. But Rado was himself in difficulties with the Abwehr. He had met a former Soviet agent, now working for the Abwehr, in a restaurant, and was quite certain that Abwehr agents were watching him. He was equally sure that they were also watching Margaret Bolli, and had taken her radio away from her for the time being.

Rado was quite right in his surmises. The Abwehr decided that Rado's mistress would pay the best dividends and set out to seduce her through the medium of a young agent named Hans

Peters. Because of her nature, since she could no longer receive the consolations of Rado's apparently skillful love-making, she was quite ready to accept the attentions of the handsome young man whose acquaintance she made, apparently fortuitously though actually through the cunning manipulations of the Germans, and within a short time Rado's difficulties were heading toward disaster.

Added to the activities of the Abwehr, the Swiss BUPO had also begun to take an interest in Rado's affairs. Quite by chance a member of the radio staff at Geneva airport had picked up a strong Morse signal operating amateur procedure. As amateur radio transmissions were forbidden in Switzerland, the airport operator informed the authorities, who were compelled to investigate. They traced the transmitter to Geneva. This had been Bolli's set, but during the investigations a second set—the Hamels'—was also operating from Geneva.

These discoveries had been made almost a year before Rado began to suspect that he was being watched, but the Swiss took no action until the Abwehr began to apply pressure on them to do so, threatening to make a diplomatic scandal if they did not do so. In September 1943, therefore, they went into action in earnest. Early in October the Hamels and Margaret Bolli were arrested. The Hamels had been caught working their set, and Margaret had been torn from the bed she had been sharing with Abwehr agent Hans Peters.

Rado himself had had a narrow escape. Once more breaking security rules, he had gone to the Hamels' flat unaware that they had been arrested and while the police were still searching it. Fortunately he was warned by a prearranged danger signal which the Hamels had been able to set.

The arrests threw Rado into a state verging on panic. He telephoned Foote's flat and confessed that shortly before the Hamels' arrest, fearing for his own position, he had deposited in their flat, in a secret hiding place, all his financial records, copies of messages *en clair* which had been sent to Moscow—they ought to have been burned—and worst of all, his code book. It is difficult to find in the records of espionage anywhere an agent who broke so many of the rules as Rado.

The BUPO were skillful in their job, and found all these vital papers. If it were not bad enough that the financial records revealed to them all the names of the network's agents, they also found details of a new Swiss Oerlikon cannon still on the secret list. This information could have come only from their own agent Rössler. Thus both Rado and Rössler were guilty of working against Swiss national interests.

But the BUPO did not yet know of the existence of Rado. They believed that Foote was directing the network. But this time, they were not far out in their assumption, for Rado had gone into hiding in Berne, and Foote had been instructed to take over the Resident Directorship.

Before going into hiding, Rado had put Foote in contact with Otto Pünter, of the Pakbo Group, but he had refused to do so in the case of Rahel Dubendorfer, though Foote later discovered that she had asked to be put in touch with him. Rado suggested that he and the whole network should take refuge in the British Legation. This would naturally mean that the British would have to be told all, but they were Russia's allies. Foote asked the Center's permission to do this, and received an unequivocal No, which rattled Rado still more; and an incident which happened when Rado had arrived for a rendezvous with Foote in a public park—his taxi driver had recognized him—brought Rado's fears to a climax. Thereafter he refused to leave his hiding place, and from this time was virtually inactive.

Foote, who was now leading the network, did not realize his own jeopardy. He carried on quietly as before, but on the night of November 19–20, 1943, as he was in the middle of his regular transmission to Moscow, the door of his flat was broken in. The door was stronger than the police had gauged, and it took more than one assault to move it. This gave Foote a few brief but precious moments, in which he was able to burn all his papers and damage his transmitter so that it would no longer work.

At first Foote believed it was the Abwehr who had taken the matter into their own hands, but he soon recognized the visitors as Swiss. Except that he would now be *hors de combat*, Foote was unworried by what was taking place, for after the arrest of the Hamels and Margaret Bolli he had prepared for the worst and had destroyed every document he possessed.

Inspector Knecht, Federal Police Chief for the Geneva Canton, was in charge of the interrogation. He told Foote that the Hamels and Bolli had confessed and incriminated him and Rado, but he honestly added that there was no evidence that Foote had spied against Swiss interests. The Inspector therefore urged him to make a full confession and he would do all he could to see that he received a light sentence.

Foote replied that he could say nothing. On the other hand, he said that if he were given only a light sentence, Moscow would interpret it to mean that he had confessed, and this would ultimately bring him before a Russian firing squad. He therefore insisted that he should be given a longer sentence than any of the others. He would much rather, he told the Inspector, spend two or three years in a Swiss prison than meet the fate awaiting him in Russia.

The BUPO were not used to this line of approach, and were perplexed by it, but since he continued to answer none of their questions and reiterated his request for a long sentence, they put him in prison while they made further investigations. These lasted ten months. He was then told that as there was no evidence against him that he had worked against Swiss interests, he could apply for bail pending his trial before a court martial.

From prison, Foote went to Lausanne, and in a hotel there considered the future. When he had made sure that he was not being watched, he began to scout the various rendezvous, hoping to make some contact with Rahel Dubendorfer, or Otto Pünter or Pierre Nicole, Léon Nicole's son. His first contact was with Nicole, who was able to tell him that Rado and his wife had never been found. Only a few days before they had left for liberated Paris, where, Rado had said, he intended going to the Soviet military attaché.

Foote also re-established contact with Otto Pünter, who had not been compromised and had been left in peace. Pünter told him that his sources were still available, and that he was anxious to get going again.

Finally, Rahel Dubendorfer made her appearance. She had been arrested with her lover, the former prominent German Communist, Paul Boettcher, and her daughter Tamara, in May 1944, but had been released after three months. Her sources were also intact, but she, too, like Pünter, was desperate for money. From what Rahel told him, Foote saw that it was absolutely imperative that he should have an interview with Rössler, who had also been arrested at the same time as Rahel. A meeting was arranged, at which Rössler told him that despite the purge after the July 20 attempt on Hitler's life, his main sources were still able to supply information, and he was anxious to start again as soon as possible.

As a result of this meeting, Foote decided that he must go to Paris to make contact with the Center through the Soviet Embassy if the network was to operate once more. This he did, and after initial difficulties, he was instructed by the Center to go to Moscow for consultations.

Rado now came on the scene, though he had actually arrived in Paris a month before Foote. He too was ordered to return. Foote had nothing to fear from an investigation; his story could be checked at every point; but Rado's position was much more serious, for he had more or less deserted his post.

Foote and Rado left Paris in a Russian aircraft on January 6, 1945. As the battle for Germany was still raging, the aircraft was routed via Cairo. During an overnight stay there Rado decided that by returning to Moscow he was literally putting a gunbarrel to the nape of his neck, and when morning came he was nowhere to be found. So Foote went on alone.

The Center was not long, however, in discovering Rado's whereabouts, and they applied to the Egyptian Government for his extradition as a deserter officer of the Red Army. After a protracted battle to resist extradition, he was eventually returned to Russia in the summer of 1945.

From the moment of his arrival there, it became a struggle for existence between Foote and Rado. Since Foote was able to prove the truth of much of his case, and the more Rado's case was probed the more apparent did it become that he had played havoc with the network's finances to his own personal advantage, Foote eventually won the struggle and was vindicated. Rado was tried secretly, and executed.

His treatment in Moscow had, however, wrought a change in Foote's attitude to the Soviet Union. As each day passed, he became more and more disillusioned, until he reached the decision that he had had enough both of Communism and Russia. But he realized that if he was to escape with his life, he must go on pretending to be loyal and in some way prevail upon the Director to give him another assignment abroad.

His chance came when the Canadian Spy Case brought in its train yet another purge. When this was complete, every available agent of proved loyalty was pressed into service, and Foote was assigned to Mexico.

So it was that in March 1947, a Major Granatov of the Red Army arrived in the Soviet Sector of Berlin, and three months later crossed into the British Sector to reveal himself to the authorities as Alexander Foote.

Today, this man, who proved himself to be a first-class agent mainly because he used his native common sense, lives a quiet, inconspicuous life in England as a clerk.

☐ The Canadian Networks

It would appear that until Canada entered the war and began to manufacture munitions, there was little in the country to attract the attention of Soviet espionage. There was another factor, too, which would have made the operation of full-scale espionage difficult—the Communist ideology had proved to have as little appeal to the Canadian proletariat as it had had to the British, with the result that although there had been a Canadian Communist Party from the early twenties, it was not numerous enough, or virile enough, to fulfill the role allotted to the national Communist Parties in the scheme of Soviet espionage.

Nevertheless, there were at the head of the CCP two men who were later to become prominent agents, brought to the attention of the world by the part they played in the acquisition of atomic secrets. They were Sam Carr and Fred Rose.

These two had carried out minor espionage work, indeed the only espionage in Canada almost from the inception of the CCP in the early twenties. Their information consisted chiefly of reports on the internal squabbles of the CCP itself, though now and again they did acquire some quite unimportant official views emanating from Ottawa, but this was not very often.

During the thirties there was an increase in general interest in Communism in Canada, and for a time the membership of the Party rose steeply, with a consequent upsurge in information relating to Canadian industry; that is to say, at the height of Soviet activity in the field of industrial espionage in Europe, Canadian industry did at last attract some attention. The main sources of the information supplied came through the formation of so-called study groups, a traditional method in Soviet technique, as we have seen.

This activity continued until the signing of the Ribbentrop-Molotov Pact, when even the Canadian Communists could not, like Alexander Foote's first leader, Sonia, understand the ethics or the logic of Stalin's *volte face*. This led to a great falling off in CCP membership, which was further increased when the government outlawed the Party.

The invasion of Russia by Hitler, however, brought about yet another change. Not only did public feeling toward the Communists become more sympathetic, but the government also relaxed its strictures. In this, of course, the government was motivated by reasons of logic. Canada and Russia were now allies, and it would have been odd for Ottawa to have continued its long-standing refusal to accord diplomatic recognition to the Soviet Union. This recognition, it would seem, was regarded by the Soviet leaders as quite unimportant, except for one thing—it would permit them to send a trade delegation to Canada and to establish an embassy in Ottawa, both with a view to stepping up espionage operations.

The trade delegation arrived first, in 1942. Listed among the clerks, though not by his rank, was a certain Major Sokolov, who was an agent of the GRU, and whose task was to organize a network. A little later he was joined by Sergei Kudriavtsev, ostensibly First Secretary of the delegation. These two men went to work in the Soviet conventional way, and their first move was to contact Fred Rose of the CCP. Progress was slow, however, and in the first year the number of agents recruited was small, probably less than ten altogether in two groups based respectively in Ottawa and Montreal.

In mid-1943, however, the embassy had become fully established, and there arrived to join its staff Colonel Nicolai Zabotin, with the rank of military attaché, but actually sent to take over the leadership from Sokolov. Among his various clerks was a cipher expert, Igor Gouzenko.

With Zabotin's arrival, recruitment was speeded up, and by the end of the following year a network of some twenty local and fifteen Soviet operators had been established. The latter filled the traditional roles of Tass correspondents, clerks at the trade delegation and in the embassy, chauffeurs and doormen. This was still not quite large enough, in Zabotin's view, to carry out the tasks which had been assigned him, and a further plan for enlarging the network was formulated based on an expansion of the trade delegation.

Before this could be done, however, and before the network had really got into its stride, the end of hostilities in both Europe and Japan had come. The activities of Zabotin's agents will, therefore, be described in detail in Part IV, Atomic Espionage.

☐ The Sorge Network
in the Far East

In the course of forty years of spying, the Soviet espionage agency has produced two or three really outstanding agents. Until the advent of Lonsdale in the Portland Naval Spy Case (1961), all such agents were of foreign nationality, and with the exception of Alexander Foote, all were Germans. Rudolf Rössler must rank among the great spies of all time from the point of view of the value of his information, but for the same reason and for the audacity and indeed impudence of his manner of operating, Richard Sorge must be considered his peer.

Richard Sorge was born in 1895, the second son of a German oil-driller who had emigrated to the Baku oil fields, where the pay was good. By the time he was of school age, Richard's family had returned to Berlin and before very long his German masters were commenting on the high level of their pupil's intelligence.

When the First World War broke out, Sorge joined the Kaiser's army, and within a short time had been wounded in the leg. In 1916 he returned to the front line, where he found that much of the confidence with which his companions had marched in the early days had been replaced by fear. Again his career as a combatant was cut short by a second and much more serious wound.

Sorge's paternal grandfather, Adolf Sorge, had for several years been private secretary to Karl Marx. To kill time while waiting for his wounds to heal, Richard Sorge began to study Marx's writings, and found that the ideas set out in *Das Kapital* attracted him.

When he had joined the army, he had been studying political economy and history, and when he was demobilized at the end of the war, he enrolled in the universities of Kiel and Hamburg, graduating from the latter in the spring of 1920, as a Doctor of Political Science. The same day that he graduated, he joined the German Communist Party.

For a time he taught in a Hamburg school, but was dismissed when his headmaster discovered that he was not only teaching Communism, but recruiting members to the Party in school hours. He then became a coal miner, and continued his evangelizing at the coal face with such effect that production was slowed up and he was again dismissed.

While studying at Kiel he had taken part in the disturbances there which accompanied the famous mutiny of the German navy. This, and his more recent activities, brought him to the notice of the Communist leaders as a competent agitator, and he was marked down for special consideration.

On the day that he left the coal mine, and made his way back to his lodgings, he found waiting for him in his room Henry Tollman, the secret chief of Communist security in Hamburg. Tollman proposed to him that he should go to Moscow for a course of training. He arrived in Moscow three weeks later, but before he left he had become involved with a woman—this was to be typical of his behavior throughout his long career—who, by chance, was a police agent, and to whom, between bouts of love-making indulged in merely to relieve the boredom of waiting, he talked about his attraction to Marx and the Communists.

The day following his arrival in Moscow, Sorge was seen by Dimitry Manuilsky, then head of the Foreign Intelligence Division of the Comintern. Like Foote, Sorge had been given no hint of what the Russians had in store for him. His interview with Manuilsky put an end to his speculations—he was to be trained as a spy.

Few spies have been so thoroughly trained as Sorge. For the next five years he passed from one school to another until he was thoroughly imbued with every aspect of espionage technique. During this time he was sent to Scandinavia and the Balkans to gain firsthand experience under expert guidance. He had a remarkable flair for languages and by 1928 he spoke Russian like a native, and he was also fluent in English and French.

As a test, he was sent by himself for a year to Los Angeles to discover all he could about the American film industry. This test he passed *summa cum laude*. After a brief visit to Moscow, he was given a final test, and in 1928 he landed in England, where he took a room in a Bloomsbury boarding house.

On all his travels he had used his own name, and the cover of a student of political science. Neither in Scandinavia, the Balkans nor California had he ever encountered anyone who recalled his agitating days in Hamburg and Kiel. But not long after he arrived in London, he was visited by Special Branch officers—he had forgotten to register as an alien—who, in the course of questioning, asked him if he had ever lived in Hamburg.

Sorge was much impressed, and reported to Moscow: "England knows more about spies than any other nation." He also realized that the officers had not been convinced by his denials, and cut short his visit.

The following year, Sorge was transferred from the sevice of the Comintern to the Secretariat for Foreign Affairs. This was merely a cover, for he was passed on almost at once to the GRU.

By this time, Sorge had gained such a reputation with the professional chiefs of Soviet espionage, that after a brief interview with the Director of the Center, he was appointed Resident Director for the Far East, with headquarters in Shanghai. So great was the confidence in him of his superiors, that, contrary to all usual practice, the Center gave him carte blanche. All he was required specifically to furnish was information about Chiang Kai-shek's growing Nationalist army. Other than this, whatever else he submitted was to be entirely at his own discretion.

This was not the first infiltration of the Far East by Soviet agents. There had been a small network in China for three years before, but it had lacked leadership and had produced little worth-while information. Now the indications were that the importance of the area was about to increase, and this automatically required a well-organized network imaginatively led.

Sorge was allowed to choose the men who were to work for his new China Unit. He retained those agents already in the area who would, in his opinion, be of assistance to him, disbanded the rest and, from a list supplied by the Center, selected two first-class radio technicians to accompany him. Early in 1930 the China Unit had become firmly established in Shanghai. For the first and only time in his career, Sorge abandoned his own identity, and became William Johnson, an American journalist.

Among his useful contacts in Shanghai he found Agnes Smedley, the American Communist writer, and with her help the network was able to go into instant operation, for she permitted the radio operator who had come with Sorge to set up his transmitter in her flat, and so saved him the trouble and time of finding a "safe address." But more than that, she arranged for him to meet certain residents of Shanghai who, though not Communists, were prepared to provide him with military information. Among them was a brilliant young Japanese scholar and journalist, Ozaki Hozumi.

Ozaki came from a wealthy family, and had graduated at Tokyo University. He had studied Marx, Lenin and Engels, but filial duty had prevented his making his belief in Communism public. He was in Shanghai as the correspondent of a Tokyo newspaper, and had made the acquaintance of Agnes Smedley.

One of Sorge's great assets was his personal charm. He was not physically handsome. A flat nose, a deeply lined forehead, small, widely set eyes, deep indentations from the nose to the corners of his mouth and full lips gave him an un-Teutonic appearance. Yet despite his bohemian behavior, his drinking and his concupiscence, there was much about him that was socially attractive. He was well aware of this asset, and never hesitated to use it when he felt that it would help him to get what he wanted.

Almost from the first moment of meeting Ozaki, he decided that he wanted the young Japanese in his network; so he turned his charm on him and the young man fell instantly. For the first time he agreed to engage in active espionage, and soon he was to render such service to the China Unit that he was scarcely to be surpassed by Sorge himself.

With Shanghai organized, Sorge went on a tour of his region, and at the end of six weeks came to Harbin, in Manchuria, where he was joined by a German businessman, Max Klausen, the finest radio operator in the Center's employ. By the time Klausen arrived in Harbin, Sorge had already made friends with the young American vice-consul there, and had persuaded him to rent a German friend of his two rooms in the consulate. So, under the protection of the Stars and Stripes, Klausen set up his radio transmitter. Sorge also engaged an agent to assist Klausen, and with the cell firmly established he returned to Shanghai, and continued building up his organization.

Within two years of arriving in Shanghai, the China Unit was functioning at full strength. It covered Nanking, Hankow, Canton and Peking, while individual agents worked as far south as Malaya and as far north as the Siberian border. They supplied the Center with reports on the support given by the various classes to the government, the Communists and to Chiang; they knew exactly the respective military strengths of these three aspects of the Chinese situation, their equipment, supplies and reserves, and they listed the details of the large business interests which would be prepared, in return for certain concessions, to support the Communists when they organized their revolution.

With the accession of Hitler, the traditional friendliness of Germany toward China began to shift away from that country toward Japan, and, becoming aware of this, the Russian leaders thought they could see also a comparable shift in the danger which they always believed existed for their Siberian territories.

Determined not to be caught out if this really was so, the

(*Above*) Lavrenti Beria, at right, in black hat, at Stalin's funeral in 1953. In front at left is Georgi Malenkov, who led the ouster of Beria later that year. (*Right*) Official photo of Beria.

(*Above*) Sergei Kruglov, Beria's successor.
(*Below*) Spy master in prewar Japan, Dr.
Richard Sorge, one of the greatest spies.

(*Above*) The Swiss ring's Alexander Rado.

(*Below*) Rudolf Rössler (left), the Soviet Union's master spy of World War II, leaves his 1953 Swiss trial followed by Doctor Xavier Schnieper, his contact.

(*Above*) Lydia Stahl with her lawyers. (*Left*) Juliet Poyntz, who quit Soviet espionage in the United States. Her body is believed to have been disposed of in New York's East River.

(*Above*) The New York offices of Amtorg, the Soviet trade organization.

(*Below*) This picture taken at Communist headquarters in Yenan, China, in 1937, according to the late Senator McCarthy, shows Owen Lattimore (right) and Philip Jaffe (center), editor of *Amerasia*.

(*Above*) Whittaker Chambers testifying before the House Un-American Activities Committee. In the second row behind Chambers, third from the left, smiling, is Alger Hiss, who had just testified that he had never been a Communist. (*Left*) Alger Hiss is taken off to begin serving sentence.

(*Above*) Senator Joseph McCarthy listens to a witness.

(*Below*) Secretary General of the United Nations Conference on International Organization, Alger Hiss shakes hands with President Harry S. Truman. This was in 1945.

UNITED PRESS INTERNATIONAL PHOTO

(*Above*) Julius and Ethel Rosenberg after being indicted as the "aggressive" members of the Klaus Fuchs spy ring.

(*Below*) Klaus Fuchs' American contact man, Harry Gold.

UNITED PRESS INTERNATIONAL PHOTO

(*Above*) Dr. Klaus Fuchs, after having served his British prison sentence, being escorted to a flight to East Germany by agents from Scotland Yard.

(*Below*) David Greenglass at N. Y. Federal Court.

KEYSTONE

(*Left*) Professor Bruno Pontecorvo in Moscow after his escape from Britain.

WIDE WORLD PHOTOS

(*Right*) Dr. Alan Nunn May.

(*Above*) Judith Coplon (at left) and Valentin Gubitchev (right), her Russian contact man, at the time of their trial in N. Y. (*Right*) Elizabeth Bentley.

(*Above*) Defector Igor Gouzenko during an interview.

(*Above right*) Once Soviet Resident Director of espionage in Australia,
Vladimir Petrov walks with security guards following his defection.
(*Below*) Mrs. Vladimir Petrov, wearing a light suit and minus one shoe,
is hustled to an airplane at Sydney airport by Soviet Embassy people.

(*Above left*) Former Captain in the Division for Terror and Diversion, Nicolai Khokhlov, after recovering from a poisoning attempt. With him is an official of the anti-Soviet NTS. (*Above right*) Khokhlov greets Georgi Okolovich, the leader of the NTS, whom he was ordered to kill.

(*Below*) Anna Maria Knuth, ill and in a deck chair, talks to her lawyers.

(*Above*) Soviet master spy Colonel Rudolf Abel, with U.S. Marshals.

(*Below*) Colonel Abel's studio apartment on Fulton Street in Brooklyn. The paintings, including a self-portrait, are by Colonel Abel himself.

(*Above left*) The Drive, Brent, London, Vassall's place of rendezvous with a Russian contact man. (*Above right*) George Blake at Berlin on his hero's return home from captivity in a North Korean prison.

(*Below*) John Vassall relaxing in his luxury apartment in London.

(*Above left*) The man called Gordon Lonsdale, before his arrest.
(*Above right*) Harry Houghton, former Navy man and Admiralty clerk.

(*Below*) Peter and Helen Kroger, or, in U. S., Morris and Lorna Cohen.

Center promoted its Director, Colonel Beldin, to General, and put him in charge of a special section for Far Eastern affairs. Beldin's first act was to recall Sorge to Moscow for consultations.

Sorge and Beldin consulted for several months, and by the end of their talks had drawn up a plan to extract all the secrets from the Japanese Government. Once more, Sorge was given the pick of all Soviet agents, and he chose the two men most likely to be of use to him. Ozaki was to ask for a transfer back to Japan, and Klausen was to move the scene of his cover business there also. To complete the network, he selected two others: Branko de Voukelich, a former officer in the Royal Yugoslav Army, and now a foreign correspondent for several newspapers, and a Japanese artist, Miyagi Yotoku, whom Sorge had met while he had been in California.

Before he himself returned to embark on building up the Japanese network, Sorge returned to Germany. How he was able to ingratiate himself with the Nazis to the extent that he was given Party membership and accredited Far East correspondent of the *Frankfurter Zeitung* still remains something of a mystery. Germans abroad with whom he had made friends certainly helped by giving him introductions to leading Party members, but this still does not fully explain how, within a short time after arriving in Germany, to build up his cover for Tokyo, he came to be invited to functions attended by the most intimate associates of the Party leadership, and even of the Leader himself; or why, on the eve of his departure for Tokyo, the Nazi Press Club gave a dinner in his honor which was attended by Bohle, chief of the Nazi Foreign Division, and by Josef Goebbels. This dinner was certainly to be of great use to him both on his arrival in Tokyo and in the years that followed.

The fact that his reputation had preceded him and that he was the *bona fide* accredited correspondent of the *Frankfurter Zeitung*, the *Bergen Kurrier*, the *Tächnische Rundschau* and the *Amsterdam Handelsblatt* automatically made him *persona grata* with the German Embassy officials in Tokyo, from the Ambassador down.

Of the five men who formed the network, Sorge and Ozaki were undeniably the most successful. There was little to choose between their respective brilliance, though it derived from different qualities. While Sorge was capable of assessing the value of the information that came to him with such penetration that he sent nothing to Moscow that was useless, he also missed nothing that was of value. Ozaki, on the other hand, besides being an expert interpreter of political trends throughout the Orient, and China in particular, also had contacts which brought him into the highest Japanese political circles.

The fact that Sorge, Ozaki and Voukelich were accredited foreign correspondents made it possible for them to meet without rousing the suspicions of the Kempeitai, the counterespionage. Sorge did not rush the initial operation of his network, but by meetings in cafés, restaurants and bars, at first casual and then arranged, he allowed it to appear that the relationship which ultimately developed had done so gradually.

Sorge's legal occupation automatically took him frequently to the German Embassy, where he made it appear that he was meeting Max Klausen for the first time. It seemed to onlookers, too, quite natural that the eccentric correspondent should take pity on the lonely German salesman and invite him to join his circle.

Miyagi was introduced in much the same way. Sorge and Voukelich were in the Ueno Art Museum one day, when Voukelich recognized a Japanese artist friend. He introduced him to Sorge, a discussion between the two men developed concerning the merits of Eastern and Western art, and Miyagi was invited to continue it at a café frequented by artists and journalists.

A base from which to operate is essential to any espionage network, and it must be a base to which all members may go openly, with ostensibly legitimate reasons for their visits, and yet safe and secure from eavesdroppers, if they are to meet at all, and not use go-betweens. Sorge had decided to keep his ring to the minimum, and had to adopt this method of making contact, so he chose as his base a ramshackle house, the rent of which was well within his salary as a foreign correspondent.

As soon as he was installed in his house, Sorge gave a party which shocked both his respectable neighbors and the members of the diplomatic corps, who had been invited along with journalists, artists, young Japanese Army officers and a sprinkling of Japanese businessmen. When the less intimate guests left at about ten o'clock a number of geisha girls were summoned to the house, and for the next few hours the noises emanating from the rickety structure testified to what was going on within.

The neighborhood listened unhappily until the early hours, when the girls left accompanied by the remaining guests, except for Voukelich, Ozaki, Klausen and Miyagi, whom Sorge had pressed to finish the last bottle with him. In the comparative quiet that followed, and before the four guests eventually left with the first light, Sorge had given his spies their first briefing.

Sorge's parties soon became the talk of Tokyo, and if watching Kempeitai agents noticed that his four best friends always stayed after the other guests had left, they saw nothing suspicious in that.

A spy normally draws the least possible attention to himself. Sorge worked from the other extreme. Not only were his wild parties the talk of Tokyo, but his relationships with women became notorious. His need for sexual gratification was truly much above normal, but his attitude toward the unfortunate women who fell under the spell of his great charm and consummate wooing was fundamentally one of contempt. He soon grew bored with a partner, and within a few weeks of the opening of an affair he cast her off and looked around for new excitements.

This reputation served him as valuable cover. The argument seems to have been that any man who attracted so much attention to himself could not be a spy.

With his ring well established, Sorge went to work, and it was not long before he was justifying the confidence which General Beldin had placed in him by a series of brilliant coups.

The first of these was achieved by the agency of Ozaki, whose reputation as a political commentator had now brought him to the attention of the Japanese government, so much so, indeed, that when, toward the end of 1935, the Foreign Minister pre-

pared a report for the Cabinet on Japan's economic and political
aims for 1936, Prince Konoye, the Prime Minister, readily
agreed to a proposal that Ozaki should be allowed to see a draft
copy in order that he might state his views on those sections
referring to China.

Ozaki was permitted to study the document for the greater
part of a day in a private room at the Foreign Office. Completely
undisturbed, he photographed it page by page. The report made
it quite clear that Japan had no intention of attacking Russia in
the near future, and that the invasion of South China would
depend on the development of heavy industries in Manchuria.

In search for confirmatory evidence, Sorge obtained a private
interview with the German Ambassador, Dr. Herbert von Dirksen,
on the excuse of writing a report for his newspapers. By clever
questioning he learned that the Japanese High Command had
hinted to the German military attaché that the withdrawal of
German officers instructing the Chinese armies would be taken
as a sign of friendship in Tokyo.

At the same time, Miyagi discovered from a Japanese staff
colonel, whose portrait he was painting—he was very popular
with army circles for his skill in portraiture—that large-scale
models of certain parts of South China were being constructed
for practice purposes.

All this information, taken in conjunction, satisfied Moscow
that their agent had supplied them with information of the utmost importance; and if, before, they had acknowledged him as
a master, they now considered him a miracle worker.

Such a coup so early in his career might have influenced another spy to rest on his laurels. For Sorge it merely set the standard for his future activities.

Realizing the importance of Ozaki's contacts in high political
circles—he presently became the private and confidential adviser of the Prime Minister himself—he set about acquiring similar contacts at the German Embassy. There, he soon became the
confidant of the military attaché, Colonel Eugen Ott, who was
later to become ambassador in the place of Dirksen.

Voukelich also consolidated his own position at the French

Embassy, while Miyagi extended his friendships with the younger military clique.

Sorge's path was not always smooth. His involvement with women at times threatened his security. Klausen, though a first-class radio operator, was not good agent material, and on more than one occasion narrowly escaped arrest. But in some strange way, the Kempeitai remained deceived, and for seven years Sorge and his tiny network operated, pulling off coup after coup, each more brilliant than the last. He warned Moscow of the impending attack on her by Hitler, having received the information from Ott and confirmation from Ozaki. He crowned his career, and brought it to an end, by obtaining the approximate date of the Japanese attack on Pearl Harbor.

This happened in such a dramatic, even melodramatic, way, that it is worth recording here.

As long ago as 1939 the Kempeitai had become aware that an illegal radio transmitter was operating from Japan, but the direction-finding techniques available were not such as to be able to locate its whereabouts. Colonel Osaki, chief of the Kempeitai, had, however, developed suspicions about Sorge and his associates, and even went so far as to ask the German Embassy to check on Sorge and Klausen with the Gestapo.

The Gestapo cleared both, and though Osaki knew how thorough the Gestapo was, yet he had an instinctive feeling that Sorge was not all he appeared to be, and he began to pay him special attention. He had never met Sorge, but arranged to do so through the good offices of a member of the German Embassy staff.

Sorge's favorite haunt at this time was the Fuji Club in Tokyo, and there the two men were introduced. Sorge found Osaki to be a typical Japanese with a taste for *sake* and women. During their discussions on the latter subject, Osaki said that in his opinion one of the most beautiful girls in Tokyo was a dancer due to make her first appearance that night in that very club. At first Sorge was not interested, but the Colonel praised her qualities so insistently and so extravagantly that his curiosity was at length aroused.

Presently the cabaret was announced and the dancer Kiyomi performed. She wore the traditional mask so that the beauty of her features could not be judged, but the rest of her body was sufficiently striking to impress itself on Sorge's consciousness.

For the next week or two, Sorge visited the Fuji Club every evening. Each evening he sent Kiyomi flowers and notes begging her to meet him. Each evening Kiyomi tore up the notes and returned the flowers.

Then one evening, Sorge's table was unoccupied. Frightened that she had gone too far, after her performance she hurried to her dressing room to telephone Osaki and ask what she should do now. But when she came into the dressing room she saw Sorge sitting there waiting for her. Within a few minutes she had capitulated.

Meanwhile, in Germany, though Hitler had been disappointed by the Japanese refusal to launch an attack on Siberia simultaneously with his own on Russia, he had not given up hope of persuading the Tokyo government to distract the Russians there by such an attack. Throughout the summer and autumn of 1941, he was cajoling Konoye and his ministers constantly. Moscow also believed that a Japanese attack on Siberia must come, and Sorge's chief task now was to collect information from which the timing of the attack might be calculated. In gathering this information Ozaki and Miyagi were chiefly responsible, but so far they had produced nothing which pointed in that direction.

As the autumn began to merge into winter, the fantastic German advances in European Russia made the Japanese Government more undecided than ever what they should do. The Russians had deprived their European armies of reserves by keeping two million men, first-line troops, in Siberia. The Nomohan Incident, which was really only a large-scale frontier clash though it lasted several days, appeared at first to the Russians to be the long-awaited Japanese attack, despite the fact that Sorge had told them that all his information was to the contrary.

It made the Russians hesitate more than ever about bringing desperately needed troops back from Siberia, but in October,

Ozaki delivered information that the Japanese had at last made up their minds. All thought of invading Siberia had been abandoned. The Japanese armies would march to the south. In confirmation, all Japanese men between twenty-five and thirty-five were called up; and for good measure, Ott admitted that the Japanese had resisted all German pressure to move against the Russians. Sorge, believing that this was his finest hour, watched Klausen transmit the message that was to change ultimately the fortunes in the Russian war.

One of the reasons why Colonel Osaki had been unable to track down the whereabouts of the illegal radio transmitter which was giving him so much trouble was due in part to its siting. Sorge, besides his ramshackle house in the city, also rented a villa in a seaside suburb of Tokyo. Here he kept a fishing boat, to navigate which he hired an illiterate ancient Japanese fisherman. Sometimes he would entertain parties of friends on fishing expeditions, who, while they were pursuing their sport on deck, were quite unaware that down in the cabin Klausen was transmitting his messages to Moscow.

Though Sorge had achieved his object with his last message to Moscow, and had worked superbly for eight years, he set himself one final objective. He would discover where and when the Japanese were to launch their attack to the south, and then the network would disband, for he had become aware during the last two or three weeks that Osaki was stepping up his surveillance of all foreigners in Tokyo, which indicated to the spy master that he had become conscious of the fact that foreign agents were operating in his territory.

But while he was waiting for the information he wanted to come to hand, he also decided that he could do no harm by continuing his dalliance with his latest mistress, Kiyomi. Of all the strange things about Sorge, it is perhaps the strangest thing of all that he had not perceived that Kiyomi had been planted on him by Osaki, for the Kempeitai chief had not been excessively cunning in bringing her to Sorge's notice. If Sorge had a fundamental flaw at all, it was his overactive sexuality.

Two evenings after he had sent the decisive message to Moscow, he was at his usual table watching the dancer go through the performance he had seen her enact a score or more times. But his thoughts were far away. He was worried. Miyagi had not made contact with him for a week. Voukelich was in a highly nervous state, for he had discovered that he was being watched everywhere he went.

During the dance, a waiter approached Sorge's table and un-obtrusively dropped on to it a tiny ball of rice paper. But not unobtrusively enough. Sorge smoothed out the paper and saw written on it was a message from Miyagi. He was also being watched by the Kempeitai.

Behind her ornate mask, the sharp eyes of Kiyomi had seen the waiter drop the paper ball, had watched Sorge smooth it out, read what was on it, and put it into his pocket. As soon as she had finished her dance, she hurried to her dressing room and telephoned Colonel Osaki.

A check on the waiter was made immediately and revealed that he frequently visited the office of Ozaki in the headquarters of the Southern Manchurian Railway, of which Ozaki was now the chief, and had also been seen in the company of Miyagi. The Colonel already knew that Sorge and Ozaki were friends.

No one meeting Sorge next day would have known that he was now a desperately worried man. He breakfasted with Ambassador Ott as usual, then went about his business as a foreign correspondent.

In midmorning, however, everything changed. He received a message from Ozaki. The coming Japanese offensive was to be directed not against the Chinese but against the Americans at Pearl Harbor; and the date, probably December 6.

At lunch with Klausen, he warned the radio operator to be on board the fishing boat that evening to send the last message to Moscow.

In higher spirits than he had been for some time, Sorge put on his dinner jacket that evening and went to the Fuji Club, where he sat down at his permanently reserved table on the edge of the dancing floor. While Kiyomi danced, she saw the waiter approach Sorge again, and again drop a ball of paper on the table.

Again Sorge read it, and put it into his pocket. The message was from Miyagi, and told him that the Kempeitai was now close on his trail and that Sorge and the others should make their escape as soon as possible.

When the dance was over, and Kiyomi had changed, Sorge told her that instead of going to his town house, they would prepare dinner for themselves in the villa on the Izu Peninsula and stay the night there. This proposal took Kiyomi by surprise, for this was the first she knew about the villa.

After they had left the city, Sorge suddenly stopped the car by the roadside and began to make love to her. Gratified, he drew from his pocket two squashed cigarettes, his lighter and the piece of rice paper. As she watched him flick the lighter Kiyomi's heart sank. She was certain that when he had lit the cigarettes, he would burn the paper, and Osaki had given her firm instructions that if ever she saw Sorge receive another message she was to obtain possession of it at all costs. But the lighter would not work, and Kiyomi pretended that she had left hers in her dressing room.

With a sharp gesture of annoyance, Sorge threw the cigarettes out of the car window, and tearing the paper to small scraps, threw them out after the cigarettes, then drove on.

Now, Kiyomi was a dancer and not a trained counterespionage agent; nevertheless, she was an intelligent girl, and at the next telephone booth they came to, she asked Sorge to stop while she told her parents that she was staying the night with a girl friend. Sorge sat in the car while she called Colonel Osaki and quickly explained what had happened, and where he would find the scraps of paper.

Arrived at the villa, Sorge left Kiyomi to prepare some food, saying that he had some private business to attend to. He went to the beach and rowed in a dinghy out to the boat, where Klausen was waiting. There he gave Max two messages, the first telling Moscow the intelligence Ozaki had given him, the second that the network was compromised and that he was disbanding it forthwith.

When Max had finished, the two men shook hands, hoped

they might meet again some day, and went their ways. At the villa Sorge ate what Kiyomi had prepared, and immediately took her to bed. Whether he had a premonition that this was to be his last night of freedom he never revealed, but the dancer later deposed that that night he made love to her with a ferocity and frequency she had not believed humanly possible. It was dawn before he was satiated and fell asleep.

And while he slept Colonel Osaki moved.

Agents were already waiting for Klausen when he arrived back at his house in Tokyo. Voukelich was dragged from the embraces of his former Japanese mistress, who had lately become his wife. Miyagi tried to stab himself to death as agents broke down his door; he was rushed to the hospital, treated and recovered. Ozaki, dressed in his finest robes, was awaiting the agents with oriental fatalism.

Sorge did not sleep long. The new day, October 15, 1941, was only a few hours old when he awoke Kiyomi, made love to her briefly, and then went through into the lounge, where he mixed himself a stiff drink. As he raised the glass to his lips, there were knocks at the door. When he opened it, Colonel Osaki and two assistants bowed themselves inside.

The Colonel said nothing. He merely handed to Sorge a piece of paper on which the scraps of Miyagi's message, scattered by the roadside, had been pasted together.

Without a word or a glance at Kiyomi, who, he realized suddenly, had betrayed him, he swallowed the drink, dressed and went out with the Colonel.

Miyagi broke down first under the Kempeitai's torture; Klausen gave way not long after. But neither of the two men knew what the last message contained. Voukelich behaved with all the courage and loyalty of a former officer, and no torture could make him talk. Sorge and Ozaki were not tortured, but when they were shown Miyagi's and Klausen's confessions, they realized they had no hope and set down their own confessions, though withholding the last message.

Eventually the cases against them were completed. Miyagi was too ill to face trial, and was kept indefinitely in the prison hospital. Voukelich was sentenced to life imprisonment and Klausen was recommended to mercy and his death sentence was commuted to life imprisonment. Sorge and Ozaki were sentenced to death.

Though it is customary in Japan for death sentences to be carried out within six months of pronouncement, for no reason which has yet been revealed the executions of the two men were delayed for two years. But on October 9, 1944, both men died on the same gallows within half an hour of each other.

☐ The American Networks

The fact that the United States and the Soviet Union were allies and that the former was, like Britain, denuding herself of vital war material in an attempt to help the more hardly pressed Russians apparently did not, in Stalin's view, preclude the Soviet Union from indulging in what is normally considered the unfriendly act of espionage. Indeed, alliance seemed to be the excuse for an expansion of espionage activities, which during the three years 1942 to 1945 reached a peak never before, and probably never since, achieved.

It will be recalled that up to 1938–39, the networks in the United States had been extremely active and flourishing. But like most Soviet networks everywhere, with the exception of Richard Sorge's in Japan, they were very greatly affected by the great Purge of 1938. It took most networks two or three years to become reorganized, as we have seen in Western Europe, but by 1941, fortuitously coinciding with the launching of Operation Barbarossa and the assault on Pearl Harbor, the American organization was beginning to find its feet again.

That the United States had been chosen for what may be called an espionage blitz even before either of these two shattering events occurred may be gathered from the fact that after a period of some years the post of military attaché at the Soviet Embassy in Washington had at length been filled and its occupant was none other than General Ilya Sarayev, a professional spy master, who was to play a very large part in the feverish Soviet espionage activity which was to make the United States the number one target until the explosion of the Canadian Spy Case three or four years later.

The ground in which the ploughs of espionage were required to work could scarcely have been easier. The FBI and the Office of Naval Intelligence were still the only two American agencies engaged in counterespionage. Neither was well equipped in manpower, expecially the ONI, and in any case the main efforts were directed against the really colossal espionage activity of the Japanese, who at the beginning of the 1940's were estimated to have tens of thousands of spies operating on the West Coast and in Central America, and the Nazi spy ring of Count von Keitel.

On the other hand, a certain naïveté was displayed by the American authorities. They should have realized, from past experience, what the Russians were planning when the embassy staff in Washington, the consular staffs strategically placed throughout the country, and in particular the staff of the new Purchasing Commission, were suddenly increased early in 1942. This naïveté seemed to have persisted for a long time, for in December 1943, General "Wild Bill" Donovan, chief of the baby Office of Strategic Services (OSS, the equivalent of the British SOE) visited Moscow with the proposal that his organization should co-operate with the equivalent Russian organization. In his discussions with high-ranking officers of the GRU—he did not apparently meet Alexander Erdberg—General Donovan gave particulars of the American *modus operandi* for putting agents into enemy-occupied territories and details of the equipment, including the latest models of portable radio transmitters, and even went so far as to suggest that a small unit of the Russian organization should be brought to Washington for liaison purposes. The Americans were only saved from the foolishness of their childlike simplicity—it would seem that, of all the top planning experts in the United States, only Admiral Leahy was opposed to the idea—by political considerations. 1944 was election year, and President Roosevelt decided that the implementation of the scheme might spark off a press campaign against it, and imposed his personal veto.

This, however, did not shut down all co-operation between General Donovan and Moscow. The OSS continued to make available to the Russians a great deal of information about conditions in the Nazi-occupied countries together with much useful intelligence gathered by American agents there; but there came a time when the Americans had to admit that the *quid pro quo* they were supposed to receive from the Russians was not forthcoming, at least not in the bulk which would have justified the Russian contribution being termed a *quid pro quo*.

Yet another factor which greatly eased the Russian effort in the United States was the characteristic warmheartedness of the Americans. The Russians were now their allies. Whatever relations might have been in the past were now wiped out by the fact that they were now fighting on the same side against a common enemy. Everywhere Russians went they were welcomed with every facet of traditional American hospitality. This included passing on information which previously would have been jealously concealed from Russian eyes. Such information naturally did not satisfy the vast maw of the Russian needs, and the situation still required a great espionage effort to fulfill those needs; but this effort was made all the easier by the friendly contact that was possible with the men who knew the secrets.

It is obvious, from the revelations which have been made before various investigating committees of Congress in the last two and a half decades, that by far the greater effort was made in the field of industrial espionage, and particularly in the industries responsible for producing war material. Experts in artillery and weapons, in aircraft and submarines were all to be found on the staffs of the Purchasing Commission, which was the chief agency in this sector of espionage endeavor, and on the staffs of the embassy and consulates. But nothing was without interest to the Russians; and how much vital information was acquired by them during the war years will certainly never be assessed.

But if the effort in the industrial field was truly stupendous, the effort in the field of political espionage was not negligible either. Indeed, when the Russian achievement in the way of infiltration of the Administration itself is considered, it is difficult not to be moved by an emotion which has some of the characteristics of fear in it. It is not proposed to say more about political espionage here, as it was tightly bound up with events of the immediate postwar years, and formed the basis of McCarthyism. It will be described in greater detail in Part V.

Probably no other country in the world has been subjected to such an espionage assault as that which Russia inflicted on the United States during the war years.* It is estimated that about eighteen separate rings were operating at the same time at the peak of activity, which in itself is no mean achievement in any espionage agency. But the results obtained by these professional rings represented only a fraction of the total achievement, and for it Americans have only themselves to blame.

*Though the Japanese effort was great, its achievements were negligible. It was brought to a sudden end when, in the days following Pearl Harbor, every Japanese in the country was interned.

PART IV

Atomic Espionage

☐ Atomic Espionage

Exactly when Soviet espionage became interested in the atomic secrets of others it is not possible to say. At all events it was before the end of 1943, for one of the charges later brought against Klaus Fuchs was "that at some time in 1943 you did pass information to representatives of a foreign power in the City of Birmingham."

The first great breakthrough in nuclear physics came when Rutherford and Chadwick succeeded in "splitting the atom" in the Cavendish Laboratories in Cambridge in 1931. Rutherford, a New Zealander by birth, had always been interested in atomic structure, and he had carried out his first work on radioactivity while Professor of Physics at McGill University, Montreal, between 1898 and 1907, and had been awarded the Nobel Prize for Physics in 1908 for his work in the field of atomic structure. In 1919, he had been appointed Professor of Physics at Cambridge, and here his work, and that of his collaborators, eventually proved what he had long believed to be true, that atoms could be artifically disintegrated.

Perhaps we may be forgiven if, for the sake of clarity, we state here very briefly and in very rudimentary form, the basis of atomic energy. A very small mass of matter represents an enormous amount of energy. A mass of one ounce if it could be entirely converted into heat would be sufficient to transform about a million tons of water into steam. In order to release energy the bringing about of nuclear fission is necessary. This is achieved by bombarding the atoms with neutrons. Until Rutherford succeeded in breaking the nucleus of certain light elements by bombarding them with what are known as alpha particles, which are given out spontaneously by the nucleus of specific elements, how nuclear fission could be achieved eluded the scientists. Thereafter Rutherford's colleagues in the same field, John Cockcroft and his collaborator Walton, devised a kind of artificial alpha particle—electrified particles which were given a high speed in a vacuum tube.

The results of Cockcroft's and Walton's experiments brought about the next significant step forward, and from this it was not long before the Italian physicist Enrico Fermi succeeded in breaking uranium atoms into the comparatively small atoms of lanthanum. Fermi's work in this connection led to the discovery that neutrons—particles having the same mass as protons, but having no electrical charge—could easily penetrate the nucleus of heavier atoms, and so bring about atomic transformations, at the same time releasing energy.

The problem facing the physicists at this point was that so much effort was required to provoke the change in a very few atoms that no use could be made of the process, although it was of the highest scientific interest. The point was that Fermi did not recognize the significance of his experiments with heavy uranium, but believed that he was merely repeating Rutherford's experiments of chipping off small pieces from the atomic nucleus.

But the bringing about of nuclear fission in a material which was easy to split and which at the same time released the greatest amount of energy had, by the mid-thirties, become for physicists a kind of alchemist's search for the philosopher's stone. In consequence, physicists in America, France, Germany, Russia and Japan, as well as England and Italy, were all working to achieve this. As there is a scientific tradition that information regarding experiments successfully carried out is made available (in peace-time) to all other scientists of no matter what nationality, what-ever was discovered in the West became known to Russian sci-entists.

The Russian physicists were as much alive to the tremendous possibilities that would accrue from the comparatively easy crea-tion of nuclear fission as were any of their Western colleagues, and they were able to impress these on the nation's leaders. This they did with such effect that new laboratories were built for them, and expensive instruments were acquired from abroad. Be-tween 1934 and 1939 Russian nuclear physicists achieved great prominence as a result of their experiments; and the names of these great pioneer Russian physicists are D. D. Ivanenko, G. N. Tamm, N. K. Semionov, D. V. Skobeltsyn and several others. But none was so outstanding as Peter Kapitsa.

Kapitsa was Russian-born, but he had come to England at an early age, and in 1921 had joined Rutherford at the Cavendish laboratories. By 1933 he had become so greatly admired for his experiments with the effects of high magnetic influence on the properties of water that he was specially equipped by the Cam-bridge authorities with facilities in the new Mond laboratory. He was not a political refugee, and the Russian authorities placed no obstacle in his way when he wished to travel to his homeland. In 1935 he went to Moscow for a scientific conference, but this time he was refused an exit visa, the Russian authorities explain-ing that they needed his services. Though it is said that he would much have preferred to return to Cambridge, he accepted a post in the Institute of Physical Problems in Moscow, taking with him his extremely extensive knowledge and know-how in nuclear physics which he had acquired at Cambridge. It would be quite wrong, therefore, to claim—as is sometimes done—that Russia was a tyro in the field of nuclear physics and had to steal all her information from the West.

The year 1939 saw yet another very significant step forward toward solving the problem on which all nuclear physicists were working. In Germany Otto Hahn discovered what is known as the chain reaction. By bombarding uranium with neutrons the nucleus was split into two parts, which rushed apart with great energy; at the same time neutrons were given out, which in certain circumstances were capable of splitting other atoms. The possibility of splitting all the atoms in a lump of uranium, which would mean the release of an enormous amount of energy, was thus at hand. The investigation of these possibilities made it apparent that, as soon as a method of controlling this operation could be found, an atomic bomb could be an actuality; and this at a time when the greatest war of all time had just broken out.

Uranium consists of three isotopes—that is, atoms of different mass having the same chemical properties—and the next discovery was that only one, Uranium 235, would be suitable for the bomb. The separation of this isotope is a most tedious and costly process. The problem now facing the physicists was, therefore, to separate from uranium a sufficiently large amount of isotope 235. The work on this was, by now, being carried out largely in the United States.

Uranium itself is derived mainly from pitchblende, of which there are large deposits in Canada, and in what was then the Belgian Congo. In 1940 an investigating committee of scientists was set up in Great Britain with Sir George Thomson as chairman. In the middle of 1941 the Thomson Committee reported that the feasibility of a military weapon based on atomic energy was established. Endorsed by the War Cabinet, the project was then entrusted to the Department of Scientific and Industrial Research. In October 1941 President Roosevelt suggested to Mr. Churchill that the work should be carried out jointly by Great Britain and the U.S. An American mission visited England in November 1941, while British scientists went to America in February 1942. As a result of these goings and comings, agreement was reached on the sharing of the project to manufacture atomic bombs, and vast plants were set up in the U.S. and Canada; the Atomic Energy Project at Montreal and Chalk River in the latter, and at Oak Ridge, Tennessee, Los Alamos, New Mexico and elsewhere in the former. British scientists now crossed the Atlantic to work at both the Canadian and American establishments, and so well did the collaboration progress that the final stages of the manufacture of the bomb were reached by 1943.

At the same time, German and Japanese scientists were attempting to beat the Anglo-Saxons at the game. The Germans were impeded by the destruction of the heavy water plants in Norway by the Norwegian Resistance under the direction of SOE. The Japanese were too far behind in their researches to be a serious threat. The Russians, too, had suffered serious setbacks from the effects of the war. The chief laboratories had to close down when, within a few weeks of the outbreak of the Russo-German conflict, Leningrad, where they were situated, was besieged. The Kharkov laboratories were overrun by the Germans, though the Russians did manage to evacuate their equipment before the Nazis arrived; but this did throw out their schedule. For the first six months, when Moscow was threatened, the laboratories there were paralyzed; and all in all, the effect was to put Soviet nuclear research far behind that of the West.

Whose wisdom it was from which emanated the decision not to make available to the Russians the advances made by the American and British and Canadian scientists it has not been possible to discover. The Russians themselves were not long in finding out that they were being kept out in the nuclear cold, and from that moment—as has been suggested, about mid-1943—rather than waste time in what they must have considered would be useless attempts at persuasion, steps were taken to obtain the information, which was being kept from them, by espionage. A special department was established, known as the Atomic Division, to organize the gathering of atomic secrets.

Whether this method would have been used if the Soviet espionage agency had not realized that already its infiltration of the scientific circles in both England and America would make the task a comparatively easy one seems to be answered by the technique adopted from the very beginning. No new networks were set up specifically to tackle the task; the existing networks in both Canada and America were used. All that needed to be done was to intensify the activities of the Canadian rings, and for this purpose they were connected up with the American networks. Major Sokolov, responsible for the Canadian organization, was himself directed by Pavel Mikhailov, operating from the Soviet Consulate in New York. (He had done more than any other to establish the Canadian network in the very early period, for he was equipped with a transmitter, and acted as the channel of communication between Ottawa and Moscow.) It was easy for Mikhailov to be in contact with the Soviet Embassy in Ottawa, for he was also involved in the organization of the Canadian Mutual Aid Program to the U.S.S.R.

The director of military espionage was Sergei Koudrivtzev, whose cover was the post of First Secretary of the Legation, and it was he who gave Sokolov his orders in the early period, until the arrival of Colonel Zabotin as military attaché in 1943, which corresponded with the decision to expand the networks, and with the removal of the British scientists to Canada. It was Zabotin who was to emerge as the real villain of the Canadian piece.

With the extension of the Canadian network's role, the old faithfuls Sam Carr and Fred Rose came into their own at last. The latter was now a Member of Parliament, and was thus of even more use than he had been before, for he was in a better position to acquire official information without attracting attention. It was Rose who brought to Zabotin's notice David Lunan, editor of *Canadian Affairs*, a journal devoted to military topics, and Lunan was to prove invaluable in suggesting recruits for the network. In a very short time through the efforts of Lunan aided by Rose, a cell of scientists had been formed, among whom was the greatest expert on explosives on the American continent, Professor Raymond Boyer of McGill University.

It was Boyer who reported to Moscow that a new plant was being built at Grand Mere* in Quebec for the production of uranium. The engineers for the plant were to be recruited from McGill, and experiments had already shown that uranium could be used "for filling bombs."

It was this information, which reached the Center very early

*Whether this was an intentional error on Boyer's part it is not possible to say. The plant location was at Chalk River, and not at Grand Mere.

in 1943, which prompted Moscow to apply quite openly to the United States government, through the Soviet Purchasing Commission, for sixteen tons of uranium, which was desperately needed by the Russian scientists so that they might carry on with their experiments. The United States authorities refused this request, explaining that the material was in short supply and that none could be spared. This did not deter the Russians, who again repeated the request at intervals throughout the year, until in April 1944, the U.S. Secretary of War, Stimson, replied to the head of the Purchasing Commission:

Dear General Rudenko,
I regret that we find ourselves unable to comply with the request contained in your letter of March 31 for certain uranium compounds.
We have made a very careful review of the situation and this review indicates that our supply of this material is not sufficient to comply with your request.
I assure you that I will remember your need and will inform you of any change in the situation.

But the governments of the United States and Canada did not control all supplies of uranium, and inquiries in the industrial markets of both countries revealed that supplies of the precious material were available. For reasons which are now extremely difficult to credit—that the prohibition of exports of uranium would unduly arouse Soviet curiosity—there was no official embargo on the shipment of uranium. In fact, as early as the time at which the first Russian request was made for sixteen tons, a request had simultaneously been made to the director of the American atomic establishment, for four hundredweight of uranium, and this had been granted, as was a second request; while in Canada, the Purchasing Commission was also successful in buying nearly half a ton in the same way. All of which gives a fairly clear picture of the confusion which existed in the Western official attitudes, which helped to make the task of the Atomic Division of the Center so much easier.

But what made the task easier still was the fact that in both the Canadian and American plants there were high-ranking scientists who were either Communists or who had sympathies with the Communists, and were prepared to hand over any secrets to which they had access.

First, there was the Englishman, Dr. Allan Nunn May. Nunn May had been born in 1912, and by the time he had reached early manhood, the world-wide depression of the thirties was having a disastrous effect in England, as elsewhere. The depression affected men in different ways. Some gave up all hope of recovery and went under; some fought back and rehabilitated themselves and the nation; Nunn May became a secret Communist.

He was a brilliant physicist, a Doctor of Philosophy of Cambridge, where he had been an undergraduate at Trinity College. In 1942 he became a member of the team working in the Cavendish laboratories in connection with what was known as the Tube Alloy Project—nuclear fission. In January 1943 he had accompanied a party of British scientists led by Dr. Halban—a former colleague of the noted French scientist, Joliot-Curie, later revealed as a Communist—to Canada. Later he visited America, where he collaborated with American scientists working on the Bomb.

Secondly there was Dr. Klaus Fuchs, who had fled from Germany because he was an anti-Nazi. He had come to England, and because of the great shortage of physicists there in the middle thirties, he was recruited into one of the British atomic teams, working first in Glasgow and later in Birmingham under another German refugee, a former acquaintance of his, Rudolf Peierls.

Naturally, Fuchs had been checked out by the British authorities before being allowed to work on these highly secret projects, but for some reason, Security did not discover that as a young student Fuchs had been a member of a secret underground Communist group of professional men in Germany; nor did they discover that he had not been in England long before he made contact with Semion Kremer, secretary to the Russian military attaché in London.

The two men first met as early as May or June 1942, and during the eighteen months until Fuchs was sent to work in the

United States, he handed Kremer copies of his monthly reports. Fuchs arrived, with British clearance, in America in December 1943 and was assigned first to Columbia University, New York, and then to the atomic plant at Los Alamos. In America Fuchs maintained contact with Soviet espionage through a member of the American network, Harry Gold of Philadelphia, and until he returned to England in 1946 he regularly passed on top-secret information,

Third, there was Bruno Pontecorvo, an Italian, a pupil of the famous physicist Enrico Fermi, until, in 1927, he went to France to work under Joliot-Curie, and another Communist scientist, Longevin. In France he joined a group of extreme left-wing Italian refugees. When the German invasion of France was imminent, Pontecorvo fled to America, where he arrived in the summer of 1940. In 1943 he was sent to Canada to work on the atomic projects there, and remained in Canada until 1949.

Now, despite the fact that theoretically the American and Canadian networks were separate entities, in the field of atomic espionage they worked in collaboration, which was the naturally sensible thing to do. While Zabotin remained in control of the Canadian network, he worked very closely with the man whom the Center sent to New York early in 1944 to take over the direction of atomic espionage in America. His name was Anatoli Yakovlev, and he was given the cover of vice-consul in New York. Yakovlev took over from the man who had shown tremendous vigor and judgment in organizing the American *apparat*—Semion Semionov—to whose work the success of the Atomic Division owed a very great deal.

Yakovlev's network in America included four outstanding American Communist spies—Harry Gold, David Greenglass, and the husband and wife team of Julius and Ethel Rosenberg. This quartet were Communists and agents of long standing, and it was probably as much due to their experience as to their situations, which well placed them for the work, that they were assigned to Yakovlev.

Harry Gold had been born in Berne to Russian parents. His family emigrated to America while he was still a child, and the family name was changed from Golodnotzky to Gold. Harry received a good university and technical education in the U.S., developed left-wing tendencies, and in 1935 was approached by the Soviet espionage agency in America and agreed to work for them. During his heyday his specialty was the theft of industrial chemical secrets. He was chosen by Yakovlev to act as go-between with Fuchs.

David Greenglass had been a member of the Young Communist League of America in his youth, a point which also seems to have eluded the FBI, for when America entered the war in December 1941 he was called up, given technical training and in July 1944 assigned to the Manhattan District Project at Oak Ridge, Tennessee. His sister was Ethel Rosenberg, under whose influence he readily undertook to divulge the secrets of his work.

Julius Rosenberg had been a Communist, and an extremely ardent one, from the early days of Communism in America. He was also one of the espionage pioneers in that country, and had already achieved great successes in obtaining radar secrets before he was ordered to go underground, after his brother-in-law's assignment to Oak Ridge, in order to concentrate on atomic espionage. It was he who had converted Ethel Greenglass to Communism and then married her; and she was to prove invaluable in persuading her much younger brother to pass on his vital secrets.

Attached to the Rosenberg ring were also Abraham Borthman, Miriam Moskowitz and Morton Sobell. But this ring was only one of three rings in the American network.

At the University of California's Radiation Laboratory, Vasili Zubilin of the Soviet Embassy in Washington had organized a ring of Communist Party groups and secret Communists, which he placed under the direction of two officials in the San Francisco consulate—Grigori Kheifets and Peter Ivanov. Among their outstanding agents were Steve Nelson, who led the ring at the Radiation Laboratory, whose chief source of information was Joseph Weinberg, a research physicist. He even tried to enlist the services of Dr. J. Robert Oppenheimer, who was to be the future director of Los Alamos, the most important of all the American atomic plants. Oppenheimer refused categorically, and informed the director of the Manhattan District Project of the approach, with the result that the FBI began to watch Nelson, though no move was made for a considerable time.

The third ring was concentrated in Chicago, where atomic research was also in progress. In the absence of a consulate here, the Russians put in a professional agent as leader, Arthur Adams. Adams was a spy of very long experience, but by 1942 he was approaching his sixties, and suffered extensively from rheumatism, and thus was somewhat handicapped. His chief source was an American Communist, Clarence Hiskey, a chemist working in the Metallurgical Laboratories on the large-scale production of plutonium for atomic bombs.

In 1944 Hiskey's espionage activities came to the notice of the FBI. It seems incredible today, but all that happened to the chemist was that he was called up for active service in the army, and sent to Alaska. Before he went, he managed to persuade John Chapin, another chemist in the Chicago laboratory, to take over his spying duties from him. In his turn also, Chapin was compromised, and this led to Adams' activities being revealed. But in those days, the U.S. Administration did not prosecute known Soviet spies, and he was allowed to leave America.

Up in Canada, Zabotin, with the assistance of Major Rogov, a member of his staff, had organized a small, compact ring consisting of four Canadian government officials. Leader of the ring was Durnford Smith, a research engineer in the National Research Council; Ned Mazerall, a member of the same body; Isador Halperin, an artillery expert who had access to secret information from the Canadian Army Research and Development Establishment; and David Lunan, already mentioned, who was editor of *Canadian Affairs*. Lunan collected the information provided by the other three, and passed it to Rogov, who passed it to Zabotin.

Among the contacts of these four were Raymond Boyer, also mentioned earlier, who was considered the star of the ring by his superiors. There was also James Benning, who was employed in the Department of Munitions with the task of preparing the quarterly forecast of war production, and Benning's brother-in-law, Harold Gerson, who worked with a Crown company engaged in the production of chemicals and explosives. In addition there was Eric Adams, who filled a confidential post in the Bank of Canada investigating industrial plans for finance purposes; Matthias Nightingale, who could supply information about all Canadian air bases; David Shugar, an expert in radar; and in the lower echelons, Agatha Capman, an employee of the Bank of Canada, who acted as go-between.

With the exception of Agatha Capman, all those mentioned above were, like Nunn May and Fuchs, not members of the ring as such, but extremely valuable sources, from whom all the important information was derived.

It is yet another of the mysteries of the whole strange affair that the activities of none of these people, either in Canada or in America, became known to the counterespionage agencies in either country, and might never have done so but for an equally strange incident, to which reference will shortly be made. They worked with unremitting devotion to their task and completely undisturbed, and by the time the atom bomb was detonated over Hiroshima they had passed to Moscow every scrap of significant information on the composition of the bomb with one or two possible exceptions.

Not until the end of the war could the Russian effort in the atomic field take advantage of this information. Nevertheless, it is estimated that at least ten years' research and effort were cut from the Russian scientists' work as a result of this highly successful espionage. This period might have been reduced still further but for Igor Gouzenko.

On September 7, 1945, the authorities in Ottawa became aware of Igor Gouzenko's existence. He was merely a cipher clerk at the Soviet Embassy, and they only became aware of him because he pleaded with them to grant him, his wife and small son, their protection. When he was asked why he should need their protection he replied that he was in possession of documentary evidence which proved beyond a shadow of doubt that there was an atomic spy ring operating in their country, and when his masters became aware that he had filched this evidence from their secret files, they would require his life and the lives of his family.

Gouzenko had been in Canada for two years, during which time it would appear that he had become converted to the Western ideals of democracy. This had brought about in him a sincere change of heart and he had made up his mind to have nothing more to do with the Russians and their secret works.

When he left the Soviet Embassy on the evening of September 5, 1945, it was for the last time. He had already planned what he was going to do; and he took with him a brief case full of secret files all appertaining to the atomic spy ring which had been operating over the last three years.

From the Soviet Embassy he went straight to the offices of a leading Ottawa newspaper, told them his story, and offered his proofs. They did not believe him, and showed him the door!

He then went to his flat, and being well aware of what would happen as soon as the Soviet officials noted his absence coupled with the absence of their files—which could only be a matter of hours—he spent the next day going from government department to government department, only to meet with the kind of humoring that is usually shown to a man who claims he is Napoleon. Late in the afternoon he visited the newspaper once more, and met with the same rebuff.

Now at his wits' end, he locked himself and his family in the flat. He had scarcely done so when there was a knock on the door. He signaled to his wife to be quiet and to pretend they were not at home; but their little four-year-old son ran with a clatter across the parquet floor. The man at the door called out, and Gouzenko recognized the voice of one of the chauffeurs at the embassy. The man went away when he received no reply.

When he had gone, Gouzenko went out on the balcony and there made contact with his next-door neighbor, a Sergeant Main of the Royal Canadian Air Force. He told the sergeant he was afraid for his life, described what had happened and asked Main to give him and his wife shelter for the night.

Main believed him, and took the Gouzenkos in. Later they were transferred to the flat of another neighbor. Then Main went in search of the police. Two police officers came and questioned Gouzenko, and agreed to keep the block of apartments under observation.

About half-past eleven that evening, Main heard voices outside in the corridor. Thinking it was the police returning, he went to his own door and saw four men in the act of breaking into Gouzenko's flat. He gave the signal for help which had been prearranged with the watching police, and when the latter arrived they found the four men ransacking the Gouzenkos' home.

When questioned, the men said that they were officials from the Soviet Embassy, and that they had the permission of a colleague, who was away in Toronto, to enter the flat to get some important papers. The policemen sent for their Inspector.

The Inspector arrived and asked to see the men's papers, which they showed without protest. Asking them to remain where they were he went outside to make some inquiries. While he was gone, the men left, the watching police making no attempt to stop them.

On September 8, the Canadian Department for External Affairs received a note from the Soviet Embassy explaining the visit of the embassy officials to Gouzenko's flat, stating that Gouzenko was a common thief who had stolen a sum of money from the embassy, and complaining of the behavior of the police who had refused to recognize the diplomatic immunity of the officials. The embassy requested the Canadian authorities to take all measures to arrest Gouzenko so that he might be deported to Russia as a "capital criminal."

On the morning of the day before, however, Gouzenko had told his story to the Canadian Mounted Police, and handed over his documents. This time he was believed; and the authorities, considerably shaken, found themselves in possession of particulars of what has been described as "the largest and most dangerous spy plot ever known in the Dominions in peace or war."

Gouzenko's disclosures revealed, for the first time, the method and technique of Soviet spying. The details were made public in the Report of the Royal Commission which the Canadian government subsequently set up to probe the affairs.

But the other equally important result of Gouzenko's action was to compromise practically the whole of the Canadian atomic espionage networks. The general roundup of the agents concerned began on February 15, 1946, the day on which Commander Burt, chief of the Special Branch of Scotland Yard, called on Nunn May at Shell-Mex House, in London.

After the dropping of the atomic bombs on Japan, the British and Canadians began to play less significant roles in the joint atomic project, and Nunn May had been recalled to London. Zabotin had been aware of his impending departure, and had informed the Center, who, not wishing to lose sight of the man who had been of such great service to them, arranged for the Englishman to be contacted in England.

At his first interview with Nunn May, Commander Burt had merely asked him if he thought that there had been a leakage of atomic information while he had been in Canada. Nunn May replied that he had never heard of such a leakage and denied that he had ever been approached by Soviet agents.

Burt knew better, for among the documents Gouzenko had taken with him were the following telegrams from Zabotin and the Center.

31.7.45
To the Director.
We have worked out the conditions of a meeting with Alek (Nunn May's cover name) in London. Alek will work in King's College, Strand. It will be possible to find him there through the telephone book.

Meetings: October 7.17.27 on the street in front of the British Museum. The time, eleven o'clock in the evening. Identification sign: A newspaper under the left arm. Password: Best regards to Mikel (Maikl). He cannot remain in Canada. At the beginning of September he must fly to London. Before his departure he will go to the Uranium Plant in Petawawa district where he will be for about two weeks. He promised, if possible, to meet us before his departure. He said he must come next year for a month to Canada. We handed over 500 dollars to him.

To Grant (Zabotin).   22.8.45
Reference No 244.
The arrangements worked out for the meetings are not satisfactory. I am informing you of new ones.

1. Place:

In front of the British Museum in London, on Great Russell Street, at the opposite side of the street, about Museum Street, from the side of Tottenham Court Road, repeat Tottenham Court Road, Alek walks from Tottenham Court Road, the contact man from the opposite side—Southampton Row.

2. Time:

As indicated by you, however, it would be more expedient to carry out the meeting at 20 o'clock, if it should be convenient to Alek, as at 23 o'clock it is too dark. As for time, agree about it with Alek and communicate decision to me. In case the meeting should not take place in October, the time and day will be repeated in the following months.

3. Identification signs:

Alek will have under his left arm the newspaper *The Times,* the contact man will have in his left hand the magazine *Picture Post.*

4. The Password:

The contact man: "What is the shortest way to the Strand?"

Alek: "Well, come along, I am going that way."

In the beginning of the business conversation Alek says: "Best regards from Mikel."

Report on transmitting the conditions to Alek.

18.8 Director 22.8.45

Grant.

Burt did not stay long with Nunn May, but he had him watched for the next five days, during which Nunn May did nothing to betray himself. In the meantime, however, more information reached the Commander from Canada, and he paid a second call at Shell-Mex House. Quite bluntly he told Nunn May that he had reason to believe that he should have met a Russian contact near the British Museum, but had not gone to the rendezvous. At this, Nunn May, even before any mention could be made of arresting him, said he wanted to confess everything.

He was tried at the Central Criminal Court at the Old Bailey, in London, March 1946. He pleaded guilty to the charge of having "communicated information to unauthorized persons" and was sentenced to ten years' imprisonment.

Now, although most of the Canadian agents had been rounded up, nothing in the Gouzenko disclosures or in the statements by the arrested spies connected Dr. Klaus Fuchs with the networks, and he might never have been discovered but for a very bad blunder made by the Soviet delegate at a meeting of the United Nations Atomic Energy Commission, who let it be known that Russia had access to secrets which the United States believed to be absolutely safe. The hunt was at once on.

It was clear, from the admission of the Soviet expert, that the information had not come from Nunn May, and this being so, it was equally clear that the Gouzenko disclosures had not uncovered all the Soviet agents working under Zabotin. By a process of elimination, the FBI narrowed its search down to two or three possibilities, one of whom was Fuchs.

Fuchs had returned to England in the middle of 1946, and had gone to work at the Atomic Energy Establishment at Harwell under Dr. Cockcroft. He had reopened his contacts with the Soviet network in Great Britain, and continued to hand over vital information.

Late in 1947, however, he began to have doubts about Russian policy and intentions, and soon he was failing to keep appointments with his Soviet contacts. But by then the wheels of fate were beginning to turn against him.

It was not until 1949, however, that the FBI was able to put the British on his trail. He was watched but, like Nunn May, did not betray himself. When, however, Special Branch officers did eventually confront him, he too made a full confession. He was sentenced to fourteen years' imprisonment.

But still the third of this most dangerous trio of scientists, Bruno Pontecorvo, was at large and operating. At the time of Fuchs's trial he was still working in the United States, but shortly afterward was returned to England. He had not been back long, however, when a reformed Communist friend in the States reported to the American authorities a full statement of Pontecorvo's activities and connections. The United States took no steps beyond warning the British, who, for some totally inexplicable reason, remained inactive.

Two years later, while still working on secret assignments at Harwell and passing information regularly to the Soviet network in Britain, he applied for permission to take his family to the Continent for a holiday. The Pontecorvos traveled by automobile through France to Rome, where they took an ordinary civil airlines aircraft to Helsinki. There they were met by Soviet officials and were taken to Russia.

These three men among them must share a large part of the responsibility for Soviet Russia's progress in nuclear physics. Much of the recent international tension stemmed from the spying of Nunn May, Fuchs and Pontecorvo.

Now, despite the fact that there had been close collaboration between the Canadian and American networks, Gouzenko's disclosures failed to give any indication of the existence of the latter. This was almost entirely due to Yakovlev's absolute insistence on the observance of security procedures at all times. Probably no better example can be found of the present writer's contention that "security is the spy's staff of life"—for which he was frequently teased by former professional colleagues—than what happened in the outcome to Yakovlev's network, for ironically enough, it was the very first failure to observe security procedure which brought about the end of the network.

Harry Gold had already attracted the attention of the FBI in 1947, and they had even interviewed him at his home in Philadelphia. But he had been able to assure them that they were mistaken and they were prepared to take his word for it. It was not until Fuchs was arrested and talked that Gold again came into the picture; and this would not have been possible but for the security slip which Yakovlev had made some four years earlier.

A few days before the explosion of the first atomic bomb in 1945, David Greenglass, at the Los Alamos plant, had prepared a highly important report, which Yakovlev desperately wished to forward to Moscow. A courier, Ann Sidorovich, was detailed by Yakovlev to collect this report from Greenglass, but for some reason or other she was prevented from carrying out instructions. Instead of waiting until she could, and apparently having no other courier available, he instructed Gold, who was the courier for Fuchs, to undertake the assignment.

When Fuchs was eventually arrested, he named Gold as his go-between. Gold was arrested, and because of this one trip to

Los Alamos, was able to name Greenglass. Greenglass also talked and named Julius and Ethel Rosenberg.

The FBI now swooped. With the Rosenbergs they also arrested most of the lesser members of the network. When the trials were finished, the Rosenbergs had been sentenced to death and were executed in 1953; Gold and Sobell were sentenced to thirty years' imprisonment; Greenglass to fifteen years; Abraham Borthman to seven and Miriam Moskowitz to two.

As for the Russians who had been involved, Zabotin remained in Canada for some time after the Gouzenko defection. He did not know how many papers Gouzenko had taken with him, because a great number of the records had been marked up in the registers as officially burned. For their part the Canadian authorities were prevented from acting quickly, because in all the Gouzenko documents agents were referred to only by their cover names, and these took many months to identify. Not until arrests began did the Center close down Zabotin's headquarters staff of fifteen, and recall them all to Russia with their chief, when he was subsequently imprisoned for four years.

In America, as soon as Gold was arrested, Yakovlev fled. He was, however, indicted along with Gold, as indeed was his predecessor, Semion Semionov. But it was a pure formality.

Whatever may be one's personal outlook, whether sympathetic toward, or in opposition to, Soviet Russia and her works, in honesty one must admire the achievement of Soviet espionage in this one field of endeavor.

PART V

The Basis of McCarthyism

☐ Spies in High Places

The junior Senator for Wisconsin, Joseph McCarthy, was undoubtedly a nasty man. That he was a little mad and completely unscrupulous is equally true. That he was in the grip of an obsession that a Russian spy lurked behind every desk and in every cupboard of every department of the Administration of the U.S. was apparent to all who saw or heard him conducting his scandalous investigations.

While he remained unexposed for what he really was, no man or woman, however highly or lowly situated, was safe from his dangerous accusations, which he made wildly without proof or which he backed by false evidence. From an outside vantage point, it seemed that while he ranted, everyone from President down to the most junior official trembled; and the world wondered why the great American people put up with him and his minions.

Perhaps part of the answer to this last question can be found in reality, for, strange though it may seem, McCarthy based his campaign on proved truths. As we have seen, Soviet espionage in America had, by the end of the thirties, reached both an extraordinary volume and a wide field of activity. In the field of

industrial espionage, of military espionage and later of atomic
espionage, the achievement was a fantastic one by any standards, though it owed much of its success to the official government attitudes, which are pinpointed by just one example. When
the Russians applied for supplies of uranium toward the end of
1942, and had the application rejected by the War Department,
it will be remembered that they moved into the industrial market. They placed orders for small quantities, and when an export
license was applied for, and the strongly anti-Russian Director
of the Manhattan District Project was required to give it his
blessing, he did so, as he explained to the House Committee on
Un-American Activities' Hearings Regarding the Shipment of
Atomic Material to the Soviet Union during World War II,
"rather than be pointing a finger at the material if the license
was refused." That is to say, he naïvely hoped that by granting
the license the Soviet Union might be misled into thinking that
uranium had no great significance for the United States. It was
on a similar kind of logic, so childish as to be scarcely credible,
that the United States authorities suffered the extensive theft of
their industrial secrets, and their war production secrets.

Or again, when Major General Donovan, chief of the OSS,
suggested co-operation between his organization and the equivalent Russian organization, for which purpose a Russian liaison
office was to be set up in Washington, not even the chief of the
FBI objected. The reformed Communist agent Elizabeth Bentley said of this situation, in her book *Out of Bondage*, "The
opinion in Washington seemed to be: The NKVD have been
wandering round the United States for years. It probably would
make it a lot simpler for us if they came already labeled."

It was a most extraordinary reaction. For what happened because of it, the Americans have only themselves to blame; and it
really deprives them of the right to criticize the British when a
Blake or Vassall crops up, though they do not hesitate to do so.

What had happened in the industrial and military fields had
happened also in the political field; but here the achievement can
be seen with a clarity not usual in espionage endeavor. This is
due, in some small part, because the network engaged in politi-

cal espionage was many times greater than the networks in the other fields; and also because the extent of the penetration was much more diffuse, this in turn being made possible by the wide scope of government administration. Nevertheless, when the picture *as known* is presented, it is somewhat breath-taking.

James Burnham, an American expert on Soviet espionage in America, in his book *The Web of Subversion,* lists the following departments of the Administration which had been penetrated during the war:

> The administrative staff of the White House; the Departments of State, Treasury, Army, Navy, Defense (under the present organization), Justice, Agriculture, Labor, Commerce; six congressional committees; the office of the Manhattan District Project (atomic energy); Office of Strategic Services; National Labor Relations Board; Works Progress Administration; National Research Project; Office of Defense Mobilization; War Production Board; Foreign Economic Administration; North African Control Board; Bureau of Standards; Bureau of Census; Civil Service Commission; Coordinator of Information; Office of Education; Office of War Information; Coordinator of Inter-American Affairs; Federal Emergency Relief Administration; Federal Public Housing Authority; Federal Security Administration; Government Printing Office; Library of Congress; Maritime Labor Board; National Archives; National Youth Administration; OMGUS (Military Government in postwar Germany); SCAP (Military Government in postwar Japan); Office of Price Administration; Railroad Retirement Board; Reconstruction Finance Corporation; Resettlement Administration; Securities and Exchange Commission; Social Security Board; War Manpower Commission; U.S. War Assets Administration; War Shipping Administration; Veterans Administration; Tariff Commission; U.S. Information Services. In addition, the web has been spun over the important international organizations to which the U. S. Government belongs or has belonged: United Nations Relief and Rehabilitation Agency (UNRRA); the United Nations itself; the International Monetary Fund.

Mr. Burnham compiled this list from the various reports of the investigating bodies which went into action after the war, when the Administration and Congress became aware that there had been serious Soviet penetration of government agencies.

Another great expert on Soviet affairs, David Dallin, in his book, *Soviet Espionage,* though proceeding more cautiously than Mr. Burnham, gives the names of known Soviet agents in a

number of the departments listed by Mr. Burnham. On page
441, he writes:

During the war years the Soviet *apparat* had its men in at least the
following agencies:
Office of Strategic Services (Duncan Lee, Leonard Mins, Helen
Tenney, J. Julius Joseph)
Counter-Intelligence of the War Department (Donald Niven
Wheeler)
War Department (and, indirectly, the FBI) (William Ludwig Ull-
mann)
Air Force (Abraham George Silverman)
State Department (with access to the secret cable room of OSS)
(Alger Hiss, Maurice Halperin, Robert T. Miller, Donald Hiss)
Coordinator of Inter-American Affairs (Joseph Gregg, Bernard
Redmont, William Z. Park)
Justice Department (Norman Burster)
Treasury Department (Harry Dexter White, Nathan Gregory Silver-
master, Harold Glasser, Solomon Adler, William Taylor, Sonia
Gold)
Foreign Economic Administration (Frank Coe, Allan Rosenberg,
Lauchlin Currie, Philip Keepey, Michael Greenberg, Bela Gold)
War Production Board (Irving Kaplan, Victor Perlo, John Abt,
Edward Fitzgerald, Harry Magdoff)
Department of Agriculture (Harold Ware, John Abt, Nathan Witt,
Lee Pressman, Henry H. Collins, Bela Gold)
Office of Price Administration (Charles Kramer, Victor Perlo)
UNRRA (Solomon Leshinsky)
Department of Commerce (William Remington, Nathan Witt)
This list is not complete, however. It was only by accident that
three of the Washington "cells" became known after the war; the
accident was the defection of persons who had served as liaison
between the cells and Soviet intelligence. There is no doubt that, in
addition to these, there were others, probably more numerous and
no less important. . . .

The extent to which even this short list goes makes it apparent
that there was very little which passed in the enclaves of official
Washington that was not passed to Moscow. Not much of the
information could have been of really significant value, but
some of it was intelligence of a very high order. Take for instance Harry Dexter White, who as a prime mover in the
Morgenthau Plan—designed to restrict German industry after
the war and encourage German agriculture, in order to prevent
a resurgence of German militarism—was in the inner counsels

of those responsible for postwar planning, and could inform the Soviet of Allied intentions well in advance. Or Maurice Halperin, who supplied official reports emanating from the State Department, and secret reports from the U.S. Ambassador in Moscow commenting on Russian internal affairs, from which a measure of the activities of American Intelligence inside Russia could be assessed. Or Major William Ullmann, who obtained through the Army Intelligence U.S. war plans and FBI reports. These three alone could and did supply information of the highest quality.

There is insufficient space at our disposal to give here a detailed account of the ramifications of the political espionage activities of the Soviet Union in the United States at this time, but an impression of its effects may be obtained from consideration of the conclusion of the Whittaker Chambers case. We have already given the early career of Chambers, and we left him a disillusioned Communist and a discreet defector, trying to ward off the attentions of the Division for Diversion and Terror by going into hiding. After ten years of clandestine existence, in 1948 he discovered that the official American attitude toward Soviet espionage had changed, and he found that he could expect protection if he divulged what he knew.

It will be recalled that, when he decided to cut short his association with Soviet espionage in 1938, he had gone to Washington in an attempt to warn the Administration that some of the government departments had been infiltrated; and that two years later he had got in touch with the FBI. But on both occasions he had held back the full story, with the result that his auditors were not impressed, and no action was taken. Now he was prepared to tell all.

Shortly before he had become inactive, Chambers had been "the contact man between a powerful Soviet espionage apparatus in Washington and my superior in New York City." Though Chambers did not then know him by that name, his superior was "Colonel Boris Bykov, a Russian officer of the Fourth Section (military Intelligence) of the Red Army." Among his American contacts were Harry Dexter White, then assistant to the Secretary of the Treasury; Abraham Silverman of the Railroad Retirement Board; Dr. Gregory Silvermaster of the Department of Agriculture; and Alger Hiss of the State Department.

By 1948, Hiss had left the State Department, and Harry Dexter White had recently been appointed to a high post in the International Monetary Fund, where he had taken with him two other Soviet sympathizers, Frank Coe and Harold Glasser. Chambers was now prepared to give the authorities all he knew, particularly about Hiss, and the conflicting testimony of Chambers and Hiss at the hearing of the House Committee on Un-American Activities provided the world with a dramatic spectacle.

The two men were highly placed. Chambers was now an editor of *Time*; Hiss was president of the Carnegie Endowment for International Peace. There were also spy-fiction elements which added to the popular interest, such as the so-called Pumpkin Papers, which Chambers hid in a hollowed-out pumpkin on his farm. Hiss defended himself vigorously, and was believed to the extent that in August 1948 the Department of Justice was preparing to indict Chambers for perjury. However, in December a New York grand jury returned a true bill against Hiss, and he was brought to trial. At the end of an outstanding *cause célèbre*, he was found guilty of perjury and sentenced to a term of imprisonment.

As will have become obvious, the Soviet spy masters had relied chiefly on American nationals with Communist affiliations or sympathies for their agents in this field. The fact that none of these men had been suspected even of such affiliations or sympathies was as great a blow to American confidence, as the extent of their activities represented a serious threat to the national security. For the first time it dawned on those responsible for security and on the general public that the greatest danger from Soviet espionage came not from the professional agents but from the secret Communists who were prepared to betray their country's secrets, not for money or any material reward, but for ideological beliefs.

This new kind of spy—the ideological spy—was believed to be a novel manifestation arising solely out of the evil machinations of the Russian Communist régime. This is still a widely held view.

Once the situation had been seized by both authorities and public, there began a great campaign of putting the American house in order. Exposure followed exposure, but sincere, genuine intellectual beliefs—as the Christian martyrs demonstrated so well—cannot be uprooted by administrative action. The authorities might probe and smoke out and expose; but for each man or woman they brought into the glare of the public gaze, who could say how many secret enemies of the State remained completely concealed behind the screen of their most secret thoughts?

Senator McCarthy believed there were many scores still. There may have been, but if there were, his methods of trying to seek them out—the methods of the witch-hunters—in the end reacted more in their favor than against them. Nevertheless, vile though his operations were, in their fundamentals they were based on solid foundations. They had one good effect, however; they made very clear that there is little that can be done to guard against the ideological spy except a constant, unremitting vigilance, which, in its turn, should act as a safeguard, not only against this kind of spy, but against the operations of spies of all kinds.

It is one of the bemusements of our times that this axiom of existence is most frequently forgotten.

☐ The "Amerasia" Case

The case which startled America and the world, and which lifted
a corner of the curtain on what had been going on during the
war, broke in 1945. Though it had been allowed to take no
action, the FBI had maintained a watch over several of those
suspected of spying for Russia who were in the service of the
government. On this account, when a magazine called *Amerasia*, in February 1945, published the slightly changed text of a
report on British policy in Thailand—which could only have
come from the files of the OSS—and the British government
complained, official notice had to be taken, and the FBI was
better equipped to deal with it than the Administration had any
right to expect it to be.

Amerasia had been launched in 1936 after the announcement
of the United Front "course" in China, which implied the acting
in unison of the Chinese Communists and Chiang Kai-shek's
Kuomintang for the purpose of resisting Japanese aggression.
The editor of the magazine was Philip J. Jaffe, a Russian-born
American and successful businessman, under whose direction
Amerasia devoted itself to attacks upon Japan and to the sup-
port of the Communist-Kuomintang rapprochement. In the State
Department the magazine was read with great attention, and
many leading officials praised and recommended it.

Co-owner of *Amerasia* with Jaffe was Frederic Vanderbilt

Field, and among regular contributors to it were Andrew Roth, who had been appointed to Naval Intelligence against the advice of Security and who had access to many secret documents; Emmanuel Larsen, of the Office of Far Eastern Affairs of the State Department, who had also worked in Naval Intelligence; and Mark Gayn, a Manchuria-born free-lance journalist. Larsen, for example, supplied Jaffe with documents from the State Department, Naval and Military Intelligence, the OSS and the Office of War Information.

Among the secret papers passed to *Amerasia* was a report of the disposition of Chinese Nationalist troops, secret reports on the private life of Chiang Kai-shek, a report on the decline of Chiang's prestige and on criticism of and oppostion to his leadership, and an order-of-battle report showing the disposition of the Japanese fleet before the Battle of Leyte.

When the British complained of the publication of their secret report on Thailand, the OSS began an investigation, which culminated in a raid on the offices of the magazine on the night of March 11. In four drawers were found photostats or originals of 267 documents from the State Department, 50 from the OSS, 58 from the Office of War Information, 34 from Military Intelligence, and 19 from Naval Intelligence.

This was as far as the OSS could go, so they handed over their haul to the FBI. The latter watched Jaffe and his staff for three months.

Despite the fact that all these government documents had been found where they should not have been, the first reactions of the Administration were those that had obtained on all previous occasions when the FBI had asked permission to move against spies. A prime mover in this embargo on FBI action was Secretary of the Navy James Forrestal, though Naval Intelligence documents were among those seized. Forrestal even went so far as to appeal to the Department of Justice to issue instructions to J. Edgar Hoover, head of the FBI, enjoining him to refrain from action. The Department of Justice complied with Forrestal's request, but only for the time being until the first meeting of the United Nations at San Francisco should have been completed.

President Truman, however, reversed this decision and on June 6 the FBI arrested Jaffe, Roth, John S. Service, a Far Eastern expert of the State Department, Gayn, Larsen, and one other. In the *Amerasia* offices they found another seventeen hundred government documents which the OSS had overlooked. However, there was no evidence that the documents had been "passed to a foreign power," and the charges laid—against Jaffe, Roth and Larsen—were that they had removed confidential documents from government offices. Jaffe pleaded guilty and was fined twenty-five hundred dollars; Larsen entered a *nolo contendere* and was fined five hundred dollars, which Jaffe paid. The charge against Roth was later dismissed.

The case itself, which took on the nature of a *cause célèbre*, and the comments of the press and leading members of the community, made it impossible thereafter to curb the probing of the FBI, even if the Administration had wanted it, which the new President, Harry S. Truman, had so clearly shown that he did not.

In any case, public opinion was fully roused, and began to demand, in an ever increasing crescendo, for every step to be taken to discover exactly how deep Soviet espionage penetration of the Administration had gone. At frequent intervals over the next five years, more and more revelations were made—among them the disclosures of Chambers and Elizabeth Bentley—and produced such a wide field of infiltration that, in September 1953, General Bedell Smith, director of the Central Intelligence Agency, was constrained to state, "I believe the Communists are so adroit and adept that they have infiltrated practically every security agency of the Government."

Special committees of Congress worked incessantly in an attempt to discover the extent of the penetration, and now under pressure the FBI went into action with all the suddenly released pent-up frustration of the past half-dozen years refurbishing the reputation which they had originally won in the great days of the G-men's struggles against Al Capone and his ilk. This time, however, the nature of their task set limits to what they could achieve; but no agency could have achieved more.

☐ Judith Coplon

Within a few weeks of General Bedell Smith's making his observation, the Chief of the Internal Security Division of the Department of Justice reported that 766 espionage cases and 261
sabotage cases were being investigated at that time. He was
closely followed by the head of the FBI, who said, "Enemy espionage rings are more intensively operating now than at any time
in the history of the country."

A long series of espionage cases was brought before the courts
of the United States. Among these cases, one of the most important was that involving Judith Coplon, for it demonstrated very
clearly that although the methods and the extent of their espionage were almost daily being compromised, the Soviet Union
was not embarrassed by them in the slightest degree, nor saw
any reason to lower its sights in any direction. It must be remembered, of course, that while the Americans were conducting
their anti-espionage operations, in England, France, Scandinavia and elsewhere other Russian networks were being discovered, particularly in the field of atomic espionage, which tended
to make the American political espionage pale almost to insignifi-
cance. But this does not seem to have had any effect on Soviet

espionage policy either, unless it was the realistic view that everyone knew everyone spied, so why stop because a few spies have been caught.

At all events there was no retrenchment by the Center, and Judith Coplon was caught up in the new web.

In December 1949, it came to the knowledge of the FBI through a thoroughly reliable source, that the Soviet Embassy in Washington had come into possession of a number of top-secret documents emanating from the FBI itself and from the Department of Justice. The information was incomplete and the only idea that could be given of the nature of the documents was that they contained particulars of certain known foreign agents, diplomats and American Communists. The information also gave an indication that the supplier of the documents might be a woman who worked in the Foreign Registration Office of the Department of Justice, and who had formerly been employed in the office of the same department in New York.

Only one woman in the Foreign Registration Office in Washington fitted this description. The FBI therefore began investigations to eliminate or convict her.

Judith Coplon, a college graduate, was twenty-seven, attractive to look at, keen on her work, which dealt with external and internal security matters, and had been marked out for promotion. This came her way when she was appointed to a forty-nine-hundred-dollar-a-year post in May 1948, after she had received a commendation from the Attorney General for a piece of brilliant political analysis.

She came of good family. Her father was a well-to-do manufacturer, who was also something of a philanthropist. Mrs. Coplon was quiet and retiring.

Judith had earlier lived in an apartment at 2634 Tunlaw Road, Washington, where her landlord and neighbors described her as a quiet, intellectual young woman who never brought men home. Recently, to be nearer her work, she had moved to a one-room apartment in Jefferson Hall, McLean Gardens, where her neighbors made the same observations.

After a month of probing and surveillance all that the FBI

could discover was that Judith saw many men, and it was with one of them, a clever lawyer employed by the Department of Justice, that she spent the first weekend of January 1949 at the Southern Hotel, Baltimore, registering as the wife of her escort. Nevertheless, all that FBI agents were able to achieve from their latest equipment for listening and looking through walls, from their post in the adjoining room, was a practical demonstration in the art of love-making. But this did, however, give them a new slant on Miss Coplon.

The following week she asked her chief, William Foley, to let her see the top-secret report on Russian agents in America, as she needed it in her work. Foley knew that she was being watched by the FBI and stalled, and immediately telephoned the Bureau.

Hoover, the chief of the FBI, called on Foley, bringing with him a faked letter marked Top Secret, in which it was stated that three Soviet agents working in the Amtorg Trade Division were really FBI agents, who were shortly to be submitted to a loyalty test. Hoover asked Foley to give this letter to Judith and ask her to work on the case, arguing that if she were really in league with the Russians, she would warn her friends.

This was done. On Friday, January 14, 1949, Judith asked her chief to be allowed to leave at the end of the morning, so that she might have a long weekend. Foley gave his permission and when she took the one o'clock train to New York, she was shadowed there by four FBI agents.

Arriving at Pennsylvania Station, she went to the ladies' room, where she stayed three quarters of an hour, and when she came down put her bag in a cloakroom, visited a bookstall, and then went into a drugstore, where she ate a sandwich at a counter. After this she went by subway to 191st Street, Manhattan.

It was dark when she arrived there, and the street lamps were already lit. She walked down the street for about ten minutes, and then stopped and looked in the window of a jewelry store. She remained looking in the window for seven minutes, clearly employing the old espionage trick—watching what was going on in the street in the reflection of the glass.

Presently, a well-dressed, dark, well-built but short man appeared. He did not speak to her but, when he walked away, she followed him, and they went into a restaurant.

In the restaurant they occupied the same alcove, but what they said the FBI agents who had followed them in were unable to hear, because they continuously fed nickels into a jukebox, the noise from which covered their conversation.

They stayed in the restaurant for about an hour, during which time Judith talked animatedly, and she was still excited when they left and took the subway again.

As the train was about to pull out of 125th Street Station the man suddenly jumped up, squeezed through the closing doors, and was away with only one FBI man after him. His security was good. He did not know that he was being followed, but he left nothing to chance. By taking a series of taxis, trains and buses he succeeded in throwing the FBI agent off.

From his appearance the FBI men were convinced that the man was of Slavic origin, and that he might possibly be a member of the staff of the Soviet Consulate-General in New York. Working on this assumption agents were posted outside the Russian offices, and at ten o'clock they saw their man entering the building. An hour later he came out, and took the subway to his apartment at 64 West 108th Street, where, through the doorman, he was identified as a Russian engineer working for the United Nations Architectural Department, known as Valentine Gubitchev.

The FBI now advised Foley to make it impossible for Judith Coplon to have access to top-secret documents, and she was transferred to another office. She did not go without demanding why, only to receive the reply that her new job had to be done and that she was the person most suited to do it.

The reason for her strong protests seemed evident to the FBI —in her new post she would not have access to any documents of value to her espionage confederates—and they were now certain that they were on the right track. For her part, when she had accepted the inevitable, she showed a persistence which, had she been a good agent, she would have realized would attract attention to her. Every day she visited her old office, and gave much-needed assistance to her successor, in this way no doubt hoping to be able to inspect the files. Apart from this, she made no move, except for another amorous encounter with her lawyer friend.

On February 18th, however, she went once more to New York. On this occasion she took the two o'clock train. This time the New York agents took with them a woman agent, who followed Judith into the ladies' room, and then on to the subway. The woman agent, accompanied by a male agent, followed her and she led them once more through a tour of the streets. From Broadway, she turned into a side street, and it was there that Gubitchev met her. They were together for a few minutes only, and though it was too dark to see, the agents were convinced that papers had passed between them. Once again Gubitchev evaded pursuit.

On March 3, Judith once again asked for the half day off, and went to New York to spend the weekend with her father and mother. During the following week she asked if she might see some of the top-secret files. Foley asked her if she remembered the three Amtorg men who were FBI agents acting as Soviet spies; he now had more information on the case, he told her.

This information included a letter from J. Edgar Hoover to the Assistant Attorney General, purporting to set out that Amtorg had recently been making inquiries about some instruments called geophones, which measure blast pressures, a few of which had been manufactured in connection with the original atomic tests. Mr. Hoover asked the Attorney General's advice as to what would constitute a violation of Amtorg's trading regulations.

The letters were a trap devised to settle once and for all whether Judith Coplon was passing information to Soviet agents.

Very shortly after her interview with Foley she went again to New York. Again there was a repetition of all that had happened on previous occasions, with only a very few unimportant variations. But this time the FBI struck. Both Judith and Gubitchev made determined efforts to escape, but at last they were arrested at 16th Street and Third Avenue.

At FBI headquarters in New York they were searched. Gubitchev had on him $125, but nothing incriminating. Judith had nothing on her person, but in her handbag was found a sealed advertising circular for nylons. When this was opened the agents discovered copies and résumés of thirty-four top-secret documents, including Hoover's letter to the Attorney General, and a covering note explaining that she had not been able to obtain a copy or even more than a quick glance at the FBI's report on Soviet and Communist espionage activities in the United States.

Judith denied everything, but the evidence against her was too strong. At her trial she put forward a defense sometimes made by captured Soviet spies—that she was in love with Gubitchev, whom she had first met by chance in the Museum of Modern Art. He had told her he was married, but she hoped to marry him as soon as he obtained his divorce. She rather foolishly denied that she had ever made love with her American lawyer friend.

The jury believed none of her expostulations of innocence and she was found guilty under the Treason Act of stealing U. S. Government documents and of conspiracy against the United States. She was sent to prison for fifteen years. Gubitchev, who had been tried with her, received a similar sentence. Both, however, were to have the workings of democratic justice demonstrated to them in a dramatic way.

At about this time, Robert Vogeler, an American and an employee of the International Telephone and Telegraph Corporation in Budapest, had been arrested as an American spy and sentenced to fifteen years by a Hungarian court. Some Americans were also being held on similar charges in Russia. Though there had been no negotiations between the two governments, the State Department somewhat naïvely believed that if they showed Gubitchev clemency, similar clemency would be shown by Russia and Hungary, and asked the court to recommend that he should leave the United States "rather than be required to serve his sentence here." So, on March 20, 1950 he was put aboard the Polish liner *Batory*, along with his wife, who shared a first-class cabin with him, for which the U. S. Government paid.

Judith Coplon, who had been allowed bail from the time that the preliminary investigations had been completed, appealed against her sentence. (Two months after her sentence she had married one of her lawyers, Albert H. Socolov.) Her appeal was heard on December 5, 1950, and because her arrest had been effected without a warrant, her sentence was quashed. The indictment was not dismissed, however. Though freed on a technicality, her guilt before the law remained. She now lives quietly, a wife and mother.

The State Department's bid to save Vogeler was in vain. He was not freed until late in 1951, and the Americans held in Russia were not set at liberty until some time after that.

By this time, too, the Center had made a complete overhaul of its American networks; the old contacts had been put aside, perhaps to wait for another day. But though the American counterespionage agencies are now behaving more as counterespionage agencies should, they know, as everyone else knows, that it is the hidden Communist who is their greatest enemy.

PART VI

The Chief Defectors

☐ Gouzenko, Petrov
and Company

One of the greatest risks which Soviet espionage has always run has been the defection of their agents. They have been aware of this risk and have tried to guard against it by holding as hostages the families of their professional agents of all ranks. Yet they have done much, by their too-apparent lack of trust, by their attempts to inculcate loyalty and by the ruthlessness with which they have punished spies who have failed, to produce the thing they most fear.

And indeed, it has been defecting agents rather than the skills of the counterespionage service pitted against them which has led to the capture of many important networks and individual spies, and to a general understanding of Russian espionage methods and techniques. With the exception of the Central Intelligence Agency, the modern postwar espionage organization of the United States, more is probably known about the intimate details of the Center's activities than is known about all the rest of the espionage services of the world put together. Though it must be said that the knowledge of the CIA has come not from defectors, but from the Agency's own stupidities and absurdities, and particularly its lack of insistence on absolute observance of security.

In the history of the early war years, from the fall of the Belgian network into the hands of the German Abwehr, we have seen that when a Russian agent was captured he was liable to become loquacious. This happened even among the veterans, the experienced and tried old Communists, whom one would have imagined would have been prepared to sacrifice their lives rather than betray the Cause. And it would appear that there is a fundamental flaw in Communism which, when the individual is *in extremis,* fails to encourage and succor him. The same flaw does not appear to be present in what one may term the doctrines of democracy, to judge by only one example. The British SOE engaged and trained many hundreds of agents from among the nationals of the German occupied democracies, and of these hundreds, many fell into German hands. But of these many, the examples of betrayal, even under torture, were very few, and in every known case those who did talk and collaborate were men and women who had flawed characters, and who ought never to have been selected as agents in the first place.

Under a régime which enforces lip-service loyalty by fear of imprisonment at best, or death, men's natures being what they are, there must always be the desire to escape. Only among the men at the top who control and devise the punishments for disloyalty, and among the fanatics, can there be anything approaching loyalty. For such a régime, without exception, is imposed, not freely approved and accepted. There can be no connection between such a régime and the physical country over which it holds sway; there can be no faith in institutions of which one is afraid; and it is these two aspects of a man's relationship with his country which forms the basis of his loyalty.

The same is true of an ideology which is not the universally accepted ideology of a nation. There must always be the risk that sooner or later the instinct to conform will get the better of the odd man out, and particularly so when the pressures exerted by a régime on a man's day-to-day existence are absent. Disillusionment has come to many who embraced Communism in the early days with great ardor chiefly for the very reason that the freedom of the individual is curtailed to the limits of extinction by the very insecurity engendered by inherent weaknesses in fundamental doctrines. If only Communism could feel itself strong enough to give the appearance, at any rate, of allowing the individual to give the Cause his loyalty of his own volition, it would have much less to fear from disillusionment. The liberalism that began to influence the régime in the Russia of the Khrushchev era seems to be a step in the right direction. The defections of intellectuals, artists and espionage agents have been negligible compared with the defections of the Stalinist-Beria period, proportionately speaking.

The defection of foreign Communists was always a risk far greater than the defection of Russian nationals. By the middle thirties it had come to be accepted as a kind of occupational risk. But in the field of espionage the services of national Party members was essential to the working of the agency, and all that could be done to offset the risk of this type of agent's throwing up the sponge was to employ him in such a way that he could not jeopardize too greatly the network to which he was attached, though the old weapon of fear, here embodied in the activities of the Division for Terror and Diversion, was used to do what it could to dissuade potential defectors.

There have been many of this kind of defector, but the Juliet Poyntzes, the Elizabeth Bentleys, the Whittaker Chamberses, the Alexander Footes and the George and Joanna Wilmers, though bringing much useful information with them, could only compromise their own particular network. This was annoying, of course, but not a great tragedy, for almost always the Center had provided for such an eventuality by having one or more networks operating on parallel lines, each network being completely unaware of the existence of the other.

In his book *Soviet Spy Net*, the espionage specialist E. H. Cookridge has written:

It was not until January 1953, almost eight years after the exposure of the atomic spy rings in Canada and the United States, that Montreal police discovered by chance that at least one "parallel" network continued its activities in Canada quite undisturbed, when members of the Zabotin network stood trial. On 5th January 1953, a sixty-year-old native of Greece, Constantin Stathapoulos, who had lived in Canada since 1927, was found dead in his home in Montreal. He had died after a long illness, and there was no suggestion of foul play. In a well-hidden cache were found steel boxes containing hundreds of documents, which the head of the anti-subversive division of the Canadian police, Mr. Louis Champagne, described as "the most important collection of espionage documents found in Montreal." Notebooks containing references to several persons involved in the Canadian spy ring, as well as to Fuchs, were found . . . from such information as they could piece together, it became clear that Stathopoulos had in his possession part of the archives of a Soviet espionage network which was quite independent of Zabotin's, but which had pursued at least some targets related to atomic espionage.

The first defector of note was Igor Gouzenko, the cipher clerk at the Soviet Embassy in Ottawa. We have already related his story in Part IV. The documents he brought with him, and the disclosures he subsequently made, revealed not only the existence of the Zabotin network, but gave an almost complete picture of the *modus operandi* of Soviet espionage. Much was either known or suspected—no one should be deceived by the note of horrified surprise which runs through the seven-hundred-page report of the Royal Commission, particularly at the notion that diplomats, or quasi-diplomats, enjoying the privileges of immunity, could so demean their calling as to use it as a cover for espionage—but the confirmation of the old and the information contained in the new knowledge was naturally of the very greatest value.

In 1954, two other defectors of first-rate importance joined Gouzenko. In January, Juri Rastvorov, a high-ranking NKVD officer, while in Japan, asked the American authorities for asylum. Only a vague mention of his defection appeared in the press, and the general public was hardly aware of it; but his information revealed the Center's plans for Japan and the Far East.

The brouhaha which attended the defection of Vladimir Petrov, just three months later, produced quite a different effect. Every literate within range of a newspaper throughout the world was startled by the story, which not only seemed to point to a repetition of the Canadian affair, but which brought home as even Gouzenko and the Gold-Rosenberg case and the trial of Klaus

Fuchs had never done, the universal role of Soviet espionage. The great welter of publicity which attended the Petrov defection was not due to any action on the part of the Australian authorities, who would probably have preferred to have kept fairly quiet about it, but to the behavior in a very public place of a number of Soviet strong-arm agents themselves.

The Australian government had not accorded diplomatic recognition to the Soviet Union until 1942, but from that moment Soviet espionage had gone into full action in the continent. The network organized and led by Semion Makarov, and his chief assistant, Feodor Nosov, the ostensible Tass news agency correspondent, worked on the traditional lines. Communists or Communist sympathizers in government agencies formed the main sources of information, particularly a group of officials working in the Ministry for External Affairs, who passed on documents relating to Australian and English foreign policy.

The war years marked a period of great activity and equal success, but after the war, when opinions and emotions toward Japan and Fascism began to mellow, and when the *Amerasia* case in America and the Nunn May case in England suddenly awoke the public awareness to the activities of Soviet espionage, the work of the network began to encounter grave difficulties, which in turn led to the Center's expressing its serious dissatisfaction with the efforts of their agents in Australia.

After the war Makarov had been replaced by Valentin Sadovnikov, who in 1949 committed the unforgivable sin, in the Center's eyes, of staying the night at the home of some Australian acquaintances. He was replaced by Ivan Pakhomov, who proved lazy and even disinterested and was recalled, to be succeeded by Vladimir Petrov within a comparatively short time.

Petrov was posted to the embassy in Canberra with the rank of Third Secretary, but his real function was that of Resident Director. With him went his wife, Evdokia, who was also an employee of the NKVD, who acted as a clerk in the embassy.

By the time that Petrov arrived, the network had reached a very low ebb indeed, chiefly through lack of opportunity, and though Petrov explained the situation clearly to the Center, before very long they were beginning to criticize him personally. Nevertheless, they sent him another assistant, F. V. Kislitsyn. Kislitsyn's stay was short, however, because he could produce no better results than Petrov, and though they expected more from his successor, N. G. Kovaliov, their hopes were unfulfilled, and when he, too, was recalled Petrov was held to blame because "of the absence of your positive guidance."

From this time on the Center's criticism of Petrov began to mount. Probably to try to put some new life into the network, in a long instruction dated June 6, 1952, it ordered him, among other things, to prepare for the outbreak of another world war, and the measures he should take to meet the outbreak when it came.

The result of all this criticism, which should have been foreseen by a Director who knew how to handle agents, was to implant in Petrov a growing bitterness. This bitterness he expressed to a friend he had made since coming to Australia, a Polish immigrant named Mikhail Bialogusky, whom he believed to be one of the most pro-Russian members of the Russian Social Club, though in fact he was an agent for the Australian counterespionage agency.

Stalin's death in 1953 brought about the downfall also of the most hated and feared man in Russia, Lavrenti Beria, the head of all the Security forces of the Soviet Union for fifteen years, in his role as People's Commissar for Interior and State Security, and Deputy Chairman of the Council of Ministers. The mystery surrounding Beria's death has not been fully cleared up, but it has been suggested that he had organized a plot to overthrow the other members of the régime and seize the supreme power. In some equally mysterious way, Vladimir Petrov was implicated in this plot, and because of this, combined with the adverse reports upon his work by his ambassador, early in the spring of 1954 he was recalled to Moscow.

On April 3 he disappeared. For some reason he had not taken Mrs. Petrov with him, and when he had not reappeared after three weeks, the order came for her to be repatriated. The aircraft in which she was being flown home landed at Darwin airport to refuel, and she, with her bodyguard of three or four Soviet agents, was taken to the terminal building to refresh herself. Her progress had been noted by Australian counterespionage, and somehow or other her husband was able to speak to her on the telephone. At Canberra and on landing at Darwin she had behaved quite docilely, but now she changed. She cried out to Australian officials that she did not want to go back to Moscow and that she wished to be granted asylum.

The bodyguard seized her and tried to rush her across the Tarmac to the waiting Russian plane, but Australian officials intervened, and were able to free her and take her into their protection. Whether they had been forewarned, or whether they had acted on their own initiative, it is no matter; but Australian photographers and television cameramen happened to be present, and the struggle was recorded. As a result, within a few hours the world knew of the defection of this high-ranking member of the NKVD.

The Center had more or less taken Gouzenko's defection in its stride, but this, coming relatively soon after, and blazoned round the world with not very edifying photographs attached, was a little too much. Diplomatic relations with Australia were broken off, and the embassy closed, its personnel being recalled to Moscow.

The information and documents Petrov had been able to take with him when he left the embassy—the documents included letters to and from Moscow dating back to 1952 which he was supposed to have burnt—added yet more knowledge to the West's picture of the working and policies of Soviet espionage. The case did much to bring home to the man in the street the skill of Soviet espionage penetration, and it roused the authorities everywhere to yet a further tightening of their own internal security. Unfortunately, as the evidence of recent years has demonstrated, the memories of citizens and authorities alike are very short. It would seem that only constant reiteration of the dangers can produce action; and even this has its drawbacks, for a thing oft repeated in the end goes unheard.

☐ Khokhlov and Company

Between the defection of Juri Rastvorov in Japan and of Vladimir Petrov and his wife in Australia, another significant defection took place, which added information to the West's files on the Soviet espionage agency's methods of working quite different from the information supplied by Gouzenko, the Petrovs and other lesser defectors.

In West Germany there has existed since the war a group known as the Society of National Unity (NTS), organized and led by Georgi Okolovich, with headquarters in Frankfurt-am-Main. The aim of the NTS was and is to subvert Red Army men and Communist officials in Eastern Germany, and at the time of which we are writing—1954, when the Allies were still in occupation of Austria—in the Russian Zone of Austria and the satellite countries, the methods used were the secret distribution of millions of leaflets.

Apparently the NTS were having a success so considerable that the Russian authorities could not overlook it, and, judging that its leader was the NTS's greatest source of inspiration, it was decided that he must be liquidated. So, in October 1953, Colonel Studnikov, then chief of the Division for Diversion and

Terror, called to him one of his operators, a Captain Nicolai Khokhlov, and informed him that he and two other agents had been selected to put an end to Okolovich's activities.

Early in the following month, Khokhlov went to East Germany, where he met two German Communists who were to be his assistants, and flew back with them to Moscow. Khokhlov was an experienced assassin, and this was by no means his first assignment for the Ninth Section. His assistants, however, were new to it, and while he studied the layout of Frankfurt and discussed the plan which had been worked out for him, the two Germans received their basic training in the use of the firearms they would carry with them, and in unarmed combat at the Special School at Kuchino near Moscow.

By the end of December, all was ready, and on the 29th, Khokhlov, Hans Kukowitsch and Kurt Weber flew back to East Berlin. They had been instructed not to enter West Germany from the East, so they went first to Vienna. Here Khokhlov waited for the signal to go ahead, while the two Germans made their way to the little watering place of Baden.

It so happened that the foreign ministers of the Big Four had arranged to hold one of their meetings about this time, and the Kremlin, wishing to avoid the embarrassment of being accused of an assassination while the meeting was in progress, recalled Khokhlov to Moscow until it was finished.

The conference broke down, and on January 13, 1954, Khokhlov was ordered to return to Vienna, once more to await the go-ahead. This did not arrive until February 8, when Khokhlov joined his two assistants in Baden.

Following the Center's instruction, Kukowitsch and Weber traveled by train to Innsbruck and from there crossed into Switzerland, while Khokhlov flew to Zurich, where the three met two or three days later. From here, Khokhlov sent the two Germans to Frankfurt, and joined them four days later, on February 18.

On the following day, Khokhlov went alone to Georgi Okolovich's flat, and to the NTS leader's amazement told him that he had been ordered to murder him, but that he had decided not to carry out instructions. Would Mr. Okolovich, he asked, be kind

enough to get in touch with the American security forces in
West Germany and tell them that he wished their protection in
return for disclosing the plan and the methods of the Ninth Section, and anything else which they might find useful, and of
which he had knowledge.

When the Americans got over their surprise, they granted his
request, but the special weapons which the Ninth Section had
supplied for the murder were not yet in the possession of the
chosen killers. So, acting on American instructions, Khokhlov
told the two Germans to go to Augsburg, where they would be
handed the weapons by an NKVD agent. This they did.

Khokhlov, knowing the ways of the Ninth Section only too
well, was certain that a second group had been sent to Germany
to shadow him and see that he carried out instructions. He therefore insisted that the greatest security precautions should be observed in the Americans' meetings with him, with the result that
the contacts between the two sides took on the trimmings of Ian
Fleming's James Bond's activities at their most imaginative. Some
of Khokhlov's conversations with the Americans took place in a
lavatory, at a Frankfurt opera house, others in a backstage dressing room.

Though Khokhlov might defect, Okolovich could not be considered safe from this particular plot while the two Germans,
who had deposited the weapons in the cloakroom at the Frankfurt main station, were at large. Rather than arrest them,
Khokhlov was asked to try to persuade them to defect also. He met
them on February 25, told them what he had done and advised
them to do the same. Apparently their hearts were not entirely in
the job, for they agreed with little hesitation. So for the time
being Georgi Okolovich was safe.

The information which Khokhlov could provide was valuable,
but perhaps the most interesting part of the whole incident,
which certainly provoked the greatest surprise when photographs and descriptions were published, were the weapons which
had been provided by the Ninth Section. They included a ciga-
rette case which shot poisoned dum-dum bullets through the tips
of cigarettes, and a four-inch-long revolver, capable of being

concealed in the palm of the hand and of making a mere snapping noise when it was fired by a battery-operated mechanism.

Since the death of Stalin, there has been a considerable decrease in the number of mysterious deaths of men and women who had formerly held Communist affiliations or sympathies. Whether this was the result of the Khokhlov disclosures—up to this time the murders of Trotsky, of Ignace Reiss, a former Resident Director, of Renata Steiner, a Swiss Communist, of Dimitry Navachin, a former Soviet diplomat, and the disappearance of Juliet Poyntz, and of many other killings and disappearances, only gave an indication of the existence of a vengeance squad, but no actual proof—or comes from the liberalizing, more humane influence of the present Soviet leadership, it is not possible to say. But the tradition is there and, if a real need for it arose, it is possible that there would be little hesitation in resuscitating it.

PART VII

Postwar Europe

☐ Since Stalin's Death

The death of Stalin affected Soviet Russia in many ways, and the so-called de-Stalinization process which has been in progress since the all-out attack made on him by Nikita Khrushchev in 1956 has demonstrated for all to see that the Russian rulers themselves wish to make a clean break with the worst characteristics of the Stalin era. Recent visitors to Russia testify that the change which has taken place in the atmosphere itself, in the behavior and outlook of the ordinary citizens and in the opening up of many cultural and intellectual frontiers is so formidable that there can never again be a return to the old ways.

In the day-to-day existence of Soviet citizens, who have lost the frightened aspect and the aloofness from intercourse with strangers which so characterized them when Stalin ruled over them, it is said that the weakening of the power of the secret police has played a major role. And it would be difficult to argue that this is not so, for under Stalin the internal security forces had the deciding voice in every individual's destiny and his ultimate fate, and this power was vested actually in the hands of one man.

Lavrenti Beria was, like Stalin, a Georgian, and, like his master and friend, possessed all the ruthlessness and cunning and desire for power which so marked Lenin's successor. The son of a minor civil servant, he was born in Tiflis in 1898, trained as a teacher, and then joined the tsarist army. He claimed that he had incited his fellow soldiers to mutiny, been court-martialed and sentenced to death, but managed to escape. However there is no independent evidence to bear out the truth of this.

After the Revolution in 1917 he was in the Caucasus, and when the White Army overran the territory, he fled to Siberia. A little later he was back again in the Caucasus, carrying out Intelligence work. It was as a result of this work that he came to Stalin's attention, and when Dzershinsky was given the task of organizing his Cheka, he received from the Commissar of Nationalities, Josef Stalin, a letter recommending to him "a brilliant young comrade [whom] I consider completely trustworthy . . . Lavrenti Pavlovich Beria."

Within a very short time, Beria was already proving that he had a flair for secret activities as well as a flair for languages— he had an excellent command of German, French and Czech— which two qualifications gained for him a post in the Soviet Legation in Prague, where he was to report on officers of the former tsarist army in exile in Czechoslovakia.

From 1928 to 1937 he worked abroad, engaged mostly in tracking down Trotskyites. During this period, he wormed his way into Stalin's confidence to such an extent that, after the Purge of 1938, he was placed in control of Security, as People's Commissar. During the next three years he used the NKVD to increase his personal power. Like Stalin, whom he was determined to follow in the leadership, he could brook no opposition, and those who were foolhardy enough to attempt to oppose him soon discovered his ruthlessness. In the forwarding of his ambition he removed, one by one, all those who might be considered to stand between him and Stalin, with a few notable exceptions; but the rest he held in his power by the detailed dossiers which bulged in his files in which were set down every single action, whether overt or covert, committed by the subject.

He was responsible for the reign of terror at home—in which

Stalin acquiesced—for he realized that his secret police constituted the most formidable weapon for achieving power. It was
he who insisted on having his agents in every unit of the armed
forces, agents who spied on the "reliability" of every man from
general to private. When the Russo-German war broke out, the
frontiers of Russia with Germany were for the most part
guarded by NKVD troops, and it has since been discovered that
his agents in the forward zones sent their intelligence direct to
him, and that he passed on to Stalin and the High Command only
that which he saw fit, withholding much information which
would have been invaluable to the military planners in the first
six months of the conflict at least.

Yet it must not be forgotten that it was under his direction
and drive that Soviet espionage brought off its most brilliant
coups to date, that he was the master whom Rudolf Rössler,
Richard Sorge and the Red Orchestra served.

Naturally he filled all the most important posts in his organizations with men whom he could trust implicitly, men who took
their cue from him, men like Merkulov, chief of State Security
throughout the war, and Minister of State Security and Control
until 1953; Dekanosov, chief of the Foreign Department of the
First Directorate; Pavel Mesnik, chief of the Special Division
and director of the Department for Diversion and Terror (the
Murder Squad); Nicoforovich Kruglov, who saved Roosevelt's
and Churchill's lives at Teheran by discovering the German plot
to murder them, and who survived five masters, including Beria.

Only one thing Beria overlooked in his climb to the peak of
power—the opposition of the Army commanders to him; and he
made a very serious underestimate of the cunning of his closest
rival, Malenkov. Long before Stalin died, Malenkov, who had
been Stalin's closest friend and bright-eyed boy, despite his
youth, came to terms with the Army in return for their support
when the moment came; and when the moment did come, and
Stalin's body lay in state in the Hall of Pillars, Beria's fate was
already sealed.

For a month or two nothing happened, then suddenly Malenkov pounced. Beria was arrested, accused of conspiracy to over-

throw the present leadership, tried secretly and executed, and nothing was said until he was dead. Arrested and executed with him were the men whose names have been quoted above—except Kruglov—and every other who had received his appointment from Beria. This latest purge reached out far and wide, and in effect removed all the old leadership of the secret services to quite a low echelon.

The danger of the power which one man might acquire who had the sole control of all the security services had not been lost on the new Soviet leadership, and they were determined that so long as they had any influence it could never happen again.

It will be recalled that early in 1941, the Commissariat for State Security and the Interior had been split into two separate departments, though Beria had retained supreme control. After Stalin's death, he had merged the two departments into one Ministry again, the Ministry of Internal Affairs and State Security, with Kruglov as the Minister, and A. I. Serov as Vice-Minister, with Beria still in control as Deputy Chairman of the Council of Ministers. After his death, the Council of Ministers carried out a further reorganization, setting up a Committee of State Security with the task of co-ordinating the internal security services under the chairmanship of A. I. Serov, at the same time abolishing the internal secret police as conceived by Beria. Under the new setup two chief directors were appointed to the secret services, one responsible for the First Directorate, the other for the Second Directorate, and both responsible to the Committee of State Security collectively.

Now, although the horrible shadow of Beria and his secret police has been lifted from the lives of the ordinary man and woman in Russia—this is not to say, of course, that a close watch is not kept for any subversive behavior—and has wrought a little miracle, the bureaucratic reorganization has had little or no effect on espionage methods or activities. Indeed, there are many signs which point to the contrary.

For example, recent cases in Sweden and in Great Britain all point to the fact that Soviet espionage is relying still on the services of blackmailed or ideologically affected nationals. The widely cast net has certainly not been drawn in at all; in fact, if anything, an even wider net has been cast. The behavior of many compromised agents still seems to indicate that the training methods have not changed, though the agent material can often be seen to be of a much higher caliber, even if it is still prone to aberrations which eventually bring about its downfall.

Equally there are signs that in tested cases, individual agents are being given far more latitude in the exercise of initiative than would have been dreamt of in the pre-Beria and Beria eras. On the other hand, it is still evident that the Center is today keeping as firm a hand on the operations of networks as it ever did.

☐ The New Setup

The postwar reorganization of Europe brought about one great change in Soviet espionage which was important from several points of view. No longer had the Center to maintain networks in at least nine countries, which, before the war, had been potential enemies. On the contrary, it could press into its service espionage agencies organized and directed, it is true, by spy masters of experience trained by themselves, but paid for by other governments and manned by personnel of other states. The secrets of about half of Europe came too into its keeping as a matter of administrative action; the secrets of the other half could be apportioned out between the Satellite agencies, leaving the Center free to concentrate on the most important fields, like America, Great Britain, France and West Germany.

The new setup saw men whose names have frequently appeared on the pages of the preceding chapters rise to new heights. They were the proven old hands who knew how an espionage agency should be organized on the Center's pattern, and who had the experience to direct along the Center's lines. Wollweber, the great saboteur of the immediate prewar and early war years, became Minister of State Security in East Germany, Vaclav Nosek, Minister of the Interior in Prague, and Vulko Chervenkov, Minister of the Interior in Prague and now a Vice-President of the Council of Ministers.

But if the new arrangement eased the situation for Soviet

espionage, it increased proportionately the counterespionage difficulties in the non-Communist countries. For the Satellites were organized and operated on the same pattern as the Russian agency. In all the Western countries which recognized the new régimes, those régimes established embassies, overstaffed for their lawful business, and including among their doorkeepers, their chauffeurs and their diplomats high-ranking members of their espionage agencies.

It was not long before the presence of these agents became known, and in a very unpleasant way. The very many people who had fled before the advancing Russian armies and had first been herded in displaced-persons camps in Germany, and then selected for the honor of living and working in a Western democracy, were one of the early targets for the Satellite agencies. Most of them had left relatives in their own countries, and under the threat of imprisoning these relatives, they were blackmailed into becoming spies.

One of the largest national refugee groups in England, for example, were the Poles who had served in General Anders's army, which had fought side by side with the Allies. Among these men was a certain Stanislaus Badjer, who became an official of a union which protected the interests of Polish workers in England. Unfortunately Mme. Badjer and her child were still in Poland.

In 1949, Badjer received a call from two men who revealed themselves as members of a small Polish network in Great Britain. They put to him the "suggestion" that he should supply them with the names and particulars of Polish refugees in this country who still had relatives in Poland. If he would not accept their suggestion, he was told that his wife and child would be sent to a Russian labor camp. At the beginning of the war, Badjer had himself spent a year in such a camp, and knowing that the threat was not an idle one, he agreed to collaborate. He set up his headquarters in Manchester, and it was there that his activities, somewhat clumsy because he was completely inexperienced in clandestine operations, made his compatriots suspicious, the Special Branch was called in, and Badjer was deported to Poland.

Then in the early 1950's several cases of young Czech and other Satellite diplomats came up. They were accused of attempting to entice workers in certain plants engaged on secret government contracts to divulge blueprints and so on in return for money. They, too, were so inept that they very soon attracted attention—in some cases the workers refused or went to the police—and there was a small spate of departures at the request of the British Government.

Even the Russians, who had had long experience in this kind of activity, made blunders and were exposed. In May 1954 Major Gudkov and Major Pupyshev, two assistant military attachés at the London embassy, were declared by Sir Anthony Eden to be no longer acceptable to the British Government. Gudkov had been assigned to obtain designs of four military aircraft, and set about his task in the traditional way. He had been given the name of a Communist employed in the plant concerned and, as this man did not have access to the secret information Gudkov required, he was ordered to find an employee who had and would be amenable to collaborating with him.

Such an employee was produced, and Gudkov arranged a meeting with him in a public house not far from the factory. There he offered several hundred pounds for copies of blueprints, and taking the Englishman's apparent eagerness to comply for granted, arranged a second meeting. The employee, however, went to the police, and when this later meeting took place counterespionage officers were present, as observers.

Acting under instructions, the employee spun out his negotiations for about six months, during which time all Gudkov's movements were watched. Then, when enough evidence had been collected, counterespionage pounced, caught the major with planted false material in his possession, and only the fact that he had diplomatic immunity saved Gudkov from arrest.

Unknown to Gudkov, his colleague Major Pupyshev had been given an identical assignment. His approach was different. He tried to make friends with an RAF officer and persuade him to obtain the information.

The officer pretended to be willing, informed the police, and counterespionage followed the same procedure as in the case of Gudkov. Pupyshev was also returned to Russia—at the same time as his fellow attaché.

Only a couple of years before these minor incidents, the British public had been made aware of Soviet espionage activities in Great Britain by the imprisonment of a Foreign Office clerk, William Marshall. In 1950 Marshall had been assigned to the British Embassy in Moscow as a cipher clerk. Like Vassall a decade later, Marshall did not "fit in" with the rest of the embassy staff, and in his loneliness sought the acquaintance of certain Russians—though, in fact, it would be more true to say that the Russians, having been told of his unhappiness, sought him out.

In 1952 Marshall was brought home to work in the Foreign Office, and he arrived in London with a letter of introduction to the Third Secretary at the Soviet Embassy, Pavel Kuznetzov. Kuznetzov introduced the young clerk to a way of life of which he had formerly only heard—expensive dinners and so on—and gradually persuaded Marshall to hand over to him any information of importance which would come his way as a cipher clerk.

When Marshall agreed, the West End meetings were replaced by meetings in less frequented places, like Richmond Park and Kensington Gardens. It would seem that Marshall, through no fault of his own, for he was completely untrained for secret work of this kind, by his behavior attracted the attention of the security officers at the Foreign Office, and a watch was placed on him. When Counterespionage was satisfied that it had sufficient evidence it struck.

Kuznetzov and Marshall were confronted at one of their meetings in a park. The Russian diplomat immediately claimed diplomatic immunity, and was allowed to go; but Marshall was arrested. When he was searched, a copy of a highly secret Foreign Office document was found in his pocketbook. Though he denied that he had spied, the jury did not believe him, and he was sent to prison for five years.

In practically every country in Western Europe and in the

United States similar manifestations of Soviet espionage were constantly cropping up. In Washington, for example, Christache Zambeti, First Secretary at the Romanian Embassy attempted to blackmail an oil company executive, V. C. Georgescu, who had had to leave two sons behind in Romania, into handing over secret information relating to U.S. security in return for visas for the boys to allow them to join their father. Georgescu went at once to the FBI, and Zambeti was asked to leave America, the fourth Romanian diplomat to be required to do so within two years.

No country was free of Soviet clandestine activities. The counter-espionage agencies opposing them had their resources stretched to the limits; but as future events were to demonstrate, the extent of the Soviet effort was underestimated practically everywhere; not only in Great Britain, but in America, in France and in Scandinavia. The Blake and Vassall cases have all had their counterparts elsewhere, though not such an outcry has accompanied them.

MI5 was partly to blame for what happened here, but there was a general carelessness among the security agencies of the many government departments dealing with strategic secrets. Not even the revelation of the pitiable lapses of Admiralty security in the Lonsdale-Houghton-Gee case prevented Blake and Vassall from operating successfully for some time after this trio were safely in prison. Admittedly, counterespionage works from a greater disadvantage than does espionage; but a skillful spy-catching organization, well trained, and always alert can be more than a match for most espionage agencies once the first clue has been discovered; while in the case of hidden Communist agents, in practically every instance there is some indication in the early careers of the men which points to the possibility of their being a security risk and which is there for the seeing if only a close enough scrutiny is made.

Nevertheless, the volume of espionage carried out and the great increase in technical skill acquired by Soviet espionage in the postwar period presents a task of gigantic proportions. But probably nowhere has Soviet activity been so intensive as in West Germany.

☐ West Germany

Anyone who has talked to a Russian, official or private citizen, about the possibilities of a third world war breaking out cannot have failed to be impressed with the sincerity with which West Germany is held to be the most dangerous potential threat to peace. Relying on history, they are quite convinced that German militarism is so deeply and firmly embedded in the Teutonic national character that they discredit all Bonn's expostulations of disinterest in war as merely a blind for a future attempt to restore national military prestige, so very badly battered by two defeats in twenty-five years, when the time is considered ripe. It is a point of view which is not without support among sections of thinking people in the West, and though all governments will undoubtedly keep a strict watch for the slightest resurgence of a German desire to possess a military offensive weapon, with the intention of suppressing it the very first sign of life that it manifests, the Russians are not prepared to leave anything to chance in this field of international activities.

From the earliest postwar years they have concentrated on West Germany an espionage effort which far surpasses their efforts anywhere else, even including America. The main endeavor of this effort has been directed to discovering every secret which the German Federal Government may be hatching.

This assignment, however, would not justify or require such a vast effort as is exerted west of the Travemünde-Hof curve, and there are other reasons which spring from Russian opportunism. First, American and British forces maintained in the Federal Republic present a target which it would be foolish for any potential opponent to overlook. Here the latest weapons and equipment are deployed—aircraft, artillery and the hundred and one other modern fighting aids—and here, too, policy secrets are lodged in files, maneuvers are carried out in forests and on heaths, and all within reach of comparatively easily placed agents.

Then, also, half of Germany is already in the Soviet camp. The strength which would accrue to the Communist world in its efforts to realize world domination if the other half of Germany were to follow suit provides a rich incentive to prepare the ground by subversion. For the most part, however, targets have been military and political.

In West Germany we see the combination of Soviet-Satellite agencies working at its most concentrated form. There are four agencies operating; a Soviet agency directed and controlled by the Center from East Germany; an East German agency; a Czech agency; and finally a Polish agency. The efforts of the four are co-ordinated; tasks are allotted by the Center, which avoids overlapping. The results go straight to the Center, and only if the Russians so wish do any of the secrets gathered by the "foreign" agencies reach those agencies' governments.

All four agencies work to the same pattern. Trained and tested recruiting officers look for their operators among the displaced persons who still have relatives behind the Iron Curtain, but their chief reservoir is Germans whose moral standards have never been brought back to what may be termed as the "norm" after having sunk to low levels during the general demoralization of the later war years, and youthful Germans who, like young people almost everywhere, want "kicks." In the case of the German agents, the main bait is money, and their paymasters, now better psychologists than they previously were, are not mean. Because many ordinary soldiers of all the Allied forces are in daily contact with the latest weapons of all kinds, and are therefore in a position to supply information or even examples, all four agencies employ a good many women. Indeed, no other agency in the history of espionage has used so many women as the networks do in West Germany today. Often these women are prostitutes—normally put to work on American Negro enlisted men—but all are prepared to offer their bodies, as well as substantial monetary payments, as bait.

In recent years the Germans have withheld the figures of Communists arrested and convicted in their courts as spies, but in the early days the figures were available, and these show with good effect the volume of activity engaged in by the Soviet and Satellite agencies in West Germany. Between 1949 and 1955 no fewer than eighty-six cases of espionage were brought before the courts; and the defendants numbered 174. Since the spies arrested can be taken to represent only a small fraction of the total operating, it can be assumed that the numbers of active agents run into many hundreds.

Both the Allied courts and the German courts—the latter have been trying espionage cases since 1951—do not treat espionage with leniency, though their sentences are not so harsh as those meted out by Communist courts in similar cases. The average is about six years' imprisonment, but in several cases the maximum of fifteen years has been imposed. And yet there is no indication that the reservoirs of potential spies are drying up.

In fact, it is the large numbers of men and women who are prepared to spy for the quite lavish rewards offered which has led to the extraordinary scale on which the networks operate. It has further influenced the organization of the networks especially in the field of training. Very little training is given to the selected spy, and what is given is rudimentary and cursory, but the spy masters have no need to worry, for while this lack of training certainly leads to the large numbers of arrests, they know that for each agent caught there are half a dozen willing to replace him. These considerations, too, influence the quality of the agent material selected, which, taken over-all, is exceptionally poor; a fact which contributes to the number caught.

These points can be more graphically presented by recounting one or two typical cases.

In 1950, the British arrested a certain Wilhelm Klein, whom they caught spying on their airfield at Gatow near Berlin. Like practically every other agent caught in West Germany, Klein pleaded guilty to the charges, and was quite prepared to talk.

The authorities were quite surprised to find that Klein, a man of thirty-two, had a criminal record, having served several sentences for burglary and black-marketeering. He was, indeed, a type whom any self-respecting espionage agency would have shunned except for very special assignments.

Klein told the British that he had been given his assignment by a Russian officer, a certain Captain Grabowski, who controlled one of the Russian networks. During his period of activity he had obtained information about the British Army of the Rhine, about military objectives—bridges, barracks and other installations—and had taken a number of photographs which he had handed over to the Socialist Unity Party, the Communist Party in the then Soviet Zone, for forwarding to Grabowski.

Three years later a cell was discovered operating when a local blacksmith reported to the British authorities that a certain Werner Berg had tried to persuade him to gather secret information, by promising to pay him seven hundred marks a month, roughly the equivalent of $170. Berg was watched, and he led the Security forces to the other members of the cell, three men and two women, all Germans, led by Robert Koch, a commercial traveler, who frequently crossed "in the way of business" into the Soviet Zone.

Their locale was Lüneburg Heath and Brunswick. The former represented the most important of all BAOR sites in the British Zone, for here tank tests and other experimental work, chiefly on artillery, was carried out; while all the activities on the Heath were controlled from the latter.

The two women were among the most important members of

the cell. Edith Seefeld, who was engaged to marry a British officer, was in a position to supply program details; while Erika Krüger, who was a telephone operator on the switchboard at the large camp at Münster, was able to gain access to reports and photographs. Edith Seefeld talked, and for her assistance the charges against her were dropped, but Berg was sentenced to five years; the other members, except Koch the leader who managed to evade capture, to four years.

Yet a third cell was discovered operating in Kiel. The two men in the case were again Germans: Harald Freidank, who was in charge of the British-sponsored press service, and Hans Frahm, a sports writer and a Communist, who was already working for the Soviet network when he met Freidank. Frahm recruited Freidank, whom he found so useful that when the British dispensed with the latter's services in 1952 he was loath to lose him, and promised to find him another job with an East German press agency with offices in the British Zone. In the course of making the arrangements for this, Frahm took Freidank to Berlin, and there introduced him to a Russian agent, who persuaded him to carry on with his espionage. When Freidank agreed, he was given an assignment in Hamburg, where his too-searching inquiries into the activities of certain British officers attracted the attention of the Security authorities.

Frahm killed himself while awaiting trail; Freidank was given the light sentence of one year.

The Soviet agency has always held British counterespionage —as well as British espionage—in healthy respect, and in their assault in the British Zone they used agents of much higher caliber—with the exception of Klein and one or two others— than they introduced into the American and French Zones. They also seem to have had a high opinion of the loyalty of British army personnel, both commissioned and noncommissioned, for, while they did make one or two half-hearted attempts to subvert British soldiers, the effort in this field was negligible compared with the attempts made to subvert American NCOs and GIs.

In this type of operation it has been the Satellite agencies—the Poles and the Czechs—who appear to have been detailed to operate. There was, for example, the case of the extensive Czech network in Frankfurt-am-Main.

Though he resided in Czechoslovakia, this network was controlled by a Czech officer who passed under the cover name of Captain Burda. In 1950, Burda made the acquaintance of Hans Pape, the well-educated and intelligent son of wealthy German parents. Pape, however, was something of a degenerate. Unstable in character, he had flitted from job to job before the war, and during the war had contrived to spend much of his time in hospitals well away from the firing line.

He was in a hospital in the east when the Russian advance overran it before he could escape, and he was taken prisoner. Released in 1947, he returned to West Germany and obtained employment at the American Rhine-Main air base. In 1950 he was summoned to the Soviet Zone, and at Weimar met a Soviet officer who assigned to him the new task of gathering information about Germans working for the Americans in the military police and counterespionage. On this visit he first met Burda, who had a proposition for him as well.

Pape was never at any time of his life able to make what he earned suffice to support his way of life. Burda's proposition, however, opened up new horizons, for the Czech was prepared to pay him $225 a month for his services. In addition to his Soviet assignment, the Czechs required Pape to supply them with reports on the Americans, and he was given the names and addresses of a number of Germans who would be able to help him. He was also instructed on his method of working.

Returning to Frankfurt, Pape opened a studio in which girls anxious to become film stars could be given film tests at five marks a time. This ridiculously low fee—the equivalent of about fifty cents—ought to have warned anyone interested that the studio was not all it tried to appear. In fact, his *bona fide* clients were few, but he did not mind this, for the studio was an excellent front for all the women who could be seen daily entering and emerging from it.

Among these women were a number of prostitutes, whom he

had engaged to obtain information from Negro soldiers, but his outstanding agent of this type was a former mistress of his, Elisabeth Dörhöfer, a very attractive girl, employed by Pan American Airways in Frankfurt. Pape did not entice her into his organization by renewing their own friendship. Instead he introduced her to Burda when he came on a visit to Frankfurt, and she became Burda's mistress and very soon his spy.

Her assignment was to obtain information from American officers, and she appears to have entered wholeheartedly into the spirit of the game she was asked to play. She had herself photographed in the nude, and used these photographs as a means of introduction to the officers chosen for her by Burda as promising targets.

She did very well, too, until one of her regular clients, a young second lieutenant, eventually became suspicious of the many questions she put to him, and reported her to the security service. As it happened, this was not the first report that the Counterintelligence Corps had received on Elisabeth. Other officers had deposed that she had offered them sums of money, in some cases as much as $2250, for information. But not only this, Pape had also reported his own network to the CIC, with the offer of acting as a double-agent, and had named his former mistress, only to have his offer rejected and his information dismissed. (He also made the same offer to the French and the British, who somewhat surprisingly reacted in the same way.) It was only when reports from officers began to come in that the CIC began to take notice.

CIC agents were set to watch her, and discovered that she made frequent visits to Czechoslovakia, and presently it was admitted that she was probably engaged in espionage. At all events, on the next occasion that she arrived at the frontier between the American Zone and the Czechoslovakian Republic she was arrested. In her handbag the CIC found a copy of a secret map, an Army circular, photographs of mortar shells and various other highly interesting and confidential documents.

She was quite prepared to co-operate, and named her two

German contacts, Karl Lippert and Hilde Klimberg. She received seven years, Lippert three and Klimberg two. Pape, for some reason best known to the American authorities, was dismissed.

Another woman agent working with the same tactics was Margarete Pfeiffer, another of Burda's collaborators. She was tall, well-built, blonde and beautiful, and normally earned her living as a model. Given the task of obtaining particulars of an infrared gunsight, she concentrated on tank-crew personnel, to whom she offered large sums of money and her expertise in bed as a special bonus.

Since she threatened her victims with death if they talked, she was fairly successful until she met a certain Private Eicher, who was unimpressed by her threats and reported her to the CIC. The CIC used Eicher to trap her and she was arrested. She did not talk, however, and stood trial alone, receiving the comparatively light sentence of four years.

In 1948, Karl Kunze and his mistress Luise Frankenberg were instructed by the Polish agency to organize a network in West Berlin. They opened an art gallery as cover, and while Kunze went about recruiting members from among anti-Allied Germans, Frankenberg looked about for useful women.

The most remarkable success she achieved in this direction was the recruitment of Maria Knuth, childless, intelligent, a woman of forty-two, separated from her husband, the well-known airman Manfred Knuth.

When the recruiting had been successfully completed, Kunze and Frankenberg were instructed to move to Frankfurt, from where it had been decided by Polish headquarters that the network should operate. Maria Knuth was left in Berlin to act as "letter box" for the network.

Not quite satisfied with the staffing of the network, Kunze brought in two more, Hermann Westbeld and Marianne Opelt, both employed by the Frankfurt police. This done, the network went into action.

It had not been operating long, however, when Kunze killed himself. He had been well supplied with funds by the Poles, and had treated his agents liberally. Nevertheless, he had spent the greater part of his money on himself and his mistress; the Poles had discovered the fact and were about to demand a reckoning, so he chose the honorable way out for the Prussian officer he had once been.

Maria Knuth was brought from Berlin to take over the leadership of the network. Frau Knuth revealed herself to be an excellent agent and the network quickly became, under her leadership, one of the most successful of all the networks operating in West Germany.

When the decision was taken in 1950 to include West Germany in NATO, the move was interpreted by Russia to be a plan for the rearmament of Germany, the thing they most feared. It called for immediate action, and the Polish agency was instructed to assign to Frau Knuth and her network the task of penetrating the agency set up by the Allies, and known as the Amt Blank. Frau Knuth made the first attempt herself. Applying for a post as a secretary in the Amt, she was rejected because her shorthand was not sufficiently fluent.

The task, in fact, proved altogether difficult, and a breakthrough was not made until 1952, when one of Frau Knuth's agents, called Hauer, introduced her to a man called Petersen who claimed to be employed by Amt Blank. As required to do, before trying to recruit Petersen for her network, Frau Knuth reported to her headquarters. She was warned that Petersen might be a plant, but was given permission to go ahead with extreme caution. Within a short time an intimate relationship had sprung up between the couple.

This was fatal. Petersen was, in reality, a West German agent, but for a time he supplied the network with excellent false material, while he learned all there was to know about the network. In April 1953 the West German authorities decided that they had all the information they required, and the complete network was arrested.

Frau Knuth by this time, however, had developed cancer in an advanced stage. While awaiting trial she underwent two operations, but she knew that she must soon die. She made no attempt to defend herself, only explaining that she wished to prevent the rearming of Germany.

As touching the East Germany agency, controlled by the highly experienced Ernst Wollweber, as Minister of State Security, its role has been more concerned with sabotage than espionage. The experts are of the opinion that the mysterious explosions and fires that have occurred in naval vessels and civilian liners are the work of this master saboteur—the fires in the *Queen Elizabeth,* the *Queen Mary* and the *Empress of Canada* in 1953, for example, and the explosion in HM aircraft carrier *Indomitable*—aided by specially trained mobile units who receive their instruction in the Maritime School at Wustrow. But his land operations have chiefly included the smuggling of strategic material from the West.

On the other hand the East German agency has carried out a few espionage assignments, all of which have been of an extremely serious nature. One such case involved a West Berlin police officer who passed over the West's plans for preventing the numerous kidnapings of West Germans, and reports on the organization of the West German police forces. Another was a high official of the Berlin police administration, a Communist called Bruno Wricke who made no attempt to conceal his Party allegiance but was appointed nevertheless. He worked for six years, supplying the East German agency with important police documents, including lists of arrested persons, copies of interrogations and so on. And there was Margarete Schmidt, whom the *New York Herald Tribune* described in the following terms:

A very attractive girl, she established her first substantial connection with Air Force personnel in West Berlin through an intimate relationship with an important intelligence officer that began in the summer of 1953 and seems to have lasted the better part of a year. It is thought that she had a concurrent or subsequent relationship with another Air Force civilian or officer of somewhat lower rank.

The higher ranking intelligence officer got her a secretarial job with an American intelligence agency in West Berlin—possibly with his own outfit. She was later dismissed from this job. The reason for her dismissal was that she showed excessive curiosity about secret papers lying on other persons' desks.

Nevertheless she succeeded in landing another secretarial post with the Americans at West Berlin's Tempelhof Air Base. While she held this job she retained contact with persons she had become acquainted with during her employment in the intelligence field. Her arrest occurred because she attempted to high-pressure a German national working for her former American intelligence employers into providing her with counterintelligence secrets.

One of the most extensive networks was uncovered by the newly created West German political counterespionage agency, the Amt für Verfassungsschutz, one of its early successes. In 1951 an Institute for Economic Research was set up in East Berlin, and in a short time had established a branch in Frankfurt-am-Main under the direction of Ludwig Weiss, a high-ranking official of the Soviet Zone's Ministry of Trade. At the same time a supposedly private-enterprise trading company was incorporated under the title of Ost-West Handelsgesellschaft.

In theory, the Institute for Economic Research and its offshoots were to be what their title implied—organizations to explore the possibilities for trade between the West and East Zones —though, in fact, their real function was to gather information on every aspect of West German life, and particularly those aspects of West German administration which they try to conceal, with special reference to rearmament. In other words, it was merely a cover for espionage on a wide scale.

How permission was obtained from the West German authorities to set up the organizations in Frankfurt and Hamburg is something of a mystery, but the real significance of them did not escape the new political counterespionage agency. Within a short time the Amt had infiltrated both the Hamburg and the Frankfurt cells, while an agent, Gotthold Kraus, actually obtained a post in the East Berlin headquarters, and actually trained agents to operate in the West, before returning to his superiors in Bonn in 1953 with enough documentary evidence to uncover the entire network, which went under the cover name of Vulkan.

Before this happened, however, Weiss, leader of the Frankfurt cell, was arrested on the evidence of another West agent, Wilhelm Ruschmaier, who had supplied him with false documents supplied by his agency. Only when Weiss became dangerous by collecting genuine information relating to military and political secrets, was he made harmless. After his arrest the network continued to operate until Kraus returned from East Berlin in the spring of 1953. Then the West agency pounced, and scooped up the remaining thirty-five members of Vulkan.

This was the third network which the Amt für Verfassungsschutz had closed down within one year. The others were one Pole and one Czech. It was also the largest network then operating in West Germany.

Today Soviet and Satellite espionage activity has not lessened in scope or effort. As has been said earlier, the majority of spy arrests and trials in West Germany are kept secret, but there is a prison in Landsberg, Bavaria, which, apart from housing a few German war criminals, is given over entirely to imprisoned foreign agents. It is said that the prison has now reached saturation point, and that further suitable quarters must be found to give shelter to the constant stream of spies still falling into the West German net.

☐ Lucy's Return

When the war was over, Rudolf Rössler, who, under the cover name Lucy, had performed such miracles on behalf of Soviet espionage during the war, refused to continue his clandestine activities either on behalf of the Swiss or the Russians. He had been paid handsomely by the Russians, and the Swiss had not been parsimonious toward him, and the bulk of his income from these two sources he devoted to his publishing house, Vita Nova. But Vita Nova began to fall on hard times, for German Fascism had disappeared, free speech was a prominent feature of the new West Germany, and there was really no market for his particular kind of propaganda.

He still regarded Vita Nova as his special brain child, however, and when the Center, having become aware of his financial straits, which coincided with their own decision to revive the old Swiss network, he accepted their offer to become active on their behalf once more. He had retained, it would seem, his wartime contacts in Germany, who were now serving the new régime, and somehow he was able to persuade them to supply him with information again.

It will be recalled that he had been introduced in the first

place to Swiss Intelligence by a young journalist Xavier Schnieper. Schnieper, after the war, had come out into the open about
his Communist sympathies and had become the chairman of the
Lucerne branch of the Communist Party. But when the national
Swiss Party had become split from top to bottom as the result of
an internal financial scandal in 1946, he had been expelled from
the Party, and had joined a number of anti-Communist organizations.

Schnieper, however, had very expensive tastes, especially with
regard to women, and he, too, was always in financial difficulties. So when he was approached by the Soviet agency, who
suggested that he should join forces with Rössler, he agreed.

In 1948 he joined the Swiss Social Democrats, and shortly
afterward was sent to Bonn as correspondent for the Swiss Socialist Press. He has a very attractive personality, and it was not
long before he had established a large circle of friends and acquaintances who were highly placed in the Federal German administration. Like Sorge in Japan, he was able to search out information without raising suspicions in his role as newspaper correspondent, and there were many who were quite willing to tell
him what they knew. What they did not realize, however, was that
everything of importance they told him quickly found its way to
Moscow.

The third member of the cell was a Czech officer, Colonel
Volf, who was one of a Czech network operating in Switzerland,
directed from Prague and instructed by the Center, with the
veteran spy Colonel Sedlaček, military attaché at the Berne embassy, as Resident Director. Sedlaček was an old friend of Schnieper's, and had little trouble in persuading him to join his outfit.

Rössler's German contacts were still able to supply him with
truly high-grade material, and not only relating to Germany, but
to Great Britain, France, America and Scandinavia as well, not
merely in Germany, but in the countries themselves. His personal worth to the Center was therefore high, and he received
the really exceptional remuneration of roughly twelve hundred
dollars a month.

Schnieper, besides specializing in technical material—Rössler concentrated on political espionage and military intelligence—acted as the German's secretary, and typed his reports. Then as the Center began to develop the use of the microfilm, he acquired the art of microphotography, and arranged for the forward transmission of the reports in this form.

The channel of communication was the concealment of the microfilms in food parcels sent to a "letter box" in Düsseldorf. At the time, this was a practically foolproof method, for the generous Swiss were sending food parcels to their German friends by the hundreds daily. Unhappily it was this method of communication which brought the activities of the cell to an untimely end.

The Rössler-Volf-Schnieper cell worked for five years, from 1947 to December 1952. In the latter month they dispatched a food parcel to a mythical Heinrich Schwartz in Düsseldorf. For some unknown reason, Schwartz did not claim the parcel and it was returned to Switzerland in January 1953. As there was no sender's address on it, the parcel was opened, and the microfilms were discovered hidden in jars of figs and honey. They contained reports on British airfields in West Germany, on the recent American Army maneuvers and on the U. S. Air Force in Britain.

The Swiss Abwehr had little doubts about the source of this exceptionally high-grade material, and Rössler and Schnieper were kept under surveillance for a short time, and then arrested. They made no bones about revealing their recent activities, and as they had not been engaged in espionage against Switzerland, they received the light sentences of a year for Rössler and nine months for Schnieper. Both could have been deported, but they pleaded that if they were sent back to Germany they would be liable to prosecution there for espionage; and they were not at all eager to go behind the Iron Curtain, either. So "in view of their great services to Swiss Intelligence during the war, and because they are stateless persons," they were given the light sentences recorded above.

Rössler died in 1962, still denying that he had ever engaged in espionage; and without divulging who his German contacts had been, or giving any hint as to their identity.

☐ France

Certainly no other non-Communist country in Europe, and probably no other in the world, presented its secrets to the Soviet Union with such open-handedness as France between the end of the war and the advent of de Gaulle. The political situation was such that there was scarcely any need for Soviet espionage to indulge in conventional activity at all.

Numerically the French Communist Party has always been the strongest national Party outside Russia itself, though the Italian has from time to time run very close. During the German Occupation it cannot be denied that the Communist Resistance, while being the most handicapped in finance, equipment and outside assistance, was the most active, the most patriotic in the primary meaning of the word and, at the same time, the most opportunist of all the Resistance groups and organizations. The many un-co-ordinated groups, which, until late in the war, fought one another as fiercely as they fought the Germans, representing all the many political groups that seem to flourish particularly well in France, were symbolic and symptomatic of the state of French political life. Though they made an attempt to sink differences and collaborate with one another for the national good—and to a certain degree succeeded—in 1944, as soon as Liberation had overtaken them, all the old enmities rose once more to the surface and the very existence of France as a democratic entity was threatened.

Had there not been one or two among the leading politicians of France who were more perspicacious than the rest, and who were temporarily prepared to co-operate for one purpose and one purpose only—to prevent the Communists from coming to power—there is no doubt that France would have become the first Western Communist state. In any case, it was a close shave.

In the confusion with which the lack of preparation for the future swamped Paris and the country, the Communists attacked the people and the institutions with a cynical disregard for all the rights and privileges of the individual. They used the strong-arm methods of the gangster. Cunningly applying the fierce hatreds and desire for revenge which wartime behavior had kindled among the more politically active sections of the population to their own ends, they used the atmosphere of anger and bitterness to try to rid themselves of their most powerful opponents. The opponents, caught up in the almost incomprehensible chaos which the internecine struggle was creating, were not only blinded by their own hatreds and unconscious of what was happening, but were frittering away what little strength they had to fight anyone at all.

For some reason, which it will puzzle historians for some time to come to explain except in terms of metapolitics, France was saved from Communism in spite of herself. A brief outline of her political situation for the first two or three postwar years will illustrate just how near she came to disaster.

On the day that Paris was liberated, August 25, 1944, France was again proclaimed a republic, and republican legislation theoretically came into force. De Gaulle remodeled the provisional government over which he had presided in Algiers since 1943; war destruction having made communication difficult, republican commissioners, armed with full powers, represented the government in the regions. Advising the government was a consultative assembly, on which all parties and the National Council of Resist-

ance sat, its members being appointed by the Resistance Committee. The first task was to re-establish communications, organize
revictualing and bring order into the country ravaged physically
and psychologically by four years of occupation.

A purge of those who had collaborated with the Germans was
deemed to be the most important first measure which had to be
undertaken. In the early days, as we have hinted above, sum-
mary execution of collaborators took place. These were the days
of greatest danger for France, but fortunately justice presently
intervened and the most notorious collaborators were brought
before proper tribunals. Administration, journalism and the world
of letters and the arts were systematically purged by committees
set up for the purpose; search was made for economic collaborators
and illicit profiteers had their gains confiscated; tens of thousands
of death, forced labor or prison sentences were passed. Pétain and
Laval were condemned to death, the latter being excuted, the
former being imprisoned for life on account of his age—he was
ninety years old.

During 1945 and 1946 France existed under provisional governments. At the back of men's minds was the desire to design a
constitution which would prevent the political degradation of the
prewar period from being repeated. On October 21, 1945, a
constituent assembly was elected, whose principal purpose was
to draw up this constitution. The Communist Party secured 150
seats, the Socialists 139, and a new party, Catholic and democratic, the Mouvement Républicain Populaire (MRP) 149 seats,
while the Radicals won only 25.

The constitution it proposed was rejected on May 5, 1946,
and a new constituent assembly was elected. Once again the
Communists were the most numerous single party, with the
MRP the next. The constitution drawn up by this assembly was
accepted by a weak majority on October 13th.

De Gaulle, at variance with the constituent assembly over both
constitution-making and foreign policy, had already resigned as
head of the provisional government on January 21, 1946, and
had been succeeded by Gouin, the Socialist president of the
assembly. Gouin supported the constitution, which the referendum

rejected, and resigned after the election of the second constituent assembly.

Gouin was followed by the MRP leader Georges Bidault on June 23, but he resigned according to custom when the new national Party began to function on November 10. It proved difficult to form a ministry as neither the MRP nor the Socialists wished to collaborate with the strongest party in the assembly, the Communists. Finally, pending the election of a new President of the Republic, the veteran Socialist Léon Blum formed a purely Socialist ministry with its life limited to six weeks. Nevertheless, in this very short time it gave a vigorous direction to policy, stopped the tendency toward a general rise in prices, and opened negotiations for a Treaty of Alliance with Great Britain. On January 16, 1947, the first President of the Fourth Republic, Vincent Auriol, was elected.

Following the usual custom, Blum resigned, and Ramadier became Prime Minister. His government, at first a coalition of Socialists, Communists and MRP, from which the Communists later withdrew, followed its predecessors in working for financial stability and reconstruction. By the spring of 1946 considerable improvements had been made, but over the next dozen years the political situation was to run continuously into considerable difficulties, the Algerian war broke out, making the situation even more dangerously unstable, until finally de Gaulle was called out of retirement to save the nation.

Now, as the strongest single party in the governing body for the first four postwar years at least, the Communists could not be denied positions of prominence in the administration. At various times Communist leaders were Ministers for War and Air, while others, like Paul Marcel and Auguste Lecœur controlled the most important government function—industrial production—while the veteran Thorez was for a period, in the autumn of 1945, the Deputy Prime Minister.

Apart from Communists in the highest places, there were also many Communists in high places and in low throughout all the organs of administration. Among the very first diplomatic missions to the Fourth Republic to arrive in Paris was the Russian.

They came with a vast staff, which could mean only one thing—
that Soviet espionage intended to launch an all-out assault on
French secrets. Many of their intentions and planned operations
they were to find unnecessary for the first three years, for the legal
penetration of the administration by Communists automatically
gave them access to all France's secrets, and to many British and
American secrets as well.

It could be justifiably said that during the early postwar period
the activities of the Soviet espionage chiefs in France were
divided into two main categories—they received the information
passed by their open agents in the administration, and they tidied
up their espionage house in the West, clearing up such untidy
messes as that left by Alexander Rado's Swiss network, and one
or two other loose ends like obtaining the release from French
justice of the famous Petit Chef Sukulov's assistant, Waldemar
Ozols.

On the other hand, the Center seems to have worked on the
assumption that the Communist prominence in French affairs might
not last, and this easy period was used to lay the foundations of
an organization which would come into its own when the time
came. One of the most significant activities at this time was the
resuscitation of the Workers' Correspondents (Rabcor) which had
worked so well in the late twenties and thirties; and there was a
return to the scene of some of the veteran figures of those early
days, like Jean Cremet and his former assistant Pierre Provost,
while Octave Rabaté, the editor of *L'Humanité* at the time of the
Cremet scandal in 1928, sat once more at the editor's desk. Within
five years no fewer than six hundred and fifty Rabcors were operating in the Paris region, with another two hundred scattered
throughout France. Once more they were to provide Soviet espionage with a seemingly unending supply of information.

When the Communists left the government in 1947, they did
not automatically cut off their access to high secrets by their
action. Many Communists in the lower echelons remained within quite easy reach of most of the vital intelligence. But apart from
the Communists, there were now large numbers of fellow-travelers.
The experiences of the war years had wrought some truly re-

markable changes in many men, and particularly among supporters of the Right, who swung right over, and if they did not openly declare their new orientation by joining the Party—as many did—their new allegiance was wholeheartedly with the extreme Left.

Take, for example, the case of Pierre Cot, though his change of heart had begun to take place before the war. Cot had once been secretary to Poincaré, one of the most brilliant statesmen of the Right France has produced. At the time of the Spanish Civil War, Cot became Minister for Air, and even at that time was accused of handing French military secrets to Moscow. After the Liberation he again became Minister for Air, and his usefulness to Moscow during this time may be gauged by the fact that in 1953 he was awarded a Stalin Prize.

Or there was André Blumel, admittedly not a rightist, but very closely associated with the Socialists, who were as opposed to Communism as the right-wing democrats and Catholics. He had been secretary to Blum, and then became *chef du cabinet* to Adrien Tixier, Minister of the Interior, in which post he had access to most government secrets. It did not become public knowledge that he was a Communist sympathizer until 1948.

The activities of the French Communists were well known to French politicians and statesmen, and there came a time when something had to be done about it, or at least appear to be done, for even when the decision was taken there was a considerable reluctance on the part of responsible authorities of all parties to do anything which might cause an affront to Russia. Even when counterespionage produced irrefutable evidence that certain individuals were handing over France's secrets to the Soviet Union, they were instructed to take no further action beyond keeping the individuals under surveillance. This, naturally, suited the Soviet networks in France very well.

The first move of any definite consequence was taken in 1951, but even then individuals were not involved. The Soviet Union had judged that France was a highly suitable location for the new organizations which had been established after the war as fronts for Communist propaganda and espionage, and had sited the headquarters of such supposedly international bodies as the

World Federation of Democratic Youth and its allied body, the World Federation of Democratic Women, and the highly important World Federation of Trade Unions, in Paris. From here they conducted their vigorous pro-Communist propaganda and their clandestine espionage activities with tentacles spreading throughout democratic Europe. More or less under the pressure of her allies France expelled these three organizations from French Territory.

A good example of what happened when evidence of really serious betrayals was exposed by counterespionage is provided by the case involving two journals, *France d'Abord* and *Regards,* both run by Communists and dealing with military subjects. In 1949 it became apparent that someone had been supplying these magazines with military secrets. This was so obvious that action had to be taken, and when the government instructed the counterespionage authorities to act, the latter promptly arrested a number of people against whom they had been holding evidence for some time. The affair was so serious, however, that the security report was made direct to the Cabinet. This report stated, among other things, that a teacher at the Pau school for airborne troops, Captain René Azema, had handed to *France d'Abord* secret documents relating to the strength and equipment of an airborne division.

The arrests of the editors of *France d'Abord* and *Regards,* Yves Moreau and Jacques Friedland respectively, and of a number of others, were ordered. The preliminaries were dragged out over two years, however, and when the defendants were tried in January 1951, by which time public attention was diverted from the case, all were acquitted.

The establishment of NATO headquarters in France not only provided Soviet espionage with another target, but it made necessary much more vigorous action on the part of the French authorities, and in 1952 two networks were discovered in Lyons and Paris which provided as much information about Soviet methods of working as the Gouzenko affair in Canada. From seized documents it was quite clear that practically every French military secret up to this time was known to the Kremlin, while the majority of NATO installations in France had been plotted on a map found in the possession of one of the agents. Yet another ring was discovered in Toulon, the naval base—the new French navy was a priority target for Soviet espionage, particularly the submarine fleet—which numbered among its members police officers and even naval security officers.

These revelations shook the French authorities, and they did begin to tighten up their security and to deal more strictly with captured agents, but in 1954, despite these new measures, there exploded on the French scene a *cause célèbre* which shocked all France's allies as well as her own people. In October of that year, two high officials of the Committee of National Defense, René Turpin and Roger Labrusse, were arrested on charges of treason, accused of having supplied secret military documents to a Communist agent, André Baranés. This was bad enough, but within a short time of the arrest of these two officials, their chief, the Secretary-General of the Defense Committee, Jean Mons, was arrested and charged with "having damaged state security." Also implicated was a police inspector, Jean Dides, who acted as go-between for Baranés with Jacques Duclos, chairman of the Politburo of the French Communist Party. At this time, France was engaged in her war in Indochina, and the documents had all dealt with French strategy, besides highly secret information on NATO policy.

The French had to cope also with the espionage activities of the various Satellites, particularly of Poland and Czechoslovakia. The reaction of the government to exposures of the spying of the Satellites was somewhat different from that to Soviet spying. Several cases came to light between 1948 and 1950, and a number of Polish and Czech junior diplomats were arrested or expelled. This brought retaliatory measures from the Polish and Czech governments, and produced a kind of tit for tat that might have been amusing for the outside spectators had the background of espionage not been so serious.

Though the French Communist Party has lost a good deal of ground in recent years, it is quite certain that Soviet espionage has not slackened its activity in France, which still proves a very profitable hunting ground for NATO secrets. An indication of this is the recent arrest of a high-ranking French official attached to NATO headquarters who admitted that he had been in secret communication with Soviet agents for a number of years. Since the advent of de Gaulle, however, there has been a greater tightening up of French security, but if the past is anything to go by, this will have been accepted by the Center as a challenge to yet greater activity.

☐ Elsewhere

The situation in Italy was not very dissimilar to that in France. In the first general election after the Liberation a system of proportional representation gave the Christian Democrats 207 seats, the Socialists 115 and the Communists 104. The two latter parties, therefore, jointly held the balance against the Christian Democrats. None had a clear majority, so the government perforce had to be a coalition, with Communists in posts in which they had access to those secrets which the Italians might have wished to keep from Moscow. For Moscow, however, Italy had not quite the same attraction as France, and espionage activity was not so great, but there were cases which showed that the Center was active, with cells in every government office, military unit, factory and trade union. One in particular demonstrated that the Center had extended its infiltrating technique even to the Vatican. In 1952 it was made known that a professor at the Gregorian Academy, Father Aligheri Tondi, was, in fact, a Soviet agent, though how this had been brought about remains something of a mystery, since Roman Catholicism and Communism are anathema one to the other.

In Europe, after West Germany and France, the country which received most attention was Sweden. Between 1951 and 1953 a series of espionage trials in Stockholm gave some idea of the extent of Soviet spying in this country, which Russia regards as her most sinister enemy in the Baltic. Five separate networks at least were identified. They had been operating unsuspected and therefore undisturbed since 1941, and according to the Swedish Commander-in-Chief of the Navy, every defense secret of Sweden was known to the Center.

The case which exposed this very serious state of affairs was that involving a naval officer, Ernst Anderson. Early in September 1951, Anderson asked for and was granted five days' leave to attend to some urgent private matters. However, instead of going home, he went to Karlskrona, the chief naval base of Sweden, and at the end of his leave returned to Stockholm.

On September 20 he went to an ice-cream parlor, picked up a bicycle which had been left standing outside and rode it to the hospital, where he left it standing in the entrance hall. Unknown to him his movements in Karlskrona had roused the suspicions of navy counterespionage, and agents had followed him. When he left the bicycle in the hospital they examined it, and found in the tool bag and pump documents describing the equipment of certain of the latest types of Swedish warships.

They took charge of the documents but waited to see who would pick the bicycle up, and the man who did come for it fulfilled their worst forebodings. He was Nicolai Orlov of the Soviet Embassy staff.

When Anderson was arrested and brought to trial, it was revealed that he had been working for the Center since 1946, when he had been recruited by a Swedish Communist, and that the network to which he belonged was controlled by the Tass news agency chief Victor Asissimov. Anderson had been one of the most dangerous agents to operate in Sweden; during his membership in the network he had passed to the Center the details of the kingpin of Swedish defense against invasion, the fortress of Boden, all the possible landing places on the Swedish coast at which the military and naval authorities considered the Russians might attempt a landing, and of the disposition of the Swedish Navy.

In July 1952, as a result of the intensive counterespionage drive following on the Anderson case, nine more Soviet agents were arrested. They belonged to a network directed by the door-man at the offices of the Communist newspaper, *Ny Dag*, Arthur Karlsson. Among these nine, outstanding was Fritjof Enbom, a former officer in the Swedish Army and now a journalist. He had been operating since 1941 and his espionage target was to provide information about industrial plants and the iron-ore mines. But he had also been given the assignment of organizing a kind of Fifth Column which would create diversions in the event of a Russian invasion by attacking defenses, blowing up railways, and operating a secret radio transmitter which would give false news.

While Enbom and his eight colleagues were being tried, no fewer than twenty-two members of the Russian trade delegation to Sweden and four embassy officials made hurried departures for Moscow. With them went the editor of *Ny Dag*, Gustav Johansson, and a leading Swedish Communist, Seth Persson.

Since that date there have been periodic disclosures and trials in Stockholm. The most recent, involving a very high-ranking Swedish Army officer, is perhaps the most serious of all. At the time of writing, the case is *sub judice,* and specific revelations have not been made, but the preliminary announcements make it quite clear that the Swedes are still unable to protect their secrets from the Center.

Espionage activity in Norway seems to have been on a some-what smaller scale than in Sweden, judging by the results achieved by the highly experienced Norwegian counterespionage. There have, however, been one or two outstanding cases. In one a Norwegian Army officer, Earling Nordby, was sentenced to three years' imprisonment, while a former Resistance leader, Asbjoern Sunde, who was arrested in 1953, was given eight years. His worth to the Center may be judged from the fact that the Russians provided money in lavish quantities for his defense.

Finland, too, was not immune. Two big cases in 1954 demonstrated this. The defendants in these cases were reindeer herds-men from Lapland and fishermen who had sold coastal defense secrets and frontier defense information to Russia.

Scarcely a country in the Western alliance has been without its disturbing spy trials. In Greece in 1952 one large network of thirty-two agents was rounded up, and showed the great efficiency with which the Center had organized its operations there. The network, directed by Nicholas Beloyannis, was equipped with two radio transmitters and gave information about American installations in the Greek islands and on the coasts of Turkey. Two further trials, exposing two other networks, followed the Beloyannis trial, but the Greek counterespionage authorities were not certain that they had broken Soviet spying in their country.

At about the same time a large network was uncovered in Holland and Belgium. In fact, wherever one may turn—in the Near East, the Far East, the Middle East, in the unsettled countries of Asia, in the Pacific, and above all in South America, the years from 1952 have had their constantly recurring espionage trials.

The scale on which Soviet espionage operates is, to a certain degree, responsible for the undoubted successes achieved by the Center. There have been serious lapses by counterespionage agencies everywhere, but their task is a formidable one. When a vast army of spies battens on a country, the initial results can be the same as those achieved by the Russian "steamroller" on the battlefields of Eastern Europe. Only a penetrating and ceaseless vigilance can prevent any country from being swamped by the Center's vast army of spies. Though this may have been brought home to the counterespionage agencies, the man in the street has not yet fully comprehended the situation, or the fact that he, too, has a definite role to play in the constant struggle to keep his country's secrets secret, and that this is as much his patriotic duty as putting on a uniform when the fighting starts.

PART VIII

The Recent Causes Célèbres

☐ Colonel Abel

In Great Britain and America the activity of Soviet espionage since the war has been much less diffuse in effort and carried out by agents of the very first flight, though there have been weak links in some of the networks which have eventually brought about disaster. Nevertheless, the penetration of Allied secrets of the highest caliber has been effected, as one outstanding case in the United States and three in Great Britain have made all too obvious.

The chief objectives in the military field have been underwater detection devices, nuclear armaments and rocket techniques, but the political field and any other subject of strategical importance in any sphere has not been neglected. Many mistakes have been made by counterespionage agencies on both sides of the Atlantic, but where the master spies have been trapped they have dealt a blow at Soviet espionage from which it will take some time to recover, if, indeed, the ground lost can ever be made up again.

For some time in the middle 1950's the FBI and other U.S. counterespionage agencies had been aware that many American top secrets in the fields mentioned above had been finding their way to Moscow. This indicated that networks were operating, particularly in the eastern regions of the United States. But the fact that search as diligently as they might they could not pick up the trail of any Soviet agents who could be responsible for acquiring the rocket, submarine and underwater detection secrets indicated that the quality of espionage performance was of a kind never before met by the counterespionage agencies. In 1957, however, the FBI was given a break. It came to them not from their own efforts, but from the defection of a Soviet agent whose choice for the work still makes one wonder what is really in the minds of the Soviet Union's spy masters when they select their agents.

Rudolf Ivanovich Abel had been an agent for many years, and because he had a genuine appreciation of the value of security, though he had served with distinction in Germany and elsewhere before the war, he had not come to the notice of any of the counterespionage agencies. This fact, when he was chosen to operate in the U.S. after the war, gave him a tremendous advantage.

During the war he had been withdrawn from espionage and had served with such distinction in the Army that he had received high decorations. His reputation for courage and his skill as a leader on the battlefield, as well as his first-class prewar reputation as an agent, to the Center, at all events, indicated that his loyalty was beyond reproach. And this, too, was an added qualification, perhaps the highest qualification, when he came to be considered for the very important post of Resident Director of a network which was to concentrate on the highest military secrets of America.

Abel received his instructions to move to the United States in 1946. He was in his middle forties, married and the father of two children to whom he was devoted. But such was his dedication to his work that he never hesitated for a moment about leaving his family, perhaps for many years. The fact that he was equipped with such hostages, of course, made his appeal to the Center much higher than it would have been had he been single.

He was to have no connection with the Soviet Embassy or any of the consulates in America, or with any other clandestine agency working there. For this reason he was to find his own way into the United States. This he planned with great efficiency by himself, for the only assistance given him by the Center was a number of false documents describing him as a displaced person, of German-Irish descent.

Since the Canadian regulations governing the entry of displaced persons into their country were less strict than the American, Abel applied to Ottawa for an immigration permit and was granted one. He arrived in Canada in 1947, stayed there for some months, and then in 1948 he crossed the frontier into America—illegally. For almost the whole of the next year he set about establishing his network.

His agents had already been chosen by the Center and were *in situ*. Working through one cut-out only, he drew up instructions for the passing of information to him, specifying a number of "letter boxes." He then settled down to directing his network unknown to any of his agents except his cut-out.

For cover he took the name of Emil Goldfus, and the occupation of artist. Though not a talented painter, he could paint well enough and knew enough about art to be able to gather about him a set of bohemian artists and friends, nearly all of them younger than him. As an artist he could disappear whenever he wished, keep irregular hours and indulge in other unconventional behavior without comment. At his Erlington studio in New York, a clutter of canvases and junk, he was a generous host.

If he was no painter he was an artist in another field. He could play the guitar with such skill that in other circumstances he might have made his living as a musician. He was also a mathematical near-genius; his radio codes to Moscow he had devised himself using the differential calculus as a basis.

He loved company, it seemed, and except when he went off on his solitary expeditions—when he was collecting information from his scattered "letter boxes"—he was always surrounded by a noisy circle of friends. Only on certain nights of the week, at ten o'clock, would he excuse himself, and return alone to his studio. There he would uncover the powerful radio transmitter, which put him into direct contact with Moscow, from under the junk, and for the next half-hour or so he would be absorbed in tapping out high-speed Morse.

All went better than probably the Center had ever hoped, and after a year the volume of information being produced by the network was so great that Abel/Goldfus asked Moscow if he might have the assistance of a deputy Resident Director. Since the Center made the choice, the blame for the destruction of the network some years later must rest solely on them.

The man they chose was Reino Hayhanen. Though his name was Finnish, he had in fact been born just inside the borders of Soviet Russia. He had begun his working life as a teacher, attracted the attention of the recruiting division, and was drafted into the NKVD during the Finno-Russian war of 1939.

He took to the work, and by 1943 was regarded by the Center as an expert in Finnish Intelligence matters, and from that year, until summoned to Moscow in 1950, was active in Finland, searching out anti-Soviet elements among the local population.

Arrived in Moscow, he was told that he had a new assignment. There he was trained in codes and photography, given the identity of Eugene Nicolai Maki, and then sent to Finland to establish a background.

It is interesting to note the choice of cover name, for we shall find the same technique used later in another case. The Makis were a Finnish family who had lived in Enaville, Idaho—the mother was American, the father Finnish—who had returned to Europe in the late twenties and settled in Estonia, when Eugene was about eight years old. What had happened to the Makis when Estonia became a Soviet Republic, it is not possible to say, but it can safely be assumed that they were in no position to compromise the new Eugene Maki.

The latter went to Turku, the Finnish west-coast port. There he worked as a plumber, and there, although he had a wife in Russia, he married a Finnish girl, Hanna Kurikka.

In 1951, he went to the American Embassy in Helsinki, and there produced a birth certificate which showed that he had been born in Enaville, Idaho, and asked for a permit to return to the U.S. A passport was issued to him some months later, and he set off for New York in 1952, sailing from Southampton in the *Queen Mary*. His Finnish "wife" followed him a few months later.

Not until 1954 did Hayhanen/Maki meet his chief, Abel/Goldfus, and the latter had a shock at their very first encounter. The security-minded Resident Director found to his horror that not only had his new assistant forgotten most of his training in codes, but that his ideas about security were so rudimentary—indeed, they seemed to be lacking altogether—that he constituted a danger to himself and to the network.

In the circumstances in which he was placed, however, Abel had to make the best of the situation. He set Hayhanen up in a shop and gave him instructions on how to operate. But all the time he was apprehensive about the safety of the network.

By 1955 Abel had been working in the field at considerable pressure for six years, and when the Center instructed him to return to Moscow for six months' leave, he gratefully accepted, though with considerable misgivings.

When he returned early in 1956, he discovered to his horror that Hayhanen had committed every crime which a spy can commit. He had operated his transmitter from one site during all that time instead of seeking out new sites in the suburbs; he had not bothered to collect all the information from "letter boxes"; and he had closed his shop, while still retaining the tenancy of the premises.

This was too much, and Abel complained to Moscow.

The Center's wheels grind with the slowness of the proverbial legal mill, and it was not until some months later that Hayhanen was recalled to Moscow. To remove suspicion of the cause of recall from his mind, the Center promoted him in rank to Major, and when he arrived at Le Havre he was handed three hundred dollars as expenses for his onward journey.

But he had not been deceived, and now that he was back on European soil, he decided that he would not return to Moscow. So he made his way to Paris and there approached the American authorities with an appeal for asylum, in return for which he would supply information about Abel's network.

Before accepting his offer, the FBI checked all Hayhanen's information carefully, and had him examined by psychiatrists. The latter found him to be unstable and an alcoholic. Nevertheless some of his information did prove that he was not playing a game with them.

As far as the members of the network went, he could not help them at all, except in one case. He identified a U.S. Army sergeant who had been assigned for a time to the American Embassy in Moscow, where he had been recruited into Soviet espionage, and who, since his return home, had supplied important information. The sergeant was arrested—and eventually sentenced to five years' hard labor—but he could not help with the other members of the network; he could only point out some of the "letter boxes" he had used, and identify Hayhanen as the go-between he had sometimes met.

In all his dealings with Hayhanen, Colonel Abel had observed the strictest security precautions—except on one occasion. For some reason he had had to examine some material Hayhanen had brought to him in the latter's presence so that he might question him if need be. For this reason he had taken him to a storeroom which he rented away from his studio for his photographic material.

Presently Hayhanen recalled this occasion, but as he did not know his superior's cover name, he could tell the FBI only that the storeroom was somewhere near Clark and Fulton Streets in Brooklyn. A somewhat lengthy search at last revealed that there was such a storeroom rented to a man called Emil Goldfus, and gave the address of his studio. (This was Abel's only other lapse from one hundred per cent security; he ought to have rented the storeroom in another name and given a false address.) When FBI agents called at the studio they found that Emil Goldfus was out of town for a few months.

When Hayhanen had not arrived in Moscow on schedule, the Center had at once realized what had happened, and they had warned Abel. They had also instructed him to leave New York and lie low to see what would happen, and he had paid two months' rent for the studio in advance and gone down to Florida, from where, if the FBI pressure became too intense, he could escape into Mexico.

As nothing had happened at the end of two months, and as Abel was so invaluable to the Center, they ordered his return to New York to take up his work again. On his arrival, he was arrested by the FBI on charges of illegal entry into the U.S.

He was brought to trial on October 14, 1957 on charges of conspiring to obtain secrets of military importance and of illegal entry into the United States, the first charges carrying the death sentence. He was provided with the best defense attorney that the Brooklyn Bar Association could provide—the distinguished Irish-American lawyer James Donovan.

But the evidence found in the studio—transmitter, microfilm and other espionage paraphernalia—was too strong, and he was found guilty of conspiracy as charged. Sentence was to be pronounced a few weeks later.

During this period Donovan addressed to the judge an appeal for clemency, in which he said, "Who knows but that at some later date an American might not fall into Russian hands charged with similar offenses. If Colonel Abel is then still alive, maybe it will be possible to effect an exchange of prisoners."

The judge took note of this argument, and sentenced Abel to thirty years' imprisonment.

Though Mr. Donovan could not have known it, Gary Powers was to fly his U-2 aircraft over Russia three years later, be shot down and captured, and brought to trial as a spy.

When Powers had served twenty months of his ten-year sentence, what Abel's defense attorney had foreseen happened. The two men were exchanged.

The Russians had the better part of the bargain, for rarely has Soviet espionage had so skillful a spy or one so loyal—for Abel refused to name any of his network, which presumably continued to work under a new master.

☐ Gordon Arnold Lonsdale

On March 3, 1955, the United States Line's transatlantic liner *America* berthed at Southampton. Her eight hundred passengers were the usual run of tourists and visiting and homecoming businessmen, to all outward appearances presenting no special interest to anyone except themselves.

Among those who disembarked at Southampton was Gordon Arnold Lonsdale, who, because he carried a Canadian passport, was not closely scrutinized by the passport control officers. From Southampton, Lonsdale took the boat train to Waterloo, the London terminus of British Railways Southern Region, and took a room in a hotel. For the next day or two, he behaved like any tourist, visiting the sights, the museums and art galleries, taking scores of photographs with an expensive camera, and buying souvenirs.

He also became a regular visitor at the Overseas League, not unusual for a tourist, but in his case an action of special significance. The Overseas League is a kind of club, and in its building not far from St. James's Park, it provides excellent drawing rooms and writing rooms, first-class restaurant facilities at moderate prices, recreation rooms, and an information service to assist its often bewildered overseas members with help and advice.

Besides making good use of Overseas House, Lonsdale made

a special point of making friends with the officers of the League. Without ostentation he let these officers know that he was well supplied with money, and they had no reason at all for suspecting that he was not what he said he was and appeared to be—a genuine, honest Canadian.

In May he left his hotel and took a flat in a luxurious block of furnished apartments, the White House, near Regent's Park. The management required references and, as he had hoped during the time he had spent winning the confidence of the officers of the Overseas League, they were only too pleased to oblige.

At the White House, Lonsdale asked for and was given a flat on the sixth floor. He told the management that he liked to have a view from his windows, but the request had an entirely different significance. The flat consisted of a small living room, a bedroom, a bathroom and a kitchenette with facilities for simple cooking, should the tenant feel disinclined to make use of the first-class restaurant on the ground floor. It cost about twenty pounds a week, which is expensive for this type of accommodation in London.

After a tour to Scandinavia he settled in at the White House and enrolled as a full-time student in Chinese at the school of Oriental and African Studies of London University. He completed two sessions before leaving in June 1957.

He did not apply all his time to his studies, but made a wide circle of acquaintances. He was a fluent and well-informed conversationalist, and had a gay and charming manner that was well-nigh irresistible. Women were particularly attracted to him, and he apparently could not exist without their company, for he had a succession of beautiful young mistresses who all later testified to his kindness and consideration, though his performance as a lover was nothing out of the ordinary.

Though no one knew exactly what his financial resources were, he had in fact between $20,000 and $30,000 deposited in various branches of the Royal Bank of Canada. From time to time he transferred some of these funds to accounts he opened with London banks, and the bank managers were so satisfied with his financial standing that when, at one time, he required extra capital urgently, he was granted an overdraft of £2,500.

For a prolonged stay in Great Britain, Lonsdale obviously needed some occupation if he was not to attract attention. Because of certain activities to which he was committed, however, it could not be one which tied him down to one locality, or even to England.

With some ingenuity he obtained a job as a salesman for juke-boxes. He began by buying two of these machines, which he sold for a handsome profit; but much more valuable than the money he made were his contacts. Before long, in certain London business circles he became known as a man with an eye for the main financial chance and with a considerable flair for salesmanship.

Towards the end of 1957, however, an even better opportunity came his way. A Mr. Peter Ayres was planning to launch a bubble-gum machine company at Broadstairs, in Kent. Ayres had been introduced to Lonsdale by a mutual business friend, and had taken an instant liking to him, and when Lonsdale suggested some sales gimmicks which might prove successful, Ayres thought he might prove a useful partner in his venture.

As a start Lonsdale undertook only to sell the machines, but he was so successful at this that he was offered a partnership in the firm. Lonsdale accepted the invitation, and bought five hundred one-pound shares, and became a director of the Automatic Merchandising Company Ltd.

This was a great step forward for Lonsdale, for it established him well and truly in the British social complex. To be able to call oneself a "company director" is extremely useful not merely in business but in lay circles as well, for to the nonbusiness mind the term has a high status significance.

The bubble-gum machine business flourished. On Lonsdale's initiative it was decided to try to enter the European market, and he himself paid visits to France, Switzerland and Italy. Though he did not get much business he continued to make these visits, arguing that he only needed time to break down resistance. When he was not abroad he was energetically selling machines in London and elsewhere in the country.

All went well for four years. Lonsdale made many friends and enough money to pay for his now luxurious way of life. But he also became overconfident in his selling ability. He persuaded his fellow directors to expand production, and soon, his forecasts of overseas business not materializing, the company found itself in serious difficulties. In March 1960 it went into liquidation with liabilities of 30,000 pounds.

Lonsdale was clearly frightened by this turn of events, and for a time he disappeared. But he possessed extraordinary resilience, and within a few months he had straightened out his affairs. On February 24, 1960, he became a director of the Master Switch Company, which had procured the patents in a switch designed to immobilize an automobile completely and protect it from theft. But there were production difficulties and not one switch had been manufactured when he was removed from the British scene by far more serious difficulties of another kind.

At the very time that Lonsdale was forming the Master Switch Company, a naval security officer at the Admiralty Underwater Weapons Establishment at Portland had begun to take an interest in a certain civilian clerk there called Harry Houghton. Houghton was fifty-four and for twenty-three of those years he had served in the Royal Navy. In 1945, when he was forty-one, he retired from the Service with a pension of two hundred and fifty pounds a year for the rest of his life. He looked around for a job, and obtained a post as a civilian clerk in the Admiralty, where he quickly impressed his superiors.

In 1951 he was sent to Warsaw as secretary to the naval attaché there. It was an important post, for it gave him access to all the secret material sent to and collected by the attaché. Unhappily for Houghton, however, he began to run into domestic difficulties. He was a great partygoer, and his wife, whom he had married in 1934, started to object to his frequent bouts of drunkenness which resulted from the generous hospitality of their Polish hosts. This led to frequent quarrels, some of which took place in public. What was happening reached the ears of the British authorities and Houghton was recalled to England, where the Admiralty committed one of those strange actions of which governments are guilty from time to time.

Houghton had proved himself to be unworthy of a position of

trust by his behavior in Warsaw, and ought to have been given a "safe" post. Instead he was appointed to the Portland establishment with access to all the information about the latest developments of underwater radar—information for which Russian espionage would pay well.

After a time Houghton and his wife separated, and he became friendly with a colleague at the establishment, a Miss Elizabeth Gee. When the friendship developed into an intimacy which neither bothered to conceal, Mrs. Houghton obtained a divorce.

By this time Houghton had left Admiralty quarters and had bought a small cottage in a nearby village. After the divorce he began to make improvements to the cottage and completely refurnished it at a cost of some hundreds of pounds. He also bought a new car.

Now, the naval security officer and Houghton went to the same pub, and what had attracted the officer's attention was the amount of money the clerk spent on his drinks. He knew that Houghton's salary was £750 and his pension £250, but it looked very much as though he was spending on drinks in a year far more than his total income of £1,000.

The security officer could make no inquiries himself, and as he had to have definite evidence to put before his superiors he asked a friend in the local CID to investigate Houghton. Within a short time the detective reported that Houghton was indeed spending more than his income on drinks and that he had paid for the improvements to his cottage and his new car in one- and five-pound notes.

This was sufficient for MI5 to be called in.

So from March 1960 until January 1, 1961 a watch was kept constantly on Houghton and Miss Gee. This watch disclosed that at frequent intervals, usually on a Saturday afternoon, Houghton, sometimes accompanied with Miss Gee, went by train to London, where they met a man whom it was not difficult to identify as Gordon Lonsdale. Nor was it difficult to discover that Houghton invariably handed a package to Lonsdale and received a package in return.

However, for nine months MI5 gathered evidence, and when they felt they had enough, handed over the case to the Special Branch of Scotland Yard for further action. So it came about that on the afternoon of Saturday, January 7, 1961, Superintendent George Smith of the Special Branch and some of his officers arrested Lonsdale, Houghton and Gee outside the Old Vic Theatre.

At Scotland Yard, after the usual cautions, Smith turned to Lonsdale to question him, but before he could speak, Lonsdale, relaxed and smiling, said, "To any question you might ask me, my answer is 'no' so you need not trouble to ask." Through subsequent long hours of interrogation, he steadily maintained silence.

In a straw basket which Miss Gee had been carrying were found two parcels containing Admiralty documents. In Lonsdale's pockets were two envelopes, one containing forty pounds, which was Houghton's "salary," the other fifteen American twenty-dollar bills.

Since he received no help from Lonsdale, Smith decided to find out what he could from people who had been known to meet him. It was an absolute coincidence that he chose as his first call a bungalow in Cranley Drive, Ruislip, whose owners were a middle-aged couple, Peter and Helen Kroger, believed by neighbors to be Canadians who had lived for some time in Switzerland before coming to settle in England in December 1954. Kroger was an antiquarian book expert, and had established quite a lucrative mail-order business, which he operated from the bungalow.

Peter Kroger opened the door to Superintendent Smith, and when Smith identified himself, asked him in. Smith entered the bungalow accompanied by Chief Inspector Ferguson Smith and Woman Police Sergeant Winterbottom.

After a few preliminaries, Superintendent Smith asked Mrs. Kroger if she would be willing to give him a list of guests who had visited the bungalow in the last six months. Mrs. Kroger recited a list, but did not include the name of the most frequent visitor, Lonsdale. Smith knew at once from this that she was lying, and said he would have to ask them to go to Scotland Yard for further questioning. Up to this moment he had had no suspicions concerning the Krogers.

Mrs. Kroger made no difficulties. She put on a coat, picked up her handbag and said, "As I am going out for some time, may I go and stoke the boiler?"

"Certainly," Smith replied, "but first let me see what you've got in your handbag."

Mrs. Kroger refused to hand the bag over, and it was only after a short fierce struggle that Smith got it away from her. Inside the flap of the handbag Smith found a plain white envelope containing a six-page letter in Russian, a glass slide bearing three microdots, and a typed sheet of code. Smith then arrested the Krogers on suspicion of espionage.

Searches of the rooms of all five prisoners revealed large amounts of money. In Miss Gee's rooms were Admiralty pamphlets, in Houghton's cottage Admiralty charts with submarine exercise areas and locations for secret trials marked on them. In Lonsdale's White House flat were encoding pads, and other espionage equipment; but it was the Krogers' bungalow which delivered up the most fascinating evidence of all—a powerful radio transmitter hidden under the kitchen floor, encoding pads, equipment for making microdots and so on.

The five spies were tried at the Old Bailey on March 18, 1961. Lonsdale was sentenced to twenty-five years' imprisonment; the Krogers to twenty years each; Houghton to fifteen years; Miss Gee to fifteen years.

During the course of the trial the Attorney General had made some surprising disclosures concerning the Krogers. Their real names were Morris and Lorna Cohen. Up to 1950 they were having regular meetings with Julius and Ethel Rosenberg, the American atom spies executed in 1953. The FBI learned of the connection too late, for when they looked for the Cohens, they had disappeared. The FBI, in fact, lost all track of them, until Colonel Abel was arrested in 1957, and the Cohens' names came up again. In fact, they had gone from the United States to Australia on forged passports. They stayed in Australia for three

years, then moved to Switzerland and thence to England on
forged Canadian passports in December 1954.

Lonsdale refused to speak throughout, even saying nothing
about his true identity. Until some time later, all that the security
authorities could be sure of was that he was not Gordon Arnold
Lonsdale, a Canadian.

Inquiries showed that there had been a real Gordon Arnold
Lonsdale who had been born on August 27, 1924, at Kirkland
Lake, in Ontario. His father was a Canadian who had worked as
a lumberman and a general handyman; his mother was a Finn
who had immigrated to Canada with her family a short time before she married Lonsdale.

The false Lonsdale had a Canadian passport when arrested,
and it was a genuine passport. When the Canadian authorities
were asked by the British to investigate the issue of this passport
to Lonsdale in 1954, they discovered that it was obtained by
means of a birth certificate which had been issued a short time
previously at Kirkland Lake.

The real Lonsdale's father told the police that he had separated from his wife a year after the birth of their son, Gordon
Arnold. Mrs. Lonsdale had remained in Canada until 1932
when she returned to Finland with the boy, then eight. Since
then Lonsdale senior had heard nothing of his former wife and
son; nor had anyone else.

The Canadian and British authorities believe that the real
Gordon Lonsdale died sometime before his thirtieth birthday,
that is, before 1954, and that his death and background were
known to the Center.

They also believe that Lonsdale arrived in Canada sometime
before 1954, though in what guise it is impossible to say, with
instructions to obtain a genuine Canadian passport. A passport is
readily obtained in Canada on the production of a birth certificate,
and birth certificates are issued without question to anyone who
says he is the person concerned.

A somewhat bizarre circumstance told the authorities that
their prisoner Lonsdale was not the real Lonsdale. During their
investigations the Royal Canadian Mounted Police traced the

doctor who delivered Mrs. Lonsdale of her son. This doctor, Dr. W. E. Mitchell, in 1961 practicing in Toronto, remembered the occasion very well, for he had had to travel many miles of rough roads to reach the Lonsdales' lonely house. This helped him to turn up old records, and these showed that within a few days of the baby's birth it had been necessary to circumcise him.

The Lonsdale recently exchanged for the British businessman, Wynne, is not circumcised.

Though no search revealed any other members of a network besides those arrested, the British authorities are inclined to think that there were others, and that Lonsdale was the Resident Director of the network. He was certainly a skillful spy, and had he given as much consideration to security observance as Colonel Abel did, he might still be operating. He had recruited Houghton, and in this he made a serious error of judgment, for Houghton was an unstable character, and very poor agent material. But Lonsdale also made an equally serious error in going to the Krogers' bungalow with his information for transmission to Moscow. Had he used a cut-out, the Special Branch might never have fallen upon the Krogers.

His loss to Soviet espionage was undoubtedly a great blow.

☐ George Blake
and John Vassall

The exact extent of the information which George Blake, British civil servant and former military Intelligence agent, passed to Soviet espionage will probably never be known except to historians of the dim future, when Blake will have been forgotten and perhaps even the Soviet Union have ceased to spy.

That it was of the highest importance may be judged from the remarks of the Lord Chief Justice in sentencing Blake after one of the shortest espionage trials in British history, and one that was remarkable for the sentence it evoked.

"Your full written confession reveals that for some years you have been working continuously as an agent and spy for a foreign power. Moreover, the information communicated, though not scientific in nature, was clearly of the utmost importance to that power and has rendered much of this country's efforts completely useless.

"Indeed, you yourself have said in your confession that there was not an official document of any importance to which you had access which was not passed to your Soviet contact.

"When one realizes that you are a British subject, albeit not by birth, and that throughout this period you were employed by this country—your country—in responsible positions of trust, it is clear that your case is akin to treason. Indeed, it is one of the worst that can be envisaged other than in time of war.

"It would clearly be contrary to the public interest for me to refer in sentencing you to the full contents of your confession. I can, however, say, without hesitation, that no one who has read it could possibly fail to take that view.

"I have listened to all that has been so ably said on your behalf, and I fully recognize that it is unfortunate for you that many matters urged in mitigation cannot be divulged, but I can say this, that I am perfectly prepared to accept that it was not for money that you did this, but because of your conversion to a genuine belief in the communist system. Everyone is entitled to their own views, but the gravamen of the case against you is that you never resigned, that you retained your employment in positions of trust in order to betray your country.

"You are not yet thirty-nine years of age. You must know and appreciate the gravity of the offences to which you have pleaded guilty. Your conduct in many other countries would undoubtedly carry the death penalty. In our law, however, I have no option but to sentence you to imprisonment and for your traitorous conduct extending over so many years there must be a very heavy sentence.

"For a single offence of this kind the highest penalty laid down is fourteen years' imprisonment and the Court cannot, therefore, even if so minded, give you a sentence of life imprisonment."

Then followed one of the most vicious sentences ever imposed by an English court in peacetime, one which, in the view of many, and the present writer included, was completely unjustified by any action which Blake may have committed, however serious. It smacked of a political sentence; a move to placate the criticism of the Americans, who were threatening to cut off all atomic information to the British if the counterespionage house were not put in order, though America's own house was in equal disarray.

Lord Parker went on: "There are, however, five counts to which you have pleaded guilty, each dealing with separate periods in your life during which you were betraying your country.

The Court will impose upon you a sentence of fourteen years'
imprisonment on each of the five counts. Those in respect of
counts one, two and three will be consecutive, and those in respect of counts four and five will be concurrent, making a total
of forty-two years' imprisonment."

With a slight bow toward the bench, the wretched, misguided
man turned slowly and went down the steps leading from the
dock to the cells below to begin a sentence which, if he com-
pletes it, will restore him to the outside world an old man of
eighty-one.

George Blake had been born on November 11, 1922, to Albert
and Catherine Behar in Rotterdam. His father came of ancient
and aristocratic Jewish stock, his mother of equally distinguished
Dutch lineage. After a period at a Dutch school, after his father's
death in 1936, following his father's dying wish, George was sent
to live with relatives in Egypt, where he attended the English
School in Cairo.

After two years there, he returned to Holland, and became a
pupil at the Rotterdam High School, which he was still attending
when the Nazis overran Holland in May 1940. On the first day
of the invasion, Mrs. Behar and her two daughters escaped to
England. They had discussed this possibility beforehand, and
George had pleaded to be allowed to stay behind so that he
might finish his course at the school, and this had been agreed
when an uncle had undertaken to look after him.

This course George followed, and when he had finished school
he became one of the first members of the Dutch Resistance. In
this he gained a reputation for courage and cunning, but eventually the Gestapo got on his trail and he escaped to England,
going via France and Spain.

Arrived in England he changed his name to Blake, and volun-
teered for the Royal Navy. His ambition, however, was to join
Intelligence, and his efforts to achieve this end eventually bore
fruit. He was transferred to SOE, trained by them and then,
somewhat to his disgust, given a desk job.

Then in the spring of 1944 he was assigned as an interpreter
to the newly formed SHAEF headquarters, commissioned as a

sub-lieutenant RNVR, where his duties consisted mostly in translating and interpreting German documents that were constantly falling into Allied hands.

Shortly after the cessation of hostilities in Europe, Blake was ordered to Hamburg in charge of a small Intelligence unit, with instructions to seize and interrogate all the U-boat commanders he could find. He carried out this work with a ruthless efficiency. When this work had eventually petered out, he was recalled to England, and on the advice of the Foreign Office obtained his demobilization from the RNVR, and went to Cambridge, where he learned Russian for a post ostensibly in the Foreign Service, though he would in fact be a secret agent in the employ of MI6.

This course successfully completed, he was posted to Seoul, in Korea, as vice-consul to the chargé d'affaires, Captain (later Sir) Vyvyan Holt.

When the Korean War broke out and the Communist troops entered the city, Blake, with Captain Holt and other members of the British colony there, was taken prisoner. Throughout his imprisonment, his fellow prisoners have all deposed, Blake set the highest example of courage and fortitude. The arrest and imprisonment of diplomatic and consular officials was contrary to all the usages of war, and the British Government at once began negotiations for the release of Captain Holt and his companions. But the Communists were loath to let them go, and while the negotiations dragged out, attempts were made to brainwash certain of their prisoners. Again according to his friends of this time, Blake resisted all such attempts, but it is now known that this experience was the turning point of his life.

Once he contrived to escape, was caught and stood before a firing squad on the charge of being a spy. As the order to fire was about to be given, he shouted out in Russian, "I am not a spy. I am a civilian internee, a British diplomat. I went out of the camp at Man-po and lost my way."

By a stroke of good fortune, the North Korean officer in charge had been trained in Russia and could speak the language. He at once dismissed the firing party and, taking Blake on one side, held a long conversation with him in Russian on the rights and wrongs of the war. He then returned him to the camp, with the advice not to try to escape again.

Not until the cease-fire had been arranged in the spring of 1953 were the survivors of the British party set free. Arrived home, Blake was regarded at the Foreign Office as one who had upheld the highest traditions of the foreign service. Whether it was as a reward for this service has never been revealed, but his one ambition to be a secret agent was now fulfilled. He was transferred to MI6.

This appointment was an extremely odd one, for the rules stipulated that all officers of MI6 must be of entirely British parentage. How it came about that the rule could be waived in Blake's case has never been explained; that it was fatal is known.

For a time Blake worked at the Foreign Office, where he met and fell in love with a young colleague. They were married in October 1954. They had not been married long when Blake was informed that he was to be assigned to the MI6 department of British Secret Service attached to the Commandant of the British sector in Berlin.

He took up this appointment in April 1955, and here in Berlin his first son was born in the following year. In Berlin the Blakes kept themselves rather aloof from the social life that went on around them, and Blake's irregular hours, which, he explained to his wife, were necessitated by his job, soon began to have their effect on family harmony.

In fact, this was not the reason at all. He had not been long in Berlin when he became involved with a double-agent who while working ostensibly for the Russians was also in British pay. Blake himself made trips into East Berlin to contact this man. Had Blake had any effective training as a secret agent he must surely have realized how dangerous such behavior was. In the Soviet-spy-ridden Berlin and Germany of this period it was fatal.

But Blake cannot be held fully responsible for what happened, for under instructions from his superiors he also established contact with yet another supposed informer, a man called Horst Eitner. A friendship sprang up between the two men, and it was not long before Blake, who had undergone a sudden conversion to Communism while in Korea in 1951, and had planned to become an agent for the Soviets if and when the circumstances permitted, was actually a double-agent himself.

The information which he passed to the Russians was of sufficient importance at this time for them to allow him to retain the confidence of his superiors by giving him information about a number of their petty spies to hand over to the British. Indeed, the British were becoming worried by the indications that their own and their Allies' innermost counsels were obviously known to the Russians. The last person suspected of having a hand in this betrayal of political secrets was George Blake. It fact, he was not suspected at all.

So for three years Blake continued his double role in Berlin. Then he made a most disquieting discovery. His supposed informer, Horst Eitner, was also a Russian agent. From that moment, he used every effort to get transferred out of Berlin. These were resisted by his superiors because of his use to them. Eventually, however, he was able to convince them that the Russians suspected that he was a hostile double-agent and that for the sake of security he must be sent away from Berlin.

So the Blakes returned to England, and settled near Bromley in Kent, from where Blake daily traveled up to Whitehall.

Presently, Blake was told that if he wished he might be assigned to the Middle East. He accepted with alacrity, and in September 1960 he and his family arrived in Beirut, Lebanon. Here, before going on to his assignment, he was to study at the Middle East College for Arabic Studies, run by the British Foreign Office for the special training of its candidates for posts in the Middle and Near East.

Shortly before the Blakes arrived in Beirut, though Blake did not know it, his old friend Horst Eitner had at last been discovered for what he was, a Russian agent, and was arrested by the British. During his interrogations, round about the middle of February 1961, he disclosed that he knew Blake to be an agent working for the Russians, and the evidence he was able to produce in support of his claim indicated that he was telling the truth.

The Prime Minister, on being informed, ordered that Blake

should be instructed to return to London for questioning. Blake had no idea why he was being recalled and went willingly. Arrived in London he learned for the first time of Eitner's arrest and accusations, and faced with this he immediately wrote a full confession.

On April 22, 1961, the Chief Metropolitan Magistrate issued a notice to the Press stating briefly that George Blake, a government official, had been sent for trial on three charges under the Official Secrets Act.

The seriousness of the case became apparent immediately. D-notices—the security ban on the publication of all information gathered from whatever source about a specific case—were issued. This secrecy, which was maintained until Blake was sentenced, and after, gave rise to many rumors and many conjectures which by not being answered by the authorities shook the confidence of the public more than they need have done.

Though no indication of the material handed to the Russians by Blake has been given other than that it was in the political field, it is not difficult to surmise what some of it must have been when one relates the Lord Chief Justice's comment, ". . . It has rendered much of Britain's efforts useless."

The period which Blake spent in Berlin was a period of great diplomatic activity the object of which was a Summit meeting. During the preparations for this meeting, which lasted for many months, the British Secret Service in Berlin was bombarded with a constant stream of questions dealing with every aspect of the Berlin problem. Blake saw most of these questions and prepared or helped to prepare many of the answers. Ergo. . . .

But if he did render all attempts at a Summit meeting fruitless, that still does not justify the vicious sentence passed on him. In the atmosphere of the times maybe it might have been felt to be justified; on the other hand, the atmosphere of the times would have prevented the Russians from making any concessions with regard to the Berlin problem or from wanting to arrive at a solution, even without Blake's intervention.

The suggestion that the sentence was a palliative to the Americans is not without substance when the following extract from the *New York Herald Tribune* is considered:

George Blake learned of every plan, every intended tactical move and of all projects the West worked out on the problems of Berlin and Germany. . . . The United States might in future withhold from the British Government its secrets, regarding Britain as a sieve. . . .

The publisher of the *Herald Tribune* is John Hay Whitney, a former American Ambassador in London.

But British security was no more of a sieve for secrets than the security of any of her Allies, even the Americans, as the Colonel Abel case had showed, and as events in West Germany, France and indeed any of the NATO countries had showed. The British authorities yielded to a pressure which was born of fright and which had no firm backing to it. The shortcomings of her Allies' security should have been boldly pointed out. Instead the British authorities fell over themselves to offer a placebo, and in doing so committed the crime of exacting a quite unjustifiable vengeance.

Now that the fear has passed, now that other men have British destinies in their keeping, is the time for some attempt at redemption of the good name of British justice. It is fortunate that under British law espionage in peacetime is not a capital offense.

Of course Blake was guilty of betraying his country, and for that he must be severely punished. But if his sentence were reviewed and reduced to the same level as those imposed on Nunn May and Fuchs—who did far more harm to democracy by their betrayals—at least some hope could be rekindled in what must now be a consciousness without hope, a state of being far more terrible than even the knowledge that one must die within a certain time.

But above all we must do this to restore our own peace of mind.

The arrest and imprisonment of George Blake coming within five weeks of the trial and sentencing of the Portland spies brought home to everybody in England as probably nothing else could that they were under heavy pressure from Russian espionage. The cases certainly had repercussions in the Center, which had lost six of its high-grade spies within such a short time, with the result that a seventh high-grade spy was instructed to cease operating for the time being.

Among the results of the Portland case was the setting up of a Committee of Inquiry under the chairmanship of Sir Charles Romer, a former Lord Justice of Appeal, to investigate the cause for the security lapses within the Admiralty which had allowed Harry Houghton to be appointed, with his background, to the post with access to secrets of great interest to the Russians, and which had permitted him to spy for such a long time before being detected. The report of the Romer Committee sorted out the facts and placed the blame fairly and squarely in the proper quarters.

It was a coincidence that something similar had happened in the case of George Blake, though another government department was involved. Anyone who had been subjected to the treatment of brainwashing which Blake had received in Korea ought not to have been drafted into the Intelligence services, and certainly not assigned to Berlin at this particular time, until it had been absolutely proved that he had really not been affected by such treatment.

The errors committed by the investigation department of counter-espionage could be more readily excused in the Blake case, however, for the evidence available to them came from honest, worthy men who had found Blake to be a tower of strength to them at a time of great tribulation physically and of great stress mentally. Nevertheless, the processes of screening were just as much at fault in this case as they had been in the Portland case. This was realized, and when the Romer Committee came out with their findings, the security forces put their house in order with alacrity.

It would appear, however, that the changes in screening routine were to operate in the future. It does not seem to have occurred to anyone to review all the cases where a background might have produced a potential Soviet agent who might still be operating. If this had been done, John Vassall could have been put out of action at least a year, if not eighteen months, earlier than he was.

Vassall, the son of a Church of England clergyman, had spent a short time in a bank after leaving school at the age of sixteen. He did not like the bank and so he turned to the civil service, where he was accepted as a temporary Grade III clerk in the

Admiralty. This job was interrupted in 1943 when he joined the RAF, in which he served as a photographer. After demobilization he returned to the Admiralty, and from the beginning of 1948 was taken on to the establishment as a clerical officer.

He did not shine particularly as a clerical officer, and he was never to get far in the promotion lists; and it is a strange commentary upon the way things are done in certain government departments that a man of such junior rank can have access to some of the most important of State secrets. In 1953, Vassall was put into exactly this position when he was assigned to the British Embassy in Moscow to work in the office of the naval attaché.

There was one thing about Vassall which ought to have precluded him from being exposed to service in Moscow. He was a homosexual, and though a man does not go about with a label declaring his deviation from the sexual norm, Vassall was the type of homosexual whom experienced men of the world could and ought to have recognized. Because of this difference, Vassall in Moscow was a lonely man, and because he was a lonely man and a homosexual he was automatically the kind of man Soviet espionage was always searching for. They found Vassall, played upon his loneliness, had him invited to parties, precipitated him into compromising sexual situations in which they photographed him, and then threatened to expose him unless he agreed to spy for them.

That is his story, and there is no reason to disbelieve it. On the other hand, the threat of blackmail does not excuse his agreeing to spy. But the Center had sized him up perfectly. They had known about his homosexual proclivities before he arrived in Moscow even if British Security did not; and they also knew that he was a weak, vain man who tried to compensate the lacks of his life by trying to move in a social milieu which the class system describes as "above him." For the proper movement in these superior circumstances, he needed more than his fifteen-pounds-a-week salary, and the Center promised him good financial rewards provided he produced the right information.

By September 1955 he had begun to operate. He removed secret documents from the naval attaché's office, slipped out of the embassy, handed them to a Soviet agent, who photographed them at once, and handed them back to Vassall, who returned them to the files before they could be missed.

This went on for ten months, and Vassall's usefulness to the Center might have ended when his Moscow appointment ended in July 1956. But the luck of the Center was in, for not only was he assigned to a position in the Admiralty which gave him access to secret documents—the Naval Intelligence Division—the information to which he now had access was even more important than the information he could extract from the naval attaché's office.

This lasted for a year, and then followed a period when he was not so useful. He was appointed to the private office of the Civil Lord of the Admiralty, where his duties were to act as a kind of Nanny to the chief, a job which suited his temperament very well.

The Center had lived up to their promise as far as financial rewards went, and Vassall, a fifteen-pound-a-week clerk, was able to live in one of London's most exclusive and expensive areas, Dolphin Square, where he rented a small flat which he furnished tastefully with expensive antiques. This fact should have come to the notice of Admiralty Security, for he was, in fact, behaving in exactly the same way as Harry Houghton, though with much more grace. It was noted by some of his colleagues, but knowing his background, his hints that he had received one or two small legacies from dear old ladies was regarded as a satisfactory explanation, and no investigation of their truth was made.

After two and a half years of tending the Civil Lord's creature comforts as he went about his job, in October 1959 Vassall was moved once again, and this time to a department which made him even more useful to the Center. He was posted to the Fleet Section of Military Branch II, the secretariat of the Naval Staff of the Admiralty, and once again had access to most of the Admiralty's secrets. There passed through his hands information concerning radar, torpedo and antisubmarine and gunnery trials, Allied tactical and exercise publications, communications, Fleet operational and tactical instructions and so on.

With the exception that he now photographed the documents himself, for which he had been equipped by the RAF, he carried out the espionage procedures which had been explained by Moscow, and his security observation was so good that, except for a year when he stopped his operations after the Portland case on the Center's instructions, he was still carrying out the routine when he was arrested in September 1962.

Though, when some of the truth came out, the security lapses in his case proved to be much more serious than in the Houghton or Blake cases, he must have been an excellent espionage operator. For he had successfully been passing secrets to Moscow for more than six years before suspicion began to fall on him. And it might not have fallen on him then had not the Blake case called for the setting up of yet another committee of investigation, the Radcliffe Committee, to inquire into the organization and working of all the Security departments. As a result of the Radcliffe findings, and the suggestions made for the better working of the security departments, the staff of Admiralty Security did review its personnel, Vassall's background was noted, he was placed under surveillance, and was discovered.

There was no point in his attempting to deny what he had been doing, for in his apartment when it was searched were found copies of seventeen Admiralty documents, and, of course, his photographic equipment. Apparently, too, he talked about all he knew.

At his trial at the Old Bailey he was sentenced to eighteen years' imprisonment, a sentence which throws into highlight once again Blake's forty-two years.

The aftermath of the Vassall case was salutary from several points of view. It brought to people's awareness that their politicians were not always the paragons of virtue they had been taught to believe they were, and really one ought to like them better for that; but most salutary of all, it led to a further tightening of security procedures, and it is to be hoped that the lessons learned will be remembered for a very long time, though one is tempted to imagine that it is a forlorn hope, since it would appear that the official memory is as short-lived as the notoriously fly-by-night public one.

PART IX

A Few Brief Observations

☐ A Few Brief
Observations

The foregoing pages can claim to be no more than an account of
the salient activities of Soviet espionage in the first forty years of
its existence. To give a full account of all the known particulars
would require several volumes the size of this one. It is hoped,
however, that a fair picture has been presented of the development of Soviet espionage activity; and if this is true, then viewed
dispassionately it must in honesty be admitted that the achievement has been a remarkable one.

Because it has been so remarkable, this is all the more reason
for it to be constantly kept in mind that the Soviet espionage
today covers the world; that its technical performance has never
been so high; that its methods are known; that its targets can be
assumed; that it will concentrate on those targets with ever increasing diligence; and that it will continue to constitute a formidable threat to all the worth-while secrets of foreign powers.

Forewarned in this case is being only partially forearmed. In
the House of Commons during the debate on the Queen's Speech
in 1962, the Minister for Defence, Mr. Thorneycroft, said:

> The first thing I want to say is that men would not be employed as
> spies if catching them was a relatively easy matter. There has got to
> be a good chance of getting away with it before any Power would
> employ a man in a capacity of this character, and the truth is that
> men over many years have been employed in many countries in
> these capacities and have got away with it. It is very easy to assume
> **after** they have been caught and after all the evidence has been

produced, "How clever we would all have been if only we had been on the job of catching them." I say that all history indicates the contrary, that in fact it is very difficult to catch spies, and probably many more of them get away than are caught, and that goes for nearly every country in the world.

The Minister was much criticized for the lighthearted, almost jocular tenor of his speech, but in fact he spoke some of the best sense of the whole debate, and the passage quoted makes the best sense of all. Spy-catching is very difficult; not every spy is caught. These are the facts of life.

On the other hand, efforts to catch them must not be relaxed, and it is suggested that if as many people as possible know how the opposition works, there will be less likelihood of relaxation than there would be if the job were left entirely to the professionals.

The greatest danger from Soviet spying lies not in the operation of the professional agents, but in the hidden sympathizers who are in positions to pass secrets on. All men and women who hold such positions must be continuously scrutinized.

The fact remains, however, that, do all that we may, the Center is bound to extract from us a large number of our secrets. All that can possibly be done is to work so that the number is kept as low as possible.

Is this the only antidote?

We are aware that we lay ourselves open to the same criticism as did the Minister for Defence when he tried to appear not unduly unworried by what had happened, when we make the following suggestion, but we make it all the same: In our view the only effective antidote to the Soviet Union's seizure of our secrets is for us to concentrate on obtaining as many secrets of theirs as we possibly can. In this way, and only in this way, can the possession of our secrets by them be effectively counteracted; by the production of a stalemate which will operate on much the same lines as the stalemate in the nuclear weapons field.

Nevertheless, our last word must be: Here we have seen how the Center works; here we have seen the lengths to which they are prepared to go; here we have seen how they may be deprived of their agents. The latter can only be brought about, however, by the constant vigilance of the population as a whole.

Index

258; requirements of personnel, 45, 225; and contacts with Military Attaché, 50; and security, 51; and France, 60, 62, 65, 113, 115-116, 120, 264, 268; and Germany, 71-72, 124, 127; overall control exercised by, 105, 239; and Holland, 107; and Belgium, 108, 110-112; and Switzerland, 136-142, 143-147, 149, 151, 258; and the Far East, 159, 161, 224; its Atomic Division, 183, 187, 193; and the U.S.A., 187, 197, 211-212, 217; Western knowledge of its activities, 221; and defectors, 223; and Petrov, 225; and Gouzenko, 227; and West Germany, 246; and Rudolf Rössler, 257; and Italy, 269; and Sweden, 269-270; and Norway, 271; and Greece, 272; scale of activities, 272; and Colonel Abel, 276-277, 279-281; and Hayhanen, 278-279; and Lonsdale, 289; and Vassall, 300, 301

Chadwick, Sir James, 179
Chalk River, Canada, Atomic Energy Project at, 182, 184n.
Chambers, Whittaker, 95-97, 205-206, 210, 223
Champagne, Louis, 224
Chapin, John, 189
Chapital, Monseigneur, Bishop of Paris, 114
Cheka, the, 12, 21-24, 236
Chervenkov, Vulko, 240
Chiang Kai-shek, 158, 160, 208-209
Chicago, 189
China, 33, 208; Soviet espionage in, 159-161
Christiansen, General der Flieger Friedrich, 123
Churchill, Sir Winston, 85, 138, 182, 237
CIA (Central Intelligence Agency), 23, 25, 35, 210, 221
Clarac, Louise, 61
Cochelin (French Communist), 60-61
Cockcroft, Sir John, 180, 195
Coe, Frank, 204, 206
Cointe, Suzanne, 115
Collins, Henry H., 204
Comintern (Communist International), 21, 23, 25, 58, 83, 114, 157, 158
Communications Division (of First Directorate of KGB), 29

Communist Student Organization (Germany), 77
Cookridge, E. H., Soviet Spy Net, quoted, 223-224
Copenhagen, Denmark, 83, 108
Coplon, Judith, 43, 211-217
Copp, Hans, 129
Corbin, Alfred, 115
Cot, Pierre, 265
Coudon, Henri, 59
Cremet, Jean, 59-62, 264
Currie, Lauchlin, 204
Czechoslovakia, Soviet satellite agency in, 32, 246-247, 258

Daily Worker, 96
Dallin, David, Soviet Espionage, quoted 203-204
Danilov, Anton, 108
Darquier, Dr. Jean, 117
Defenders, Union of, 114
Dekabristi revolt, 12
Dekanosov (Chief of Foreign Department, First Directorate) 237
Denmark, 104, 105, 112
Deuxième Bureau (France), 23
Dienstbach, Karl, 80
Dirksen, Dr. Herbert von, 164
Disch, William, 91-92
Displaced persons, 241
Documentation service, 29
Donovan, James, 281
Donovan, Major-General Wild Bill, 173, 202
Dörhöfer, Elisabeth, 251-252
Dozenberg, Nicholas, 89-90
Dubendorfer, Rahel ("Sissie"), 136, 138-141, 149-151
Duclos, Jacques, 64, 65, 267
Duke, Sir Paul, 21
Düsseldorf, Germany, 259
Dutch Resistance movement, 293
Dzershinsky, Felix, 20-21, 24, 33, 94, 236

East Berlin, 295; Institute for Economic Research in, 255-256
East Germany, 228; Soviet satellite agency in, 32, 246, 254-255
Eden, Sir Anthony, 242
Eicher, Private, 252
Eifler, Erna, 133
Eitner, Horst, 295, 296
Empress of Canada, 254

The Author and His Book

Ronald Seth was born at Ely, England, on June 5, 1911. After his graduation from Cambridge University, he was appointed a lecturer at the University of Tallin in Estonia. When World War II broke out he returned to England and became one of the founding members of the BBC's Monitoring Intelligence Bureau. In 1941 he entered the RAF as an Intelligence Officer in the Bomber Command, but transferred to the Special Operations Executive in the following year. In the SOE, Mr. Seth parachuted into Estonia to help organize resistance against the Nazis. After the war he became first a civil servant, then a schoolmaster. Now a full-time writer, Mr. Seth has produced more than thirty books about war and espionage, two of which are novels. He resides at Ashford, Kent, in England.

Unmasked! The Story of Soviet Espionage is set in Fairfield, a type face designed by Rudolph Ruzicka. The display type is Craw Modern. The book was composed, printed and bound by The Haddon Craftsmen, Inc., of Scranton, Pennsylvania.

A HAWTHORN BOOK